D0982581

EUREKA SUMMIT

EUREKA SUMMIT

Agreement in Principle
and the Big Three
at Tehran, 1943

Paul D. Mayle

DELAWARE

NEWARK: UNIVERSITY OF DELAWARE PRESS
LONDON AND TORONTO: ASSOCIATED UNIVERSITY PRESSES

Associated University Presses
440 Forsgate Drive
Cranbury, NJ 08512

Associated University Presses
25 Sicilian Avenue
London WC1A 2QH, England

Associated University Presses
2133 Royal Windsor Drive
Unit 1
Mississauga, Ontario
Canada L5J 1K5

Library of Congress Cataloging-in-Publication Data

Mayle, Paul D., 1949–
  Eureka summit.

  Bibliography: p.
  Includes index.
  1. Teheran Conference (1943) 2. World War,
1939–1945—Diplomatic history. I. Title.
D734.T4 1943zb   940.53′14   85-40879
ISBN 0-87413-295-9 (alk. paper)

The paper used in this publication meets the
requirements of the American National Standard for
Permanence of Paper for Printed Library Materials Z39.48-1984.

Printed in the United States of America

APR 2 4 1987

To Ruth and FLM

CONTENTS

ILLUSTRATIONS

MAPS

ACKNOWLEDGMENTS

My thanks to the staffs of the Franklin D. Roosevelt Library, Library of Congress, National Archives, George C. Marshall Research Foundation, Churchill College, King's College, and the British Library. I am indebted to Mr. Christopher Catherwood of Cambridge, England, for the preliminary research he undertook at the Public Record Office and the Imperial War Museum.

Research was made possible by a grant from Mount Vernon Nazarene College and an Albert J. Beveridge Grant for Research in American History. Arrangements for my trips to Washington, D.C., Hyde Park, and England were eased by the unflagging support and timely assistance of Dr. Robert G. Lawrence, Academic Dean, Mount Vernon Nazarene College.

Professor Wesley M. Bagby, West Virginia University, directed the dissertation from which this study evolved. His thoughtful and careful reviews of the manuscript in all stages were insightful and instructional.

Governor W. Averell Harriman, who knew the Big Three intimately and was an eyewitness to most of the events herein described, graciously granted me a personal interview. I am grateful for his help.

From the beginning of the research, my wife's patient support was both encouraging and inspirational. The project could not have been completed without her assistance.

I wish to thank the following for granting me permission to quote materials to which they hold copyright: The Master, Fellows and Scholars of Churchill College in the University of Cambridge; Mr. Philip Mallet; David Higham Associates, Ltd.; Lord Alanbrooke and the Joynson-Hicks Trustee Company; Lloyds Bank; and Governor W. Averell Harriman.

In undertaking a detailed study of the Tehran Conference (alternate spelling: *Teheran*), I have attempted to resist the Cold War Era extremes that describe the Big Three as either totally villainous or entirely heroic. To be sure, the words and actions of the allies were not always above reproach. One need not look hard to find pettiness, callousness, and, perhaps, the corrupting effects of too much power. Yet it is hardly fair to lay the sins of the world at their feet. The evidence suggests to me that Tehran was a significant meeting of three mortals laboring under their individual and national concerns in the midst of the uncertainties and doubts of a war not yet won. Under such limitations, they established a working formula of agreement in principle, enabling them to survive many, but not all, of the pressures inherent in coalition diplomacy.

I have tried to tell the story in the words of the participants and, to the greatest extent possible, within the context of their "specious present." In the end, I remain responsible, however unintentionally, for errors of fact or judgment.

EUREKA SUMMIT

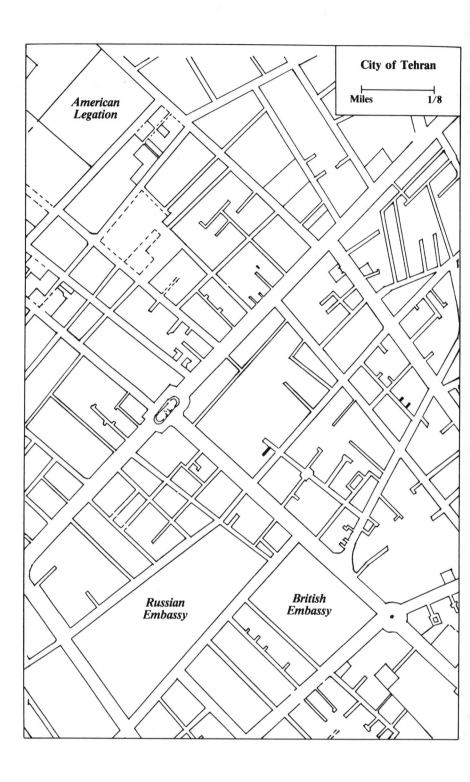

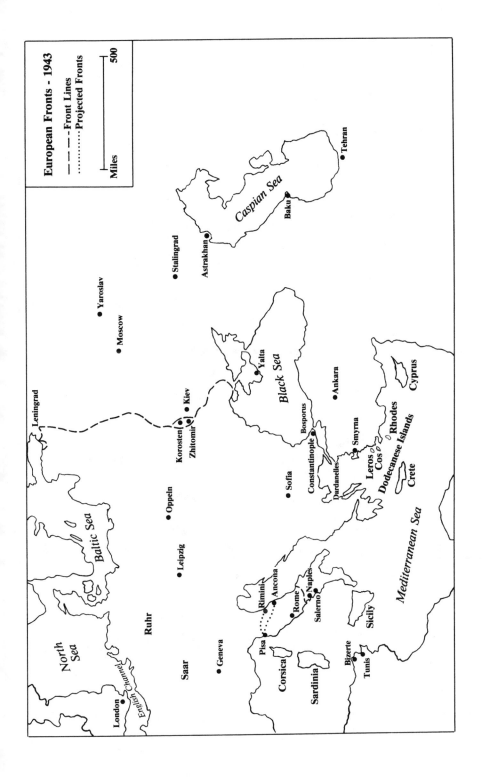

European Fronts - 1943

-- - Front Lines
····· Projected Fronts

Miles   500

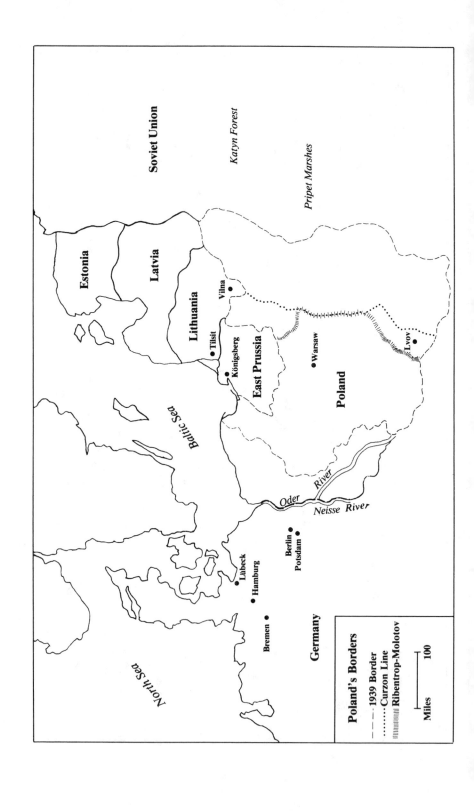

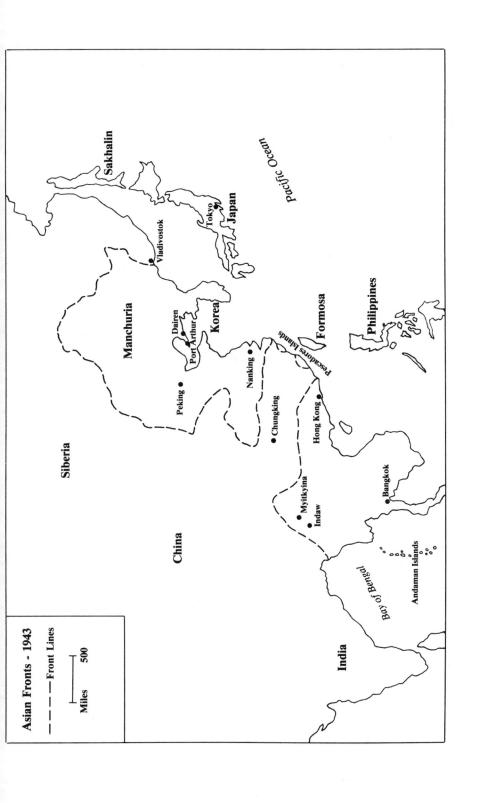

Asian Fronts - 1943

- - - - Front Lines

Miles   500

INTRODUCTION

> When a man says he approves of something in principle, it
> means he hasn't the slightest intention of putting it into
> practice.
>
> —Otto von Bismarck

Between 28 November and 1 December 1943, Prime Minister Winston S. Churchill of Great Britain, Premier Joseph Stalin of the Soviet Union, and President Franklin D. Roosevelt of the United States met at Tehran, Iran, for "one of those great occasions on which history hinges."[1] Although long wartime partners, the Big Three had not previously met in a tripartite summit. For nearly two years, they had conducted their alliance through correspondence and bilateral conferences. In August 1942, Churchill met Stalin in Moscow. And, during 1943, British and American leaders met at Casablanca, Washington, and Quebec to iron out military plans. Thus, Tehran was a milestone in Grand Alliance diplomacy.

By late 1943, although the war was far from over, the allies were reasonably confident that they would win. Wartime alliances typically disintegrate as the mutual threat diminishes, and, as Axis strength began to crumble, disagreements among the Big Three increased. They needed a summit meeting, said America's wartime Ambassador to Russia, W. Averell Harriman, "to decide how Hitler could be defeated most expeditiously."[2] In the strictly military sphere, this meant coordinating operations on numerous fronts and, from the Western perspective, ensuring that Russian forces continued to fight, even after Germany's surrender, by joining the war against Japan. Beyond immediate military planning, other issues loomed: the prospects of wooing neutrals and Axis satellites; the treatment of defeated enemies, including reparations and territorial adjustments; the future of Poland; the roles of France, China, and Iran in the postwar world; and, embryonic plans to replace the defunct League of Nations.

While a Big Three summit offered a substantial opportunity to remove obstacles standing in the way of final victory, such diplomacy was not without risks. America's often checkered performances at international meetings once prompted Will Rogers to quip that Americans never lost a war nor won a conference. So, victory on the battlefield might be thrown away through careless or inept diplomacy. Sharing the burden in winning and dividing the spoils of victory among three powerful rivals to the satisfaction of all were considerable challenges. Tehran was, therefore, the most significant allied conference in 1943.

In retrospect, it is tempting to conclude that Tehran was a seminal and decisive meeting at which the Big Three finalized their military strategies and anticipated the coming peace. Here, some would claim, is the high point of allied wartime cooperation, the shadowing of subsequent summits at Yalta and Potsdam, and the culmination of the most successful alliance in history.[3] Indeed, one of the most recent interpretations is that here the allies determined military strategy for the last two years of the war and framed postwar spheres of influence.[4]

Yet, other analysts, disappointed by the postwar breakup of the Grand Alliance and the tensions of the Cold War, paint a different picture. Critics insist that the Big Three managed to concoct a sort of temporary harmony, at best. More seriously, some scholars charge that the Western allies ignored or jettisoned the very principles for which they were presumed to have fought in order to ensure Soviet collaboration and to check veiled Russian threats of making a separate peace with Germany.[5] Or, it might be argued, none of the allies took their stated principles seriously, in which case they might be likened to greedy despots pursuing selfish national interests.[6] Tehran was a disaster, in the view of some critics, because Roosevelt naively placed emphasis upon personal diplomacy or, worse, made concessions to the Russians without counting the costs.[7] And, in hindsight, Stalin seems to have fared better than his allies at the bargaining table. But the real question is whether Roosevelt and Churchill conceded anything that Stalin could not have obtained without their consent.

Which analysis is correct? Was Tehran a success or a failure? Both interpretations tend to impose a pattern on the past. An operation carried out, even if the execution only vaguely resembled the original agreement, makes it easy to believe that the Big Three were in complete accord, at least on specific issues such as the second front. On the other hand, the bitter experiences of the Cold War era make it easy to want someone to blame.

A close study of the conference reveals that binding commitments were not reached. Divided by national interests, personal conflicts, and disagreements on strategic planning, the Big Three resorted to an exchange of views to clear the air, and, then, they created patchwork agreements to hold their alliance together. They reached agreement in principle on sufficiently ambiguous statements to allow for varying interpretations, as time or circumstances warranted. Without spelling out in detail all the steps for executing their plans, they postponed quarrels to a later date. The result was a colorful, theatrical meeting of three giants who controlled unprecedented power.

One might conclude that the allies never intended to keep their promises.

But Stalin obtained a rather innocuous pledge that the West would launch the long-awaited second front in northwestern Europe. Roosevelt proved, at least to his own satisfaction, that the Grand Alliance would remain intact through the end of the war and hopefully into the postwar era. And Churchill could take consolation in a diminished, but extant, commitment of allied resources to the Mediterranean theater. What the Big Three produced was a flexible, almost ingenious, statement of principles and guidelines. Because the promises were conditional, each of the allies could interpret the accord as he chose, and, if subsequently called to task for breaking it, could claim that his nation was fulfilling the spirit of the agreement. The Tehran Conference, which provided a good beginning for plans to end the war and establish the peace, was a fairly successful attempt to find a workable accommodation of conflicting interests.

1

THE NEED FOR A SUMMIT

We stand by what was agreed . . . but we do not feel that
such agreements should be interpreted rigidly and without
review in the swiftly changing situations of war.
—Winston S. Churchill

Strange Bedfellows

The Grand Alliance was deceptively efficient, an illusion enhanced by the
outcome of the war. Actual operations were frustrated, retarded, or ruined
by mutual distrust and grievances among the Big Three, who were rivals as
well as allies. The war effort demanded public expressions of cooperation
and kindred spirit, but the partners were uneasy co-belligerents, almost as
much at odds with each other as with the common foe.[1] Of the three, Stalin
seemed the most suspicious, and his occasionally blunt queries and accusations angered both Churchill and Roosevelt.

In signing the Ribbentrop-Molotov Pact in 1939, the Russians had apparently sought not only to avoid European war, but to enjoy the spectacle of
capitalism's self-destruction. Russian Ambassador to Britain Ivan Maisky
admitted that he added British and German casualties on the same side of the
ledger.[2] And Stalin may well have suspected that the West would delay
committing large numbers of troops to Europe after Russia entered the war
in the hope that the Nazis and Communists would destroy each other.

Western behavior did little to reassure the Russians. Churchill and Roosevelt rejected appeals for a second front, on the grounds that Soviet proposals
were impractical or that the West was not strong enough. When Maisky
pressed the British, Churchill replied angrily, "You of all people have no
right to make reproaches to us."[3] Later, Churchill wrote, "If they [Russians]
harbour suspicions of us, it is only because of the guilt and self-reproach in
their own hearts."[4] Occasionally, articles in the Western press asked why
American or British lives should be sacrificed needlessly to save Russia.

Stalin apparently had real fears that his allies would sign a separate peace.

Moscow gathered reports of many contacts between high-ranking Nazi officials and Western representatives in Geneva, of various proposals exchanged through the offices of third parties such as Rumania and Argentina, and of German inquiries through Swedish channels concerning Western peace terms. Harriman believed that a "very real chance existed for a German-Western agreement until January 1943."[5]

Stalin was not alone in fear of being left holding the bag. The Western allies worried when Russia refused to coordinate military operations with them and ignored requests for information about the eastern front. Stalin, they feared, might withdraw from the war when he was sufficiently strong enough to restore his 1939 frontiers. Stories of alleged peace feelers proliferated throughout the summer and fall of 1943. On 28 September 1943, a false rumor that Russia and Germany had signed an armistice circulated in European capitals. But, if the Germans and Russians intermittently groped for a secret peace between January 1943 and May 1944, they could find little basis for agreement.[6]

Also, the West had to consider the possible costs of rescuing or helping Russia. More harm than good, some feared, could result if the Russians profited excessively from a complete German collapse. On one hand, Westerners faced the unappealing prospects of Russian withdrawal from the war and, on the other, the disturbing possibility that Russia might win too complete a victory over Germany.

Even relations among the British and Americans were often stormy. Despite a common language, blood ties, and shared culture, the Anglo-Americans were rarely as cordial in private as they appeared to be in the presence of photographers or reporters. Each was annoyed by the other's habits and quirks. According to British standards, the Americans took breakfast in the middle of the night, lunch halfway through the morning, and dinner at teatime, while many Americans scoffed at the Englishman's tea rituals. Many Britishers were offended by those Americans who flaunted their profusion of food, clothing, and money. American soldiers tended to despise British soldiers for tolerating conditions and pay that would have caused Americans to mutiny. And the British frowned at the casual discipline of the American soldiery, who seemed to regard life as a permanent party.[7]

Both sides suspected the other of running the war to gain selfish or national advantage. To Major General Leslie Hollis, commander of the British Military Mission to Moscow, his own countrymen were "resolute, volative [*sic*], vibrant, and versatile," but Americans were "rough, ruthless, and unbending."[8] The prime minister's physician, Lord Charles Moran, criticized Americans for what he called stiff-necked pride in refusing to follow the British lead.[9] And Roosevelt and Churchill sometimes found each other's prima donna antics difficult to stomach. Americans and British often blamed each other for military setbacks and quarreled about the credit for victories.

At the summit, the Big Three, editorialized *Newsweek*, were "oddly contrasting characters."[10] One observer noted the physical contrasts between Churchill's "round, cherubic countenance," Stalin's "square, pockmarked visage," and Roosevelt's "oval, smiling face."[11] They arose from contrasting political systems and ideologies, and they sought differing, even conflicting, goals.

At age sixty-nine, Winston Leonard Spencer Churchill was in the fourth decade of a stormy and colorful career. He has been described as courageous, brilliantly imaginative and resourceful, impatient, and impetuous. He was a man of many moods, and he was often mischievous as well as solemn, boyish as well as statesman-like. To Harriman, who knew him well, Churchill was a leader of "great judgment and restraint in spite of his exuberance," and self-control led in his relationships with Roosevelt and Stalin.[12] But Major General John R. Deane, who commanded the American military mission to Moscow, called Churchill mercurial—at one moment he might be suave, pleasant, and humorous, but the next moment, rough, ill-mannered, and deadly serious.[13]

A skillful debater, Churchill was rarely at a loss for words. Once, in the White House, according to Special Assistant to the President, Harry L. Hopkins, the president caught Churchill stark naked, having just emerged from his bath. Unabashed, Churchill had announced, as Roosevelt beat a hasty retreat, "The Prime Minister of Great Britain has nothing to conceal from the President of the United States."[14] He inspired subordinates as a man who "would not be content with merely warding off the enemy's blows, but would 'give it them back' with all the power at his command."[15]

As prime minister, Churchill was committed to regaining colonies lost to the Axis and to preserving the British Empire. So intense was his devotion to imperial interests that some observers wondered if nationalism was a religion to him, and Churchill added to the speculation by confessing that he worshipped the empire. Nineteenth-century stability, he claimed, had rested upon its strength, and the twentieth century needed a similar foundation. He would never willingly allow Britain to play second fiddle to any country in the world.[16]

Churchill was anxious to win the war as rapidly as possible, without, at the same time, injuring imperial interests. He may have feared that Russia would replace Germany as a threat to Britain. And a postwar world dominated by the United States would be little better. He once described himself as being flanked by the "great Russian bear" with outstretched paws on one side and the "great American buffalo" on the other, while the "poor little British donkey was the only one who knew the right way home."[17]

The sixty-four year old Iosif Vissarionovitch Dzhugashvili, known as Stalin (man of steel), was perhaps the "most photographed man in history."[18] His reputation as a ruthless tyrant preceded him, contributing to a larger-than-life image. But, when photographed, he habitually sat forward in his chair, making those around him seem somewhat shorter.[19] This tended to mislead nearly everyone who met him in person. Those who expected a large bear-like physique were startled to find that he was only five feet, four or five inches, tall. Squat and mustached, his appearance was more Middle-Eastern than European.

Stalin was a man of few words, and his face usually showed little sign of emotion. Churchill's Chief of Staff, General Sir Hastings Ismay, called Stalin "inscrutable as the Sphinx."[20] Stalin sometimes averted his eyes and at other times gave a cold and penetrating stare. Occasionally, he doodled on a pad as if paying no attention to what was happening, but he was quick to pick up a point and was "never at a loss for a reply."[21] Customarily blunt and rude, he knew how to be courteous and even gracious, but Harriman judged that his veneer of civility was too thin for him to be called a gentleman.[22] Stalin's cold appearance hid a hard, tenacious, and driving mind. In talking to foreigners, he offered no affectations or poses and laughed readily, indicating a robust sense of humor.[23]

Stalin behaved as if he trusted no one. He was known for unexpectedly accusing even his closest associates, turning to them and saying, "Why don't you look me in the eye today?"[24] Stalin's suspicions were undoubtedly so deeply ingrained that nothing could have been done to change him.[25] This affected his relations with his allies, whom he trusted little more than his enemies.

Westerners generally knew so little about Stalin that they considered him an enigma. Some disliked him, while admitting that he was an effective ruler. But Admiral William D. Leahy, chief of staff to the president, believed that he was a "highly intelligent man who spoke well and was determined to get what he wanted for Russia."[26] Others could "not help but recognize qualities of greatness" in him.[27] Harriman described him as a cruel but "extraordinarily effective" wartime leader.[28] And General George C. Marshall, American chief of staff, called him a "rough SOB who made his way by murder and everything else and should be talked to that way."[29]

Of the three allies, Stalin had the clearest goals, the most important of which was Germany's total defeat. Insisting that postwar Germany must be weak, he sought punishment of Germany with such ardor that some Westerners concluded that he had abandoned world communism in favor of the more traditional policy of national security.[30] Also, he undoubtedly wanted to regain territory that the tsarist regime had lost in the First World War and to expand Russian boundaries.

Franklin Delano Roosevelt, at age sixty-one, was in his third term as

president. Strikingly handsome, he radiated self-confidence. Despite con-
finement to a wheelchair, his broad shoulders gave him the appearance of a
large and strong man. He construed his constitutional powers broadly and
wielded them vigorously. Nevertheless, there were always questions about
his health. The president's physician, Admiral Ross T. McIntire, insisted
that Roosevelt was in fine health and bearing the strain of the wartime
presidency remarkably well. Yet, the public was not informed as to his exact
condition, and rumors circulated that he was a sick, even a dying, man.[31]

Roosevelt chose to use personal charm as a political instrument and was a
"convinced believer in the efficacy of personal contacts between the chiefs of
state."[32] He had great assurance in his powers both to "understand and get
people to do what he wanted by argument."[33] Attempting to put relations
with foreign leaders on a human level, he expected that reasonable and
friendly men could reach mutually acceptable compromises no matter what
the problem before them. As a result, some State Department officials feared
that his faith in personal diplomacy was exaggerated and dangerous.

Roosevelt's top priority was to win the war and to prevent any further
resurgence by Japan and Germany. He wanted to continue the Grand
Alliance after the war, and, according to his wife, Eleanor, he believed that
world community would be best served by creating mutual confidence with
the Russians and by convincing Stalin that cooperation with the United
States would be advantageous.[34] He did not want the Russians to feel that
Westerners would not play fair. He agreed with Harriman, who urged
"complete frankness" and an open attitude toward the Russians.[35]

Many American leaders disapproved of such an approach in dealing with
the Russians. General Henry H. Arnold, chief of the army air staff, insisted
that the Russians respected only someone "stronger than they."[36] Ambas-
sador-at-large Patrick J. Hurley suggested that the way "to get on with the
Russians was to be tough, to go in, and say, 'What the hell is this all
about?' "[37] Some argued that the president should make no concessions to
Stalin without receiving something in return. To soothe Russian suspicions,
complained former American Ambassador to Russia, Admiral William H.
Standley, Roosevelt seemed anxious to "give and give and give."[38] Westerners scratched their heads to see what other gifts they could send to Russia,
and the Russians scratched their heads to see what else they could request.[39]

Despite the advice of his subordinates, Roosevelt pursued his own more
generous policy. When America's first Ambassador to the Soviet Union,
William C. Bullitt, warned the president that Stalin was a "Caucasian bandit
whose only thought when he got something for nothing was that the other
fellow was an ass," Roosevelt was not persuaded. He told him how once,
when he had tried to influence a policy decision, President Wilson had
admitted that FDR might be right but had refused to change his mind. So,

Roosevelt said, "That's what I say to you, Bill. It's my responsibility and not yours, and I'm going to play my hunch."[40]

Strange bedfellows were the three leaders drawn together by their common enemy. Combined, they controlled the greatest concentration of power that the world had ever seen. But it must not be forgotten that they were also rivals, each with his own view of what he thought the world should be. Their individual goals caused disagreements about how to use their military forces, and their differences made a summit conference necessary.

Friction in the Grand Alliance

Churchill could have been referring to the Grand Alliance when he said that the only thing worse than fighting with allies was fighting without them.[41] The Big Three often seemed to be fighting separate wars. The European theater was divided into the Russo-German front in the East, the air war in the North, and the Anglo-American-German front in the Mediterranean. The Russians left the war against Japan to the United States and Britain. And the contributions of the allies to the war were far from equal.

In late 1943, the Russo-German front was an irregular line stretching from the Baltic to the Caspian Sea. In the North, Axis forces controlled Finland, Estonia, Latvia, and Lithuania, and Leningrad was under heavy but diminishing pressure. To the South, Russian forces were advancing slowly against strong enemy resistance and, by the end of October, they had trapped large numbers of German troops on the Crimean Peninsula. On the central front, the Russians gradually pushed the enemy beyond the Dnieper River and liberated Kiev in November.

The Red Army carried the brunt of the land war against Germany. Some Western commentators estimated that 205 German divisions, nearly 75 percent of their total available land forces, were in Russia.[42] Stalin would insist at Tehran that the Germans had 260 divisions of 12,000 men each for a total of more than three million soldiers on the Russo-German front, and, according to Western estimates, the Russians enjoyed a three-to-two numerical superiority over Axis ground troops, a four-to-one advantage in fighter aircraft, a two-to-one advantage in bombers, and a decisive edge in artillery and tanks.[43]

In 1943, as far as Western sources could determine, Germany's total front line strength was two hundred fifty-eight German and seven depleted Rumanian divisions.[44] The German surface fleet was largely confined to port, and the once vaunted U-boats were losing effectiveness in the war for the sea lanes. Defensively, the Germans were yielding space under pressure in order to minimize losses. Anglo-American military chiefs expected Germany's allies—Hungary, Rumania, Bulgaria, and Finland—to surrender when sub-jected to sustained attack or when relieved of the fear of Germany. But intelligence sources warned that Germany might still recuperate or, failing that, seek through negotiations to split her principal enemies. Though greatly weakened, Germany was not yet vanquished.

Meanwhile, the Western allies nibbled at the edges of Europe. The Ger-mans had sixteen divisions in Norway and Denmark, forty-two in France and the Low Countries, twenty-five in Italy, and about thirty-eight in the eastern Mediterranean. Yet, the Americans and British actively engaged no more than twenty-five divisions, perhaps 300,000 enemy troops.[45] Begin-ning in 1941, the Western allies promised repeatedly to establish a land front in northwest Europe, but they did not keep their pledges. They controlled the sea lanes, but they restricted their activity in northwest Europe to air attacks. This level of fighting disappointed the Russians, who wanted the allies to land major forces in France to draw off German troops from the eastern front.

By 1943 Anglo-American troops occupied North Africa, Corsica, Sar-dinia, Sicily, and the southern third of Italy. After Italy surrendered in September, the allies advanced northward toward Rome, but Western leaders who had anticipated easy mopping-up operations were disappointed when German forces fiercely contested every inch of the mountainous terrain.

In the eastern Mediterranean, allied control was limited to the southern and eastern rims, including Egypt, Palestine, and Cyprus. Turkey main-tained neutrality. Axis troops dominated the Balkans, but both the Amer-icans and British were anxious to beef up resistance by local guerrilla forces. In November, the British gave up their Dodecanese campaign when they failed to dislodge the Germans from Rhodes, Cos, and Leros. Compared to the Russo-German front, Western contact with the enemy was peripheral.

In the Pacific, the Japanese controlled Korea, Manchuria, coastal China, Taiwan, Indochina, the Dutch East Indies, the Philippines, and northern New Guinea. The inhospitable terrain, tropical climate, and logistics hin-dered Western offensives. Japan's two-and-a-half-million ground troops posed a formidable obstacle, and many Westerners predicted that the Jap-anese would fight even more fanatically as the front approached the home islands. Moreover, Western commanders feared that resistance, continuing many months after Germany's surrender, would make the defeat of Japan costly.[46]

Consequently, the West sought help in the war against Japan. Not much assistance was likely to come from Chinese forces. Despite American train-ing and supply, the combat efficiency of Nationalist forces under Gener-alissimo Chiang Kai-shek was never very high. The American joint chiefs decided that the Chinese intended to remain "generally on the defensive pending the re-equipping and training of their army for offensive action at a later date."[47] The Japanese invasion had interrupted a civil war between the Nationalists and Chinese Communists, and Chiang, who seemed to want to conserve his forces for postwar action against the communists, would not commit all of his forces against Japan. Russia, while officially neutral in Asia, maintained approximately 700,000 ground troops near her eastern border. Western analysts believed that Russia was likely to intervene in the war against Japan at some stage, but probably not before the German menace was removed. Many planners agreed that the earlier a Russian entry could be arranged, the better.

It is now possible, of course, to tell what part of the Axis strength was an illusion and what part was real, but the allies could not be sure, at the time, how long the war would last or what the victory might cost in manpower and resources. They agreed in principle that coordinated military pressure would be most effective, but they disagreed about the specific nature and timing of operations.

When Churchill and Roosevelt met at Placentia Bay, Newfoundland, in August 1941, the United States was not yet a participant. The purpose of the meeting was to discuss American intervention in the Atlantic, aid to Britain and Russia, and the increasing menace of Japan. The major outcome, however, was that the two leaders issued the Atlantic Charter, which disclaimed aggrandizement and territorial changes that were not in accord with the freely expressed wishes of the people concerned. The charter, which proclaimed the rights of people to choose their own government, to enjoy equal access to trade, the high seas, and raw materials, and to live in freedom from fear and want, called for all nations to abandon the use of force.

After Pearl Harbor, Roosevelt cabled Churchill, "Today all of us are in the same boat with you and the people of the empire and it is a ship which will not and cannot be sunk."[48] In reply, Churchill suggested a conference to review the "whole war plan in the light of reality and new facts, as well as the problems of production and distribution."[49] Roosevelt agreed, and the prime minister traveled to America for the First Washington Conference, Arcadia, from 22 December 1941 to 14 January 1942.

At Arcadia, the Western allies established the Combined Chiefs of Staff Committee to pool resources and to decide grand strategy. Churchill's plan, named Gymnast, for the British to invade Algeria, was accepted in principle as the best way to weaken Hitler, and was revised to include American forces and rechristened Super-Gymnast. But disputes arose when the allies drafted a declaration of the "United Nations," Roosevelt's term for the countries at war with the Axis. When informed about the Arcadia proceedings, the Russians rejected any reference to *freedom of religion*, but they agreed to accept the phrase *religious freedom* instead.[50] Who, asked Churchill, could sign the paper? If only governments, the Free French could not participate, so he suggested using the word *authorities*. Both the Americans and Russians refused this change. On his part, Churchill would not consent to India signing as a sovereign power. Twenty-seven nations eventually signed the declaration, affirming the Atlantic Charter, pledging full cooperation in the war effort, and promising not to sign a separate peace.

From the beginning, the Russians asked for quick opening of an Anglo-American second front, by which they meant an invasion of France to drain enemy strength from the East. Soviet Ambassador to the United States, Maxim Litvinov, chided Westerners for their "lack of adequate and timely support."[51] After Russian Foreign Minister Vyacheslav Molotov visited London and Washington in June 1942, the Anglo-Americans, much to British Foreign Secretary Anthony Eden's dismay, announced that "full understanding was reached with regard to the urgent tasks of creating a second front in Europe in 1942."[52] The Russians interpreted this as a definite commitment, but at the hastily summoned Second Washington Conference later in June, Roosevelt and Churchill, then suffering reverses in North Africa and the Pacific, decided upon a "qualified rejection of continental operations in 1942" and a postponement of North African operations.[53] Churchill agreed to break the news to Stalin during an August trip to Moscow. When Stalin asked why his allies were so reluctant to tackle the Germans, Churchill sketched a picture of a crocodile and promised to attack the soft belly, that is, the Mediterranean, rather than the hard, northern European snout. Stalin, disappointed, growled, "May God prosper this undertaking."[54]

By January 1943, when Roosevelt and Churchill met in Casablanca, Western fortunes had improved, following successful landings in Africa in late 1942. Churchill succeeded in getting agreement that the first charge on allied resources would be to win the war for the sea lanes. The allies decided to transport the greatest possible volume of supplies to Russia, to step up the bomber offensive in Europe, and to attack Sicily in July. The combined chiefs established a planning staff to prepare Bolero, an invasion of the continent "as soon as German resistance was weakened to the required extent."[55] Concerning the Pacific, they decided to invade Burma by an operation named Anakim to begin in 1943 and also to seize Rabaul, the Marshalls, and the Carolines, "if time and resources allowed without prejudice to Anakim."[56]

The most significant Casablanca decision was the unconditional surrender policy. At a press conference, the president announced that he and Churchill were looking beyond the fighting to the allied victory and the nature of the peace settlement. Peace would come to the world, he said, only by the total elimination of enemy war power. This meant unconditional surrender and the destruction, not of German, Italian, or Japanese populations, but of their philosophies based upon conquest and the subjugation of other peoples.

Churchill, cautious of stiffening enemy resistance, disapproved of Roosevelt's public announcement of the Casablanca decisions. Moreover, the prime minister perceived disheartening signs that the Americans were adopting an increasingly independent line in strategic planning by showing less willingness than earlier in the war to accept British recommendations without qualification. Nevertheless, he retained his confidence, and, departing, he muttered, "I think it's a pretty straight road now, even the Cabinet could manage it."[57]

In May 1943, the Americans and British held the Third Washington Conference, Trident. The Western allies having drifted further apart in strategic planning, this meeting opened in an atmosphere of tension. According to the British, favorable conditions for a cross-channel invasion would not occur before 1944, and then only if the Russians drew off German strength from the western front. Following heated discussions, the combined chiefs resolved to amass forces and equipment in the United Kingdom, "with the object of mounting an operation with target date May 1, 1944, to secure a lodgment on the continent."[58]

In other areas, the allies found agreement easier to reach. Looking beyond the war, Churchill proposed a Supreme World Council—America, Britain, Russia, and possibly China—and regional councils for Europe, the American hemisphere, and the Pacific to prevent future aggression by Germany or Japan. Also, he contended, a Danubian federation should replace the Austro-Hungarian Empire, and Prussia should be separated from the rest of Germany. The Americans accepted these ideas in principle.

Meanwhile, the Russians were only interested in securing a second front. Stalin badgered his allies with such acrimony during the summer of 1943 that Churchill dropped personal correspondence for a time. And, on 11 June 1943, Stalin cabled Roosevelt, "Is it necessary to say what painful and negative impressions will be made in the Soviet Union . . . by the new postponement of the second front . . . ?"[59] Maisky insisted that America's industrial strength invalidated Anglo-American protests about the physical impossibility of such an operation, and the Russians rejected apologies for delay with "bluntness, almost to the point of insult," in messages bristling with recriminations.[60]

Many Westerners seconded Russian appeals for a second front. American Secretary of War Henry L. Stimson feared that failure to establish what the Russians wanted would weaken Western claims at the peace talks; fighting on the periphery, he said, was like trying to "hold the leg for Stalin to skin the deer."[61] From the start, Marshall took it as an article of faith that only a second front in France would enable the allies to win the war.[62]

But not until the second half of 1943 did the British and Americans conclude that German strength was sufficiently weakened to be vulnerable to an Anglo-American invasion. Learning that Hungary, Rumania, Bulgaria, and Finland wanted to leave the war, Western intelligence sources predicted that Germany was losing control of the eastern front and that her preoccupation in that area might open an opportunity for an invasion in western Europe.

The allies, however, still disagreed about the site and timing of a second front. Stalin argued that the attack should be launched only in northwest Europe and without delay. American and British leaders agreed that a second front was essential, but they disagreed on nearly every other point. The British preferred not to fix an exact date, because, they said, war was apt to take unexpected courses that made quick shifts in planning necessary. The Americans, on the other hand, favored firm agreement on major operations, which would not be aborted once set in motion. The British preferred to parry and thrust, while the Americans wanted a knockout blow; the British aimed for the enemy's vulnerable extremities, but the Americans sought his heart.[63]

Opportunism, said General Dwight D. Eisenhower, commander in northwest Africa, was often applicable in tactics, but dangerous in strategy, because major decisions would cause repercussions all the way back to the factory and training center.[64] The Americans wanted to stockpile men and materials on British soil, gain air control over the European coast, and cross the English Channel to France with overwhelming force. American military doctrine emphasized the direct approach, meticulous preparation, the power drive, the set-piece attack, and massive logistical support. The Americans codenamed their proposed cross-channel invasion Overlord.

The British were more interested in the eastern Mediterranean and the Balkans. According to some critics, British interest in these areas was entirely political.[65] A strong enemy controlling the eastern rim of the Mediterranean could potentially cut the empire's life line, the trade route through the Suez Canal to India and the Far East. And, perhaps, the British wanted to get into the Balkans before the Russians.

Americans accused the British of putting imperial interests before the immediate need to defeat Germany. Arguing that they should choose the shortest route to Berlin, and hence the quickest way to end the war, Americans favored an invasion across the European plain, where no natural obstacles greater than rivers guarded the heart of the Reichland. They preferred this to invasion from the Mediterranean, where the mountainous terrain of Italy and the Balkans stood in the way. Some, like Stimson, feared that allied involvement in the Mediterranean would immeasurably lengthen the war.[66]

In reply, the British argued that they had already committed troops to Italy and that expanding an existing front made more sense than creating a new one. Some British leaders insisted that the Russians would best be served by an Anglo-American assault on the weakest part of the German defense rather than on the heavily fortified French coast. Churchill maintained that building allied strength in the Mediterranean would draw off German forces from the eastern front. He told his chiefs, "It is true, I suppose, that the Americans think we have led them up the garden path in the Mediterranean—but what a beautiful path it has proved to be. They have picked peaches here, nectarines there. How grateful they should be."[67]

The British emphasized the inherent risks of crossing the English Channel. One of Churchill's aides pointed out that the West had "never carried out a successful combined operation in face of strong opposition *on the beaches.*"[68] According to Eisenhower, Churchill often said, "We must take care that the tides do not run red with the blood of American and British youth, or the beaches be choked with their bodies."[69] And, if the allies failed in their attempt, Churchill added, there could be no second chances.[70]

Timing was the key. Launched too early, Overlord might result in heavy loss of life with little to show for it except eroded prestige. If Overlord were launched too late, however, the Russians would gain victory over Germany and physical control of Europe. Significantly, the British never called for Overlord's abandonment.[71]

Nevertheless, British enthusiasm for Overlord was restrained, to say the least. The first logical step in assisting the Russians, claimed Churchill, was to capture Rhodes, which action would persuade Turkey to join the war. Then, the allies might establish a beachhead in the Balkans and give the Russians a true second front. Yet, under American pressure, the British had reluctantly agreed to invade northwestern Europe during the summer of 1942, but only if the Germans suffered a military collapse beforehand. When the Germans did not weaken, the British and the Americans planned successive invasions of France for summer 1943, late 1943, or early 1944.

At Churchill's suggestion, Roosevelt agreed to an Anglo-American conference, Quadrant, in August at Quebec. In line with American ideas, the combined chiefs decided to make Overlord the overriding priority, to plan it for 1 May 1944, and to transfer landing craft from the Mediterranean.[72] The British begrudgingly consented to an "Anglo-American invasion of northern France" in the "spring of 1944," without insisting that a German collapse precede the attempt.[73] Churchill offered to accept Marshall as the operation's commander. Anvil, an assault on the southern French coast, was designed to complement Overlord, but the allies neglected to set troop strengths or fix the timing of this subsidiary operation.

According to Stimson, these second-front decisions were not quite final, but from this time onward, Overlord held the inside track.[74] Yet, Roosevelt and Churchill said nothing about the operation in their report to Stalin. Instead, they listed decisions to increase their bomber offensive, to stockpile forces in the United Kingdom, to step up the pace in the Mediterranean, to supply guerrillas in the Balkans, and to accelerate operations against Japan.[75] Maisky concluded that they had devised an india rubber formula, promising to do all that they could without actually committing themselves.[76] In October, Churchill informed Roosevelt, "We stand by what was agreed . . . but we do not feel that such agreements should be interpreted rigidly and without review in the swiftly changing situations of war."[77]

The British and Americans also disagreed about what operations to undertake in the Pacific. The Americans proposed a plan named Buccaneer, to capture the Andaman Islands in the Bay of Bengal in support of a land operation, Tarzan, in North Burma, to reopen a land transportation route into China. They argued that the necessary forces were available and that this operation would boost Chinese morale, demonstrate Anglo-American support for China, and discourage Japanese hopes of a separate peace with China. Reluctantly agreeing in principle, the British accepted Buccaneer.[78]

Thus, the allies faced a series of important decisions to determine which operations should receive the bulk of allied resources. Whereas the British put the capture of Rhodes first, Overlord second, and Buccaneer a distant third, the Americans supported Overlord and Buccaneer, but they wanted to ignore Rhodes. For the British, the central issue was whether Overlord was to be preserved in its entirety, irrespective of Mediterranean developments.[79] For the Americans, the issue was whether or not the British would accept binding commitments.

Other problems troubled the allies, who were plagued by the "hard realities of logistics."[80] Amphibious warfare required specialized craft and tactics, both of which were in short supply. Establishing beachheads required landing craft to transfer men, trucks, and tanks from ship to shore. Advocates of various allied fronts vied for the available landing craft. Anglo-American planners had several options. They could assign top priority to one operation and postpone the others, dole out available supplies equally, or shuttle craft from one front to the next.

Delivery of Lend-Lease supplies to Russia was accomplished at great peril over long supply routes with scarce shipping. High losses, particularly on the northern route, which was often troubled by hazardous weather and subject to heavy air attacks, occasionally led Churchill and Roosevelt to suspend Arctic convoys. The unenviable task of so informing Stalin normally fell to Churchill. The usual Russian response was that supplying armaments and other military goods was an obligation, and Stalin's remarks suggested betrayal by his allies.

Political developments also troubled the Grand Alliance. The discovery of mass graves in the Katyn Forest, where nearly 4,500 Polish officers, once Russian prisoners, were buried, raised disturbing questions. The Russians denied German accusations that they were responsible. When the Polish government-in-exile demanded an investigation, the Soviet government broke relations with the Poles. As Russian troops approached the Polish frontier in late 1943, Churchill and Roosevelt feared that the Russians might cite their disagreement with the Poles as an excuse to establish a puppet communist government.[81]

A precedent had already been set. Without advance consultation with the United States and Britain, the Russians had formed a Free Germany Committee. In setting up a puppet government composed of "old communist wheel-horses and renegade army officers," the Russians demonstrated an apparent determination to have postwar Germany fall to Russian, not allied, control.[82]

Many of the crises within the alliance were hidden from the public. A survey of Americans between October and December 1943 indicated that 51 percent believed that Russia would cooperate with the West to bring the war to a successful conclusion.[83] Although the allies proclaimed their harmony with fanfare, serious military and political conflicts needed to be resolved. But first, the Big Three had to agree to meet, and agreement even on this point proved to be difficult to obtain.

2

OPENING MOVES

I prefer a comfortable oasis to the raft at Tilsit.
—Franklin D. Roosevelt

Stalin noted that in principle he had nothing at all against
such a meeting.
—Valentin Berezhkov

Roosevelt Seeks a Meeting

Shortly after Pearl Harbor, President Roosevelt asked Prime Minister
Churchill and Marshal Stalin for a meeting to coordinate war plans. His wish
was not fulfilled until two years of war had passed, Axis expansion had been
checked, and eventual allied victory assured. By then, his interest had shifted
from military operations to the shape of the peace and the postwar world,
but he was no less eager for a meeting. Besides, the president was somewhat
jealous of Churchill, who had already developed a personal relationship with
Stalin, and he wanted a chance to try his charm on the Russians. He may
have wanted to rebut critics who charged that he let the British run the war.
Also, the coalition seemed to be eroding, many disagreements demanded
attention, and he hoped that he could work better with Stalin than Churchill
had to achieve allied harmony.

In 1942, a number of Roosevelt emissaries sounded out the Russians. On 5
February in London, Harriman invited Maisky to lunch and asked if Stalin
would agree to a conference in Iceland or somewhere along the Bering
Straits. Archangel or Astrakhan, Maisky replied, would be better, but he
could not promise that Stalin would agree to meet. In April, Ambassador
Standley told Stalin that Roosevelt hoped to meet with him "somewhere in
Alaskan or Siberian waters during the next summer," to which Stalin replied
that he hoped it could be arranged.[1] In July, Harriman, who had accompanied Churchill to Moscow, received the impression from his discussions
with Stalin that a conference might be arranged in the winter, when the
Russians were not so busy fighting. In late July, when Hopkins broached the

subject, Stalin agreed that "big strategic questions could not be settled by soldiers alone."[2]

On 25 November 1942, Roosevelt cabled Churchill, "I feel very strongly that we have got to sit down at the table with the Russians."[3] To pave the way, proposed the president, each of the allies might send up to three military representatives to a secret meeting in Cairo or Moscow. Churchill suggested holding a summit conference without a staff meeting first, because in August Stalin had agreed in principle to a Big Three conference, was willing to meet in the winter, had mentioned Iceland as a possible site, and had spoken "with some zest of his desire to fly and of his confidence in the Russian machines."[4] Apart from the climate, according to Churchill, Iceland was a suitable location for a January meeting.

On 2 December 1942, Roosevelt telegraphed Churchill that he had been giving much thought to the proposed joint conference with the Russians and that the allies should meet about the fifteenth of January 1943, or soon after. Both Iceland and Alaska were impossible during the winter, he said, and a "secure place south of Algiers or in or near Khartoum" was better. "I don't like mosquitoes," warned Roosevelt who added that he preferred a "comfortable oasis to the raft at Tilsit."[5]

On the pretext that the conference would not deal with political questions, Roosevelt sought to exclude Secretary of State Cordell Hull from the planning. Roosevelt was not fond of the State Department, which he once described as a "haven of routineers and paper shufflers."[6] Evidently, the president did not want to be troubled by objections from Hull that he was giving the Russians too much, and he did not want to have anyone around that he should consult in advance about what he said or did. Roosevelt intended, or so it seemed, to relegate the State Department to the role of a maiden aunt, whose sole function was to worry over the "endless importunities of the numerous poor relations living on the other side of the tracks."[7]

But Roosevelt could not easily ignore Hull, who had accepted his post on the condition that he share "in every possible way in the formulation and conduct of foreign policy."[8] Hull told Secretary of the Treasury Henry J. Morgenthau, Jr., that a State Department representative, presumably himself, should accompany the president to add weight to any decisions made at a summit conference.[9] "Scarcely any large scale military operations," he argued, "could be undertaken that would not have diplomatic aspects."[10] If he were absent, it would be virtually impossible for him to keep Congress informed of foreign affairs. But Roosevelt insisted that military and diplomatic issues were separate.

Hull apparently accepted the president's explanation until he learned that his British counterpart, Eden, would attend the proposed conference. When he asked why, Roosevelt explained that the American and British systems of government were different. Hull finally gave in. For all practical purposes, the State Department was denied an effectual role in diplomacy at the highest level.[11]

Roosevelt also wanted to exclude the press. Of course, the allied leaders would need to discuss secret military plans. Without the press to seize on every word, he perhaps hoped that Stalin would warm to a free exchange of views. And he wanted to avoid giving ammunition to those who might criticize his war policies. He cabled Stalin that the more he thought about the "mutual military situation and the necessity for reaching early strategic decisions," the more convinced he was that the Big Three should meet 15 or 20 January at "some secure place in Africa, southern Algeria, or Khartoum area where all visitors and press [could] be kept out."[12]

On 3 December 1942, Churchill endorsed Roosevelt's bid for a summit with Stalin. Sending representatives to Moscow could only lead to a deadlock and "queer the pitch," he said, so nothing could take the place of a Big Three conference.[13] He agreed that Roosevelt should leave Hull and the press at home, and the minor partners in the Grand Alliance, he added, had no business attending a Big Three summit. A decision had to be reached, he said, on the "best way of attacking Germany in Europe with all possible force in 1943."[14]

Three days later, Stalin declined Roosevelt's proposal, while welcoming the opportunity to establish a common effort and agreeing in principle that a meeting was necessary. But the front against Germany was ablaze and, "This is so critical a moment that I cannot absent myself," he wrote, "even for a single day."[15] Adding that action was more important than words, he asked when the West intended to open the second front. This reply must have disappointed Roosevelt, who told Churchill on 8 December 1942 that another attempt still seemed worthwhile. He said that they should put the "responsibility for declining up to our friend," and he had sent another telegram to Stalin suggesting a meeting in Africa around the first of March.[16]

On 11 December, Roosevelt, assuming that he might not get a favorable answer from the Russians, suggested that he and Churchill meet. Because of its vile climate and icing on aircraft wings, he said, Iceland was out. He dismissed both England and Bermuda for political reasons, but he agreed to meet in Africa. If Stalin consented to meet on 1 March, he said, the allied staffs could meet "somewhere in Africa, or even as far as Baghdad, and come to certain recommendations which would at least get the preliminaries of new moves started."[17]

Churchill entered the bidding to arrange a conference. On 12 December he wired Stalin, "You ask specifically about a second front in 1943. I am not able to reply to this question except jointly with Roosevelt. It was for this reason that I so earnestly desired a meeting between the three."[18]

Two days later, Stalin wired Roosevelt that he could not leave the Soviet

Union "in the immediate future, or even in early March." He blamed "front affairs," which necessitated his "continuous presence."[19] Why, he asked, had no mention been made of agenda items? A meeting was important, he observed, only if the West was ready to reach a decision about the second front. Otherwise, the allies could handle their affairs, as before, through correspondence. Stalin's reply disheartened the president and temporarily dampened Churchill's enthusiasm. "Stalin will greet us," warned the prime minister, "with the question: 'Have you then no plans for the second front in Europe you promised me for 1943?' "[20] Stalin was reluctant to meet, per- haps, because he was "engrossed in his military command and suspicious of what he considered an Anglo-American line-up."[21]

When Stalin rejected a three-power summit, Roosevelt sought a private meeting. He seems to have believed that Stalin needed assurance that a Big Three meeting would be profitable, and the Russians might feel more comfortable if the British were absent. On 5 May 1943, Roosevelt proposed an informal visit for a few days to attempt a meeting of minds. Deciding where to meet, he wrote, was a problem, because Africa was out of the question in summer, Khartoum was British territory, and Iceland was dan- gerous and would make it "difficult not to invite P.M. Churchill at the same time."[22] He offered to meet on either side of the Bering Straits. Joseph Davies, Roosevelt's old friend and former Ambassador to Russia, hand- delivered this message.

In the meantime, on 22 May, Soviet officials announced the dissolution of the Comintern. To Roosevelt, this may have suggested that the Russians were trying to show their willingness to cooperate. Indeed, the action appeared to be a gesture of retrenchment from worldwide agitation and revolutionary expansionism. And, whether the Comintern had simply out- lived its usefulness or Stalin wanted to make a dramatic move, the timing of the dissolution was certainly auspicious.

In response to Roosevelt's proposal, Stalin agreed that a meeting was vital and should not be postponed. Hitler had already concentrated, he an- nounced, over two hundred German and thirty satellite divisions on the eastern front. If given two weeks' notice, he offered to meet in July or August at a place he would name later. This pleased Davies, who reported to Roosevelt: "There is complete agreement in principle."[23]

When Churchill learned of Roosevelt's bid for a private meeting with Stalin, he was angry. Enemy propaganda, he told Roosevelt, would make much of a meeting excluding the British who, in turn, would be bewildered and alarmed. Insisting that he would "go at any risk to any place," he called Scapa Flow, Britain's main naval base in Scotland, the "most convenient, the safest and, if desired, the most secret" place.[24] A tripartite conference "anywhere on the globe that can be agreed," he concluded, would be "one of the milestones of history."[25]

Having been caught trying to go behind Churchill's back, Roosevelt compounded his blunder by lying. "I did not suggest to U.J. [Uncle Joe] that we meet alone," Roosevelt claimed, "but he told Davies that he assumed (a) that we would meet alone and (b) that he agreed that we should not bring staffs to what would be a preliminary meeting."[26] Just the same, added Roosevelt, a private meeting was a good idea because it would give him a chance to explore Stalin's thinking "as fully as possible concerning Russia's postwar hopes."[27] And Roosevelt promised to meet afterwards with Churchill. The president also sent Harriman to smooth Churchill's ruffled feathers. On 29 June, Churchill relented.

But in late summer, Stalin retreated from his willingness to hold a summit conference. He told Roosevelt that his primary duty was to direct the action at the front and that his presence was necessary for morale. However, responsible representatives, he said, could meet either in Astrakhan or Archangel. Because he had to visit troops more often than usual, he told Churchill, he could not go to Scapa Flow or any other distant point, but representatives could make preliminary plans, raise issues, and draft proposals for a Big Three meeting.

Churchill and Roosevelt tried a joint appeal to Stalin. Insisting that neither Archangel nor Astrakhan was suitable, this time they suggested that they meet at Fairbanks, Alaska, "in the near future." Should it be impossible to arrange this "much-needed meeting of the three heads of governments," then there should be an exploratory meeting at the foreign office level.[28]

Stalin's reply was similar to his earlier excuses. Admitting that a meeting of the three leaders was important, perhaps even necessary, he stated that it was the "considered opinion" of his colleagues that he could not "without detriment to military operations leave the front for so distant a point as Fairbanks."[29] On 4 September, Roosevelt asked him to meet in North Africa sometime between 15 November and 15 December, adding, "I know you will understand that I cannot be away from Washington more than about twenty days because, under our Constitution, no one can sign for me when I am away."[30] But Stalin would not yield.

The Choice of Tehran

On 8 September 1943, Stalin cabled his allies that he would agree to a summit conference in November or December, when the eastern front would be less active. He suggested meeting in a country "where all three were represented, such as Iran."[31] The Russians controlled northern Iran, and Tehran's proximity to the Russian border made uninterrupted communications with Moscow possible. And Tehran was on the wartime route used by Westerners who traveled to Moscow.

The end of November, Roosevelt replied, would be a good time to meet, but he had grave misgivings about the site. Tehran was too far from Washington. Law required him to act upon legislation within ten days when Congress was in session, and bad flying weather over Iran might keep him from receiving and responding to bills in time. He asked Stalin to consider some part of Egypt, which, he claimed, was neutral and where he could carry out his constitutional responsibilities. Only Tehran, Stalin insisted, was suitable. And in Egypt, he noted, the Soviet Union was "not yet represented."[32]

Churchill was more receptive to Stalin's plan than Roosevelt. It was the meeting itself that was important, Churchill told Stalin, and choosing the site was simply a matter of finding a place convenient for all. While he preferred Cyprus or Khartoum, he agreed to accept Tehran, unless Stalin could think of a better place in Iran.

If Stalin refused to budge, the only choice Western leaders had was to accept Tehran or give up plans for a summit. To minimize the Russian victory on this point, they decided to make the Tehran meeting, if it came to that, the second in a series of three conferences, the other two at Cairo. At one point, Churchill offered to tell Stalin that a "very real constitutional difficulty" prevented Roosevelt from going as far as Tehran and to suggest a meeting in "Egypt or [the] Levant or possibly at Cyprus," but he changed his mind.[33] As early as 4 October, Roosevelt reportedly told Standley confidentially, "You know, it's all set. We're to meet in Tehran."[34] And Churchill suggested naming the conference Eureka ("I have found it!").[35]

But on 14 October 1943 Roosevelt again told Stalin that the choice of Tehran might cause constitutional difficulties and urged a shift of venue. After describing the merits of Cairo, Baghdad, and several eastern Mediterranean ports, he told Stalin that the hopes of the future world depended upon how well the Big Three worked together.

Stalin refused to consider any point beyond Tehran. Neither Roosevelt's constitutional concerns nor the potential advantages of other sites could sway him. He could go no farther than Tehran, he repeated, and still maintain constant communications with Moscow. Agreeing with the president that the press be barred, he proposed 20 or 25 November as possible dates for the summit.

On 14 October, Churchill, changing his mind, proposed that the three should meet in Habbaniya, Iraq, where, he said, they could confer in "comfort and security." Referring to Matthew 17:4 which tells the story of three tabernacles, one each for Jesus Christ, Moses, and Elijah, Churchill suggested to Roosevelt that three tabernacles could be erected for the Big Three. This analogy amused Roosevelt who replied that Saint Peter "sometimes had real inspiration." And a fourth tabernacle, added the president, could be built for Churchill's "old friend" Chiang Kai-shek.[36]

The same day, Roosevelt cabled Stalin, "The problem of my going to the place you suggested is becoming so acute that I feel that I should tell you frankly that, for constitutional reasons, I cannot take the risk." Among suitable alternatives, he listed Cairo, eastern Mediterranean ports, where each of the three could have his own ship, and the "neighborhood of Baghdad." The hopes of the future world, he repeated, depended upon personal and intimate contact among the Big Three.[37]

Roosevelt's bid was thwarted. On 16 October Stalin sent an offensive and brusque criticism of the Lend-Lease convoys. Condemning Western leaders for what he called ineptitude, Stalin accused them of intentionally depriving Russia of vital weapons and equipment. The telegram, said Churchill, was "not exactly all one might hope for from a gentleman for whose sake we are to make an inconvenient, extreme, and costly exertion," but he guessed that it came "from the machine rather than from Stalin."[38]

Then, on 19 October, Stalin again insisted that the Big Three meet at Tehran. All his colleagues, he claimed, believed that military operations demanded daily guidance and his personal contact with commanders. Because Tehran had wire telegraph and telephone facilities, his colleagues favored Tehran.

Meanwhile, the foreign ministers held a preliminary meeting. At the end of October, Hull surmounted age, his first airplane flight, claustrophobia, and virulent stories alleging that he was anti-Russian, to join Eden and Molotov in Moscow. This meeting laid the foundations for a Big Three summit. Western representatives promised an invasion of northern France in spring 1944, but they were evasive about the exact date which, in fact, was still unresolved. The Russians agreed in principle to cooperate in shuttle bombing, by which allied bombers would fly back and forth from bases in the West to Russian airfields, hitting Axis targets on each pass. Also, the Russians accepted proposals to exchange weather information and improve air transport. Regarding Germany, the foreign ministers proposed total disarmament, reparations in both goods and services, and punishment of war criminals. To study peace settlement issues, they set up the European Advisory Commission. They referred a Russian request for a share of the Italian navy and merchant fleet to the Big Three. And Stalin joined the conference long enough to promise that Russia would join the war against Japan soon after Germany's defeat.

At about the same time, Roosevelt sought Churchill's help in fixing the summit conference site. "The possibility of Tehran is out," Roosevelt told him, "because I find the time risks are flatly impossible to take. I hope you can find some way of having Eden back this up."[39] But when Eden tried to change the site, he was rebuffed. When Stalin offered to send Molotov in his place, Eden replied that the Western leaders would not make "long journeys except to meet him."[40] British Ambassador to Moscow, Sir Archibald

Clark-Kerr, also found Stalin unbending. While Stalin greatly regretted inconveniencing Roosevelt and claimed to be only too glad, under other circumstances, to travel past Tehran, he insisted that the "opportunities now existing in the war happened only once in fifty years."[41]

The British thwarted, the initiative passed to the American side. Hull was granted a personal meeting with Stalin and found the marshal to be extremely cordial. When Hull said that one of their most important tasks was to lay the groundwork for a meeting of the three, Stalin "noted that in principle he had nothing at all against such a meeting."[42] Hull handed Stalin a personal message from Roosevelt explaining his objections to Tehran. The mountainous approach and unstable weather conditions sometimes made flying impossible for several days. He offered to travel as far as the Persian Gulf, "not in any way considering the fact that from United States territory I would have to travel 6,000 miles and you would only have to travel 600 miles from Russian territory," but, "I must tell you," he added, "that I cannot go to Tehran."[43] His cabinet and congressional leaders agreed with him on this point, he said. Insisting that the problem was "not a matter of theory but a question of fact," he begged Stalin not to fail him "in this crisis" and urged him to consider Basra, Baghdad, Asmara, or Ankara.[44]

But Stalin refused to budge. Saying that he could not really decide without consulting his associates, he suggested that the allies postpone the meeting until spring, at which time they could meet in Fairbanks. But no city was more suitable than Tehran, he said. "It is for you alone, of course, to decide whether you can go there."[45] Harriman and Hull concluded that Stalin would have Tehran and no other, and they informed Roosevelt accordingly.

By this time, Roosevelt and Churchill seemed to be objecting to Tehran, not so much because of the site itself, but from reluctance to yield to Stalin. On 2 November, Churchill wired Roosevelt, "Uncle Joe will not come beyond Tehran," but, at the same time, he proposed trying to wheedle him into meeting at Habbaniya.[46] Failing that, he agreed to accept Tehran. When Roosevelt instructed Hull to ask Stalin to consider flying from Tehran to Basra for even one day, Stalin replied that the president must choose Tehran. On 29 October, Molotov asked why, if the meeting was so important, Roosevelt was not willing to fly "just a little further" himself?[47]

Finally, after Churchill and Harriman advised him that air travel to Tehran was not hazardous, Roosevelt gave up. On 8 November he wired Stalin that his constitutional problem could be solved. If Congress passed a bill requiring his veto, he explained, he could fly to Tunis, carry out his responsibilities, and then return to Iran. The prospects of their meeting, he said, made him "especially happy."[48]

On 11 November, Roosevelt contacted Churchill, urging that they do nothing to cause Stalin to retract his agreement and asking Churchill to accept Tehran. Churchill replied that he was willing to go anywhere his allies decided and expressed pleasure that the summit was "now definitely arranged."[49]

But Stalin was not finished setting conditions. On 12 November he insisted that participation of representatives of any other powers except the Big Three should be absolutely ruled out. Then, the following day, he instructed the Russian Ambassador in London, Fedor Rarasovich Gusev, to deliver his formal acceptance. British Permanent Under Secretary of State for Foreign Affairs, Sir Alexander Cadogan, recorded in his diary, "Frogface with message from Joe. He agrees to meeting in Tehran about the 27th."[50]

When Churchill tried to arrange a preliminary Anglo-American meeting to draft a joint strategy for dealing with the Russians, Roosevelt responded that this would be a terrible mistake, because Stalin might conclude that his allies had ganged up on him. Instead, the president wanted to let the Russians eavesdrop on Western discussions. "Let us take them in on the high spots," he told Churchill.[51] The prime minister argued that translations would create intolerable delays, and he was gravely disturbed.[52] Either the Americans were lining up with the Russians, or they were providing Stalin with a golden opportunity to drive a wedge between his allies.

Stalin had reason to be pleased with the arrangements. He had won the first round of negotiations and had the psychological advantage of having the Western allies meet him at Russia's doorstep. Moreover, the disparity in distances that each had to travel substantiated the claim that Stalin was bearing the brunt of the war and could spare less time away from directing military operations. Besides that, Roosevelt and, to a lesser extent, Churchill, showed their anxiousness to set up a meeting and thus enabled Stalin to play hard to get. And from the standpoint of convenience, Stalin came off best.

First Cairo Conference

When, on 22 October 1943 Roosevelt told Churchill that the British and American staffs should prepare an overall plan for the defeat of Japan, Churchill, more interested in reaching general agreement on European operations and anxious for joint planning before meeting the Russians, suggested that the chiefs meet 15 November and that he and Roosevelt join them three days later. Replying that he suffered from the "nuisenza of influenza" and that his doctor prescribed a sea voyage to cure him, Roosevelt proposed 20 November in North Africa.[53] When Churchill suggested that he and Roosevelt meet in their battleships at Oran while the staffs worked at Malta, Roosevelt then insisted on a meeting of both staffs and leaders in Cairo beginning 22 November. Churchill accepted Cairo for a conference to begin 20 November.

On 11 November, Roosevelt and the American joint chiefs boarded the *U.S.S. Iowa*, America's newest and largest battleship, for the voyage to Egypt. During the trip, they met several times in the admiral's cabin to discuss a wide range of topics. To avoid the risks and "inevitable losses of American lives and resources involved in a committee control of closely related operations," the joint chiefs requested separate commanders for Overlord and the Mediterranean.[54] Roosevelt proposed partitioning Germany into three, possibly five, smaller states. Staff planners insisted that Soviet collaboration in strategic bombing and agreement on zones of military occupation were the most important issues to discuss with Stalin.

For the Americans, a major purpose of the Cairo Conference was to meet with the Chinese. In the summer of 1943, Roosevelt had cabled Chiang, asking when the Chinese could meet. Any time after September would be possible, Chiang had replied, if he could have a fortnight's notice. On 25 October, Roosevelt suggested to Churchill that they invite the Chinese to join them for two or three days. In cryptic reply, Churchill said that he had the "option on Tutankhamen's tomb" for Chiang.[55] On his part, Chiang told Hurley that he was not willing to meet Stalin. When Roosevelt asked Chiang if he could reach Cairo by 22 November, Chiang agreed, on the condition that Roosevelt meet with him before meeting Stalin.

On 6 October the president had proposed to the British that they invite Russian representatives to the Cairo meeting. Churchill agreed to welcome Molotov and a military staff. When told that the Cairo talks were preparatory for the Big Three meeting, Stalin consented to send Molotov, but, when he learned that the Chinese were invited, he changed his mind. The Russians could hardly participate with the Chinese in planning joint East Asian war operations while Russia was at peace with Japan. On 12 November, Stalin told Roosevelt that he could not send Molotov, due to "some circumstances . . . of a serious character," but that Molotov would accompany him to Iran.[56] Roosevelt concluded somehow that Molotov was ill and sent his best wishes for a speedy recovery.[57]

For the British, who wanted to iron out their differences with the Americans, the presence of neither the Russians nor the Chinese was desirable. The Western allies, Churchill said, should meet both before and after the Big Three conference. Between 20 and 29 October, he worked to win American approval for a full conference, which he proposed to name Sextant, of the combined chiefs. The Russians "ought not to be vexed if the Americans and British closely concert the very great operations they have in hand for 1944. . . ."[58] From HMS *Renown*, which he had boarded on 12 November, Churchill radioed Roosevelt that including the Chinese and Russians might cause grave embarrassment and he refused to "abandon rights to full and frank discussions . . . about the vital business of our intermingled armies."[59]

On 19 November, Roosevelt, saying that his security advisers feared that Cairo was too dangerous because German planes could reach it, suggested moving the site to Khartoum. But Churchill reasoned that a brigade of infantry, eight squadrons of British aircraft at Alexandria, and "upwards of 500 anti-aircraft guns hard by" were sufficient protection. So, he sent this advice: "See Saint John, chapter fourteen, verses one through four," which begins, "Let not your heart be troubled; ye believe in God, believe also in me. . . ."[60]

At least two of the British chiefs expected hard and bitter negotiations with the Americans. In the air en route to Cairo, Chief of the British Imperial General Staff, Sir Alan Brooke (later Lord Alanbrooke) recorded his thoughts: "I wish our conference was over; it will be an unpleasant one, the most unpleasant one we have had yet, and that is saying a good deal."[61] And Hollis wrote that the allies must

> first settle the principle as to whether we are to continue with the "lawyer's agreement" system. The rigidity and complete lack of flexibility in our combined strategy has led to the present situation whereby we are being suspected, if not openly accused, of bad faith and "dishonourable" conduct.[62]

The opening of the conference was festive. Most of the statesmen and beribboned officers had met at previous conferences and their renewal of acquaintances conjured up a scene "like a mixture of Grand Central Station and a college town on the day of a class reunion."[63] By the end of the first day, they had exhausted Cairo's supply of Scotch whisky and were airlifting in new stocks. The prime minister contributed to the early carnival atmosphere by alternating between his zip-up siren suit and a brilliant white sharkskin suit with a ten-gallon cowboy hat.

The arrival of the Chinese entourage caused a sensation. British descriptions of Chiang ranged from "small and wizened" to a "formidable looking ruffian" to looking something like a cross between a pine marten and a ferret.[64] Madame Chiang left an altogether different impression. She had, according to Moran, a "certain cadaverous charm," and Brooke wrote,

> Although not good-looking, she certainly has a good figure which she knew how to display at its best. Gifted with great charm and gracefulness, every small movement of hers arrested and pleased the eye. For instance, at one critical moment her closely clinging black dress of black satin with golden chrysanthemums displayed a slit which exposed one of the most shapely of legs. This caused a rustle amongst some of those attending the conference and I even thought I heard a suppressed neigh come from a group of the younger members![65]

The British were disappointed to find the conference "sadly distracted by the Chinese story, which was lengthy, complicated, and minor."[66] Irritated because the Americans would not meet alone with him, Churchill tried to persuade the Chinese to spend their time viewing Cairo's sights, but to no avail. The result, lamented Churchill, was that the Chinese business occupied first instead of last place, and, according to Ismay, if ever there was a case of putting the cart before the horse, this was it.[67]

Roosevelt wanted to sound out Chiang's views on postwar conditions. For example, he asked Chiang about abolishing the emperor's position in Japan. What form of government, Roosevelt asked, did Chiang think was best suited for Japan? This question, Chiang replied, should be left to the Japanese people to decide after the war.

The Chinese demands were straightforward. Chiang asked the United States to take responsibility for training and equipping ninety divisions, besides delivering 10,000 tons of supplies every month, regardless of consequences to other theaters. And insisting that Burma was the key to the whole campaign in Asia, Chiang called for Buccaneer, a land offensive from India to establish a bridgehead over the Chindwin River, and an airborne landing at Indaw on the railway to Myitkyina to open a road to China. Chiang brought his chief of staff, American General Joseph W. Stilwell, to help him plead China's case.

A Burma campaign might keep China in the war, tie down Japanese forces, and prevent reinforcement of enemy-held islands in the South Pacific. But Buccaneer's main handicap was the disinclination of the British chiefs, especially Churchill, to undertake it, for reasons tangled in the dispute over the second front.[68] Churchill refused to promise that naval operations in the Bay of Bengal would "necessarily be coordinated with and linked to the land campaign in Burma."[69] And Brooke suggested that further discussion be postponed, because the Russians might have something to say about the war in the Pacific.

The Chinese performance at the conference hurt their cause. On 23 November, when Brooke asked the Chinese generals for their views and criticisms of allied planning, there ensued the "most ghastly silence." Eventually, the Chinese replied that they would rather listen. Brooke asked again for Chinese views, suggesting they take twenty-four hours to study the plans. Turning to Marshall after the Chinese left, Brooke whispered, "That was a ghastly waste of time," and Marshall replied, "You're telling me!"[70] Admiral Ernest J. King, commander-in-chief of the fleet and chief of naval operations, considered Brooke's pressure tactics to be quite insulting.[71]

After the Chinese withdrew from the room, the combined chiefs started a heated debate on Buccaneer. The spark was the British suggestion that landing craft be diverted from the Andaman Islands to the Aegean. The Americans, who wanted to withdraw landing craft from the Mediterranean for Overlord, accused the British of forgetting grand strategy in what Arnold described as "quite an open talk with everybody throwing his cards on the table face up."[72] Stilwell recorded that Brooke got nasty, and King got "good and sore," nearly climbing over the table. "God, he was mad," wrote Stilwell, "I wish he had socked him."[73] And Brooke later wrote that history would never forgive the Americans for bargaining equipment against strategy.[74]

But the chiefs dined together that evening in an atmosphere much more pleasant than the afternoon's stormy session. The British and Americans enjoyed an excellent dinner, vintage wines, splendid service, and congenial conversation. The spotlight fell on Brooke, who entertained the chiefs with his rendition of the history of the Knights of Malta.

Meanwhile, Roosevelt threw his support behind Buccaneer and promised the Chinese what Churchill called a "considerable amphibious operation across the Bay of Bengal within the next few months."[75] Churchill, flabbergasted at this decision, threw aside tact and prudence and argued vehemently, but Roosevelt stood firm.[76]

China figured prominently in Roosevelt's plans for the postwar world. On 23 November, in a private meeting with Chiang, Roosevelt offered to recognize China as one of the Big Four. The reason for such an offer is unclear. Perhaps the president wanted to stimulate greater Chinese efforts against Japan, or, less likely, he may have anticipated the day when China would be a political heavyweight and wished to win Chiang's good graces beforehand. The Chinese, said Roosevelt, should receive reparation in kind for war damages and the restoration of territories, including the northeastern provinces of China, Taiwan, the Pescadores Islands, and the Liaotung Peninsula with its two ports, Dairen and Port Arthur. Moreover, he suggested that the Ryukyu Islands be placed under joint Sino-American trusteeship.

The British were more successful when discussion turned toward the second front. They had earlier presented a detailed memorandum outlining preconditions on Overlord. Four days of fine weather must precede the landing, and air operations required a full moon. During Overlord's first month, some eighteen divisions must be landed and twelve more the second month. The British concluded that the target date should be "in the middle of June to allow for a postponement of twenty-four days in case weather conditions are unsuitable."[77] From American Ambassador to Britain John G. Winant the Americans learned that the British did not intend to abandon Overlord, but they opposed a fixed date, in spite of the Quebec decision that had named 1 May 1944.[78] Summarizing the British case, Ismay insisted that "major developments" warranted "consideration of adjustments of, if not actual departures from" the Quadrant decisions and that the target date should not "become our master."[79] While Overlord remained at the top of allied plans, said Churchill later, it should not be such a tyrant as to rule out other activities in the Mediterranean.[80]

The Americans were uneasy about the latest Overlord developments.

While not particularly shocked to find the British trying to wriggle out of the arrangements, they were troubled when they received reports that Russian enthusiasm for the cross-channel invasion had cooled. The possibility that Stalin might shift the focus of the allied effort to the Mediterranean and "indications of a hardening British attitude" raised the nightmarish vision that Russia and Britain might join together to abort Overlord.[81]

On 26 November the chiefs debated strategic planning. Brooke and Marshall had the "father and mother of a row" over the best way to win the war, but the chiefs resorted to an off-the-record discussion and began to make progress toward agreement.[82] However, Brooke insisted that Buccaneer would only be possible provided Overlord's date was put back. Retreating, Leahy stated that the Americans did "not attach vital importance to any particular date or to any particular number of divisions in the assault and follow up."[83]

But the Americans rejected British proposals to draft a joint program for the upcoming conference with Stalin. It would be unfortunate, said Harriman, to give Stalin the impression that the Americans and British were "arriving at the conference with anything approximating a cut and dried plan." The correct approach, Harriman insisted, was "perfect frankness and a willingness to weigh thoughtfully any proposals made by the Soviets."[84] A disappointed Churchill noted that the Cairo talks did not lead, as he had hoped, to a broad Anglo-American agreement.

Moreover, the British and Americans disagreed about the command structure for their invasion of Europe. Assuming that the British plan to appoint separate commanders in the Mediterranean and northwest Europe had already been accepted, Churchill reacted strongly on 25 November to an American memorandum recommending a "supreme figure who would not only plan and conduct the war in both theaters, but move the forces from one to the other as he might think best."[85] After discussion, Churchill remained under the impression that Marshall would command Overlord, that Eisenhower would become American chief of staff, and that General Harold Alexander would command the Mediterranean. According to Brooke, however, the discussion was inconclusive.[86]

Relations were easier during dinner meetings, such as the one on Thanksgiving Day, when Roosevelt invited Churchill to join the American table where two large turkeys with the trimmings were served. The president, propped up high in his chair, carved for all. "This jolly evening," wrote Churchill, "and the spectacle of the president carving up the turkeys stand out in my mind among the most agreeable features of the halt at Cairo."[87] Indeed, the atmosphere was relaxed; the speeches warm and intimate. Roosevelt later told a reporter that the evening was the most enjoyable he had spent in a long time.[88]

When photographs were taken of the delegations, the smiles and staged friendliness were not entirely wholesome. Standing and sitting about for hours, reported Eden, was a "desperate waste of time," and the combined delegations, to Brooke's eye, were "not a very attractive lot to look at!"[89] When chairs were set up on the lawn, Roosevelt offered the center seat to Chiang, who modestly declined and insisted that the president take it. Oddly, complained one of the Britishers, no one seemed to think of asking Churchill.[90]

The First Cairo Conference left behind a sour taste. The British and Americans made a poor job of bridging their differences on strategic planning. Perhaps the Americans hoped, by playing their China card and threatening to expand operations in the Pacific, to dislodge the British on the second front issue. Instead, they further postponed an already long-overdue final decision on Overlord and the Mediterranean. Indeed, the British were stirred to stiffen their resolve, and the Americans seemed to retreat on a fixed date for Overlord. Resentments and misunderstandings were bound to carry over to Tehran.

3

BRINGING THE BIG THREE TOGETHER

> If you don't know what you are going to say tomorrow, it's
> too late. . . .
>
> —John G. Winant

The Americans, Roosevelt told Stalin, could arrive in Tehran during the afternoon of 29 November if that would be convenient for the Russians. When Stalin replied that he planned to be "at the disposal of his allies" by the evening of 28 November, Roosevelt announced that the Americans would plan to arrive in Tehran on 27 November.[1] Perhaps Stalin wanted to reach Tehran first to give the impression that he was the host, because, without informing his allies, he changed his plans to arrive on 26 November.

No advance decision was made regarding how long the conference would last. The British and Americans were accustomed to lengthy meetings, but Stalin had emphasized repeatedly that he could not leave Moscow for a protracted period of time. When Roosevelt offered to stay four days, Stalin did not reply. Churchill, apparently, did not expect or request a fixed timetable.

Lying on an extensive upland plateau south of the snowcapped Elburz Mountains, Tehran mixed old and new, traditional bazaars and modern shops, burros and Lend-Lease trucks, dirt sidewalks and paved wide streets. To many, the city left a great deal to be desired. Standley described it as "whitely beautiful," but only from the air and a distance.[2] Closer inspection revealed that it was "unsuitable in almost every particular."[3] Shop windows were crammed with Persian silks and rugs, Scotch tweeds and whisky, French perfumes and vermouth, English cloth, American toilet articles, Swiss watches, and German gadgets, but Tehran was also "dirt, filth, all kinds of humanity, walking, talking, and jabbering."[4] To Harriman, Tehran was an interesting sight with beautiful mosques and not "unduly dirty to anyone used to the East."[5]

Travel Arrangements

As he had planned, Marshal Stalin was the first to arrive. The first leg of his journey was by luxury train from Moscow to the Crimea. Previously, he had refused to entrust his life to the skill of a pilot, but, at Baku, he transferred to an airplane for his first flight. Original plans called for Stalin's plane to be piloted by a lieutenant general, while the "lesser mortals would go in one with a mere colonel at the controls," but Stalin chose to go with the colonel because lieutenant generals did not get much flying practice. Three fighter squadrons escorted his plane to Gale Morghe airport on the outskirts of Tehran.[6]

Upon arrival, the Russians took up residence in the Russian embassy compound. The embassy was in an old and scenic park in the heart of Tehran, and the grounds had many pools, gardens, and rose bushes. Surrounded by bronze-leaved sycamores, the main building was a massive, yellow square, box-like structure dominated by a portico with white Doric columns.[7] "Not so hot from the outside," sniffed Major John D. Boettiger, Roosevelt's son-in-law.[8] But inside the rooms and the conference hall were of "noble proportions."[9] Above all, the Russian embassy was an armed fortress. Encompassed on all sides by a high stone wall, the compound looked like a feudal castle. Troops and plain-clothes policemen blanketed the grounds and stood double guard at every gate.

Accompanying Stalin was Molotov, who "talked a lot and said very little" and did nothing without Stalin's prior consent.[10] Representing the Russian military was Supervisor of the State Committee for Defense, Marshal Kliment E. Voroshilov, who was known as one of Stalin's "old stooges, incompetent but not dangerous."[11] Chief of the General Staff, Marshal Alexander M. Vasilevsky, did not make the trip, nor did any representative of Russian naval or air forces. Two interpreters, Ivan Pavlov and Valentin Berezhkov, completed the streamlined Russian delegation.

Churchill strained his voice in Cairo arguing with the Americans; he "talked from 8:30 till 1:35" on 26 November, and "then expressed surprise at having a sore throat!"[12] On 27 November, Eden found the prime minister feeling sorry for himself, until he had finished a stiff whisky and soda. Dressed in an air commodore's khaki drill uniform, Churchill boarded a York for the flight to Tehran, changing into blues during the trip. After an easy journey that revived Churchill's spirits, the plane landed at Amirabad airport in the early afternoon, to be followed shortly by the chiefs and other members of the party.

The British delegation was considerably larger than the Russian party. Besides Brooke, First Sea Lord Sir Andrew Cunningham, and Ismay, the British military chiefs included Field Marshal Sir John Dill; Chief of the Air Staff, Air Marshal Sir Charles Portal; Chief of the British Military Mission to Moscow, General Sir Giffard Martel; and Hollis. Diplomatic personnel included Eden; Cadogan; Clark-Kerr; British Security Chief, Commander Walter H. Thompson; Moran; interpreter Arthur H. Birse; and two of the prime minister's children, Sarah Churchill Oliver and Captain Randolph Churchill. The latter were appointed to serve as aides to the prime minister.

Churchill was nearly as security conscious as Stalin. During the planning, the prime minister had proposed that several days prior to the meeting the British and Russians each throw a brigade around the city and maintain a cordon until after the Big Three departed. But Stalin rejected the idea on the ground that Churchill's plan would give advance notice of their meeting. The Russians, added Stalin, were perfectly capable of providing adequate security. Nevertheless, Churchill did not trust the host country, did not want Iranian officials to be told of the meeting until immediately before the allies arrived, and assigned protection of the British embassy to his own troops.

The necessity of driving through Tehran's narrow alleys and streets bothered the British. Congestion could slow even normal traffic to a crawl, and British security agents noted that many buildings overhung the streets, giving potential snipers numerous vantage points. To protect the prime minister and deliver him safely to the embassy, the British devised a ruse. The surprised Eden was "instructed to get into a car and drive off on [his] own."[13] Accompanied by a cavalcade, Eden's car was supposed to draw attention. Near the embassy gates, a Persian cart and stubborn donkey blocked the way, while the police tried, at first with little success, to clear the path. Waiting in his car, Eden realized that he was a sitting duck, until the donkey finally moved and the procession swept inside the embassy wall.

Meanwhile, the prime minister traveled from the airport another way. Persian cavalrymen stationed every fifty yards for at least three miles clearly marked the road. A police car with a blaring siren preceded the car that carried him, Sarah, and the British Minister to Iran, Sir Reader Bullard. Churchill later remarked that if his security men had "planned out beforehand to run the greatest risks and have neither the security of quiet surprise nor an effective escort," they could not have done it more perfectly.[14] A crowd of inquisitive natives pressed to within a few feet of the car and blocked the entrance to the embassy. Many of them were almost close enough to touch Churchill, and some were "knocked away" by the British.[15] Extremely angry with the whole procedure, Churchill did not breathe easily until they were safely inside the gates.[16]

The embassy was an imposing building in the middle of a garden with tall, russet and yellow trees. But Ismay, unimpressed, called it a "ramshackle house," and Sarah, shivering in the embassy's dark rooms, called it "cold and cheerless."[17] With bushes and thick shrubbery growing up to the back wall, it was, recalled a British guard, a security officer's nightmare and an assassin's delight.[18]

Nearly eighty Americans went to Iran. The delegation included the joint chiefs—Marshall, King, Arnold, and Leahy. Also accompanying the president were his military aides, Major General Edwin M. Watson and Rear Admiral Wilson Brown, his assistant naval aide, Lieutenant (j.g.) William M. Rigdon, Hopkins, Winant, Hurley, McIntire, Secret Serviceman Michael F. Reilly, and interpreter Charles Bohlen. Like Churchill, Roosevelt took family members to the conference. Besides Boettiger, the president's son, Colonel Elliott Roosevelt, joined the delegation.

Heavy fog kept the Americans grounded beyond their scheduled 4:30 A.M. 27 November lift-off. Shortly after 7:00 A.M., American transport planes with fighter escorts climbed into the morning skies beginning the 1,310-mile flight. King and Arnold rode in one plane, Marshall in another, the president, Hopkins, Leahy, and Harriman in a third, while a fourth transport was crammed with secret service agents.[19]

Over Palestine, the president asked his pilot, Major Otis Bryan, to circle Jerusalem twice to give the passengers a good view. Someone commented that the "promised land" was mostly desert and that when Moses had seen it from a mountain top, he had "committed suicide rather than face the disappointments of such an arid land."[20] During the six-and-a-half hour flight, Harriman and Hopkins discussed a plan for postwar American aid to Russia, but the specific details of that conversation have been lost.

The Americans arrived about 3:00 P.M. at Gale Morghe, with little fanfare. While an elaborate escort of armed cars shielded a dummy presidential caravan, Roosevelt went "quite unguarded" another way, by "utterly unpredictable streets and byways."[21] According to one report, the president's car was driven "wildly" through the city, while a considerable force of armored vehicles followed some distance behind.[22] The Americans arrived without having to run a gauntlet of inquisitive Iranians, and Churchill praised the Americans for exercising better judgment than his own security forces.

The accommodations at Tehran were "so very limited" that neither the Americans nor the British could be housed adequately at a single, convenient location.[23] Numerous residents of Tehran were forced to make room for uninvited guests. Some Americans were farmed out to the homes of the Minister to Iran, Louis G. Dreyfus, and the Commanding General of the United States Persian Gulf Command, Major General Donald H. Connolly. Other Americans went to Camp Parker, headquarters of the Persian Gulf Command, about six miles northwest of the city. The cramped and uncomfortable rooms at the American legation were reserved for Roosevelt's use.[24]

Protecting the president while he stayed at the American legation concerned many Americans. Hurley had set up security arrangements on 24 November. Reilly had also inspected the legation before Roosevelt's arrival, and, reviewing the situation on 27 November, concluded that everything possible had been done to ensure Roosevelt's safety.

According to Sarah Churchill Oliver, her father was no sooner installed in his quarters than Roosevelt tried to arrange a private meeting. The British are supposed to have replied that the Americans had missed their chance at Cairo. And Winant chipped in, "If you don't know what you are going to say tomorrow, it's too late anyway." Besides, the prime minister was trying to recover his voice before the plenary meetings, so he retreated to bed, surrounded himself with hot water bottles, and read *Oliver Twist* until midnight.[25]

A different story is contained in Boettiger's diary. Having noted Churchill's throat problems, Hopkins called the British embassy and inquired about the prime minister's health. When the British would not give him a direct answer, Hopkins angrily hung up the telephone and cursed the "stuffy" British.[26]

More interested in talking with the Russians than with Churchill, the president actually tried to arrange a dinner meeting with Stalin. Several emissaries rushed to the Soviet embassy and they returned with both surprising and disappointing news, the former that Stalin had arrived earlier than he had informed Roosevelt, and, the latter, that the dinner invitation had been turned down on the rather flimsy pretext that Stalin was too tired.

Housing Problems

When Roosevelt had written to Stalin about housing and security in Tehran, he asked, "Where do you think we should live?"[27] Stalin replied that the Russian embassy was roomy and comfortable and the Americans could stay there if they wished. Its nearness to the British embassy, he said, would make communications easier during the conference. At about the same time, Churchill offered accommodations at the British embassy.[28]

But Roosevelt declined both offers. He told Rigdon that he wanted to be "more independent than a guest can hope to be."[29] Informing Stalin that he did not wish to choose one ally over the other, he politely but firmly said he would stay at the American legation. When the Russians reminded Hurley of the invitation, Roosevelt's trouble-shooter replied that the decision to use the American legation was final, because plans could not be changed on short notice. But he had one of his aides inspect the Russian quarters just in case.

From the beginning, Roosevelt had wanted to establish a friendship with Stalin. What better way to show his trust than to live in the same building with him under Russian security? Churchill's invitation made it difficult to accept Stalin's offer, but Roosevelt encouraged Stalin to keep trying. Hurley told the Russians that the president might be able to accept if they persisted, and, on the evening of 27 November, Roosevelt sent Brown to the Russian embassy to sound out the Russians. But, reported Boettiger, a "rat-faced *chargé d'affaires*" would not even confirm that Stalin was in Tehran, following an exchange that left Brown "testy."[30] Nevertheless, when Harriman called on Molotov to explain that it might create "some feeling on the part of the British should he go to one place rather than the other," Molotov replied that the Russian facilities would remain available if Roosevelt changed his mind, "or if difficulties arose."[31]

Stalin was apparently as eager as Roosevelt to work out something. Perhaps the marshal feared a united Anglo-American diplomatic front, suspected his allies of working to limit Russian gains, and wanted to keep Roosevelt from close contact with the British. Any such fears might have been allayed had he known the full extent of the gap between the British and Americans on military and diplomatic issues. Possibly he felt that having the president as his guest would give him some advantage. The most likely explanation is that Stalin was concerned about tightening the security arrangements.

When Iran's twenty-four-year-old Shah, Mohammed Reza Shah Pahlavi, learned, almost after the fact, that the Big Three would meet in his capital city, he was jubilant. But the allies rejected his gestures of hospitality. Conscious of the president's security, Americans declined the Shah's offer to meet Roosevelt at the airport. And when he offered Golistan Palace in Tehran as guest quarters for his distinguished visitors, Roosevelt replied that the American legation was adequate to meet his needs.[32]

However, Roosevelt spent only one night, 27 November, in his legation. Harriman, who had opposed the president's staying there, called the legation "utterly inadequate."[33] It was at least half a mile distant from the British and Russian embassies, which were "cheek by jowl."[34] Between the British and Russian embassies was a narrow alley with high walls that could be sealed off. But, if they went to the American legation, Churchill and Stalin would have to travel dangerous streets two or three times each day.

The British facilities were not large enough to house both Churchill's retinue and Roosevelt's party. The embassy did not even have sufficient space for the entire British delegation. When Harriman asked the British if they had any spare room, Churchill admitted that his quarters were crowded.[35] So, the British embassy could hardly accommodate additional guests. This makes Churchill's invitation all the more curious.

When Hurley personally inspected the Russian embassy, he found that what the Russians had to offer was impressive. He saw a suite of rooms with a large reception or assembly room, four smaller rooms that could be used as bedrooms, one large bedroom with an adjoining bath for the president, a large dining room, and a spacious conference room. The suite contained two baths, the same number available in the entire American legation. Probably alone in Tehran, the Russian embassy was steam-heated to ward off the chill of Iran's cold nights. The only work needed was to install the special bath facilities the president required. Hurley reported that the Russians "most cordially" solicited the president's acceptance and that he had given them a list of the necessary furnishings.[36]

Near midnight on 27 November, Molotov asked Harriman and Clark-

Kerr to meet him immediately at the Russian embassy. There, Molotov informed them that the Russians had uncovered a plot—German agents in Tehran had learned of Roosevelt's presence and were making plans for action that was likely to take the form of an assassination attempt on one or more of the Big Three while they were in transit between meetings. Three would-be assassins had been apprehended, said Molotov, but others remained at large. Thus, the security of the Big Three was at stake, and the allies would have to take appropriate countermeasures.[37]

Concerned that the possibility of assassination was "very real," Harriman pressed Molotov "within the limits of civility for details, but nothing of importance was forthcoming." Assuming that the president would be safer if he stayed at the Russian embassy, Harriman inspected the rooms set aside for Roosevelt and found them "over-elaborate and ugly," but comfortable and well arranged.[38]

Earlier in the day, Molotov had agreed to hold all meetings of the conference at the American legation, due to the difficulties that attended any move of the president. Therefore, Churchill and Stalin really had the most to fear from any German assassins on the loose. When Eden learned about the plot, he urged the Americans to move, and Stalin asked Roosevelt to choose between the two embassies.

Although Tehran had long been a center for German intelligence activities, the manner and timing of Molotov's revelation suggested a contrived story. Roosevelt apparently never believed the threat was real.[39] Also, Harriman bluntly asked Molotov if he had dreamed up the story. The Russians, replied Molotov evasively, knew about the presence of German agents in the city, and Stalin believed that all three of the allied leaders would be safer if Roosevelt moved to the Russian embassy.[40]

At least Molotov was telling the truth when he said that the Germans wanted to assassinate the Big Three. In August 1943, the head of the German secret police, Heinrich Himmler, had interviewed numerous magicians and self-styled mystics who tried by various means to discern where and when the Big Three would meet. The Germans were able to glean some details from the Western press, whose editors "fell all over themselves in a sort of front page strip tease in trying to let the customers in on the news without actually coming out with it."[41] By 21 November, *New York Times* correspondent James B. Reston reported from London that German radio had announced the upcoming summit conference.[42] From various sources, German leaders learned that the Big Three would meet in Tehran in late November or early December, and they may have set in motion an assassination plan named Operation Long Pounce.[43] But nothing materialized.

Some Americans, suspecting that the Russians had concocted the assassination story, wanted Roosevelt to stay in the American legation. But, in an early morning message on 28 November, Stalin emphasized the distance separating the president from the others and urged him to move closer. Security matters, he added, would be greatly eased if travel through the streets could be avoided. Staying at the legation, Reilly observed, would mean assuming unnecessary risks. Harriman warned that the Americans would be held responsible if anything happened to Churchill or Stalin, and Leahy advised heeding the Russian appeal, whether or not the plot was genuine.[44] When Roosevelt asked if it mattered which embassy he chose, Reilly replied that the security angle was the same for both, and Roosevelt decided to accept the Russian offer.[45]

When the British learned Roosevelt was moving to the Russian embassy, some of them suspected an anti-British conspiracy. Cadogan scoffed at the Russian claim to have unearthed a plot, and Moran, fearful that the British had been outwitted, perceived Stalin's apparent desire to have Roosevelt "under his eye, where he cannot spend his time plotting" with the British.[46] But Churchill informed Hopkins that he was "quite agreeable to having the president reside with Stalin." Churchill commented afterwards that he "strongly supported Molotov" in his appeals to Roosevelt to move inside the Russian compound, which was "three or four times as big as the others, and stood in extensive grounds, now ringed by Soviet troops and police," and he took credit for prevailing upon Roosevelt to accept the Russian offer.[47] The British recognized that convenience and security would be enhanced by having Roosevelt move, that the only logical choice was the Russian embassy, and that the Americans must accept. We "had the great satisfaction," wrote Ismay, "of telling the Americans that if they did not move the president to join the others, they would be assuming responsibility for the lives of both Stalin and the Prime Minister. This did the trick. . . ."[48]

Roosevelt moved to his new quarters in the early afternoon of 28 November. Even if the Americans could line the entire route with soldiers, Reilly feared, "half a dozen fanatics with the courage to jump from airplanes could probably figure out some way to get in a shot."[49] Secret Service Agent Robert Holmes rode in Roosevelt's place to accept the cheers of the local citizens.[50] Roosevelt then joined Hopkins, Leahy, and Boettiger in an army staff car that went another way.[51]

Having enjoyed his adventure immensely, the president arrived at his new residence in fine fettle. A "stiff-necked Russian lieutenant general," said Boettiger, ushered the Americans to the main embassy building about one hundred and fifty yards from the smaller house where Stalin stayed.[52] "After cleaning out part of an accumulation of dirt that must have been collecting for months or years," they arranged reasonably comfortable accommodations about which Roosevelt offered no complaints.[53]

If Roosevelt intended to show trust in Stalin, the move to the Russian embassy was perfect. He not only placed his life in the hands of Russian troops, but he also placed his daily activities under the close inspection of servants who were really secret policemen. Ismay described the president as being under the Russian microscope and wondered if the Russians had installed microphones so they could hear as well as see what he was doing.[54] But Harriman insisted that the Russians had no reason to bug the president's rooms.[55]

The Russians went through the motions of disguising the servants' true identities, but no one was fooled. They dressed in ordinary street clothes, but observers noted a suspicious bulge on their hips that could only have been caused by their "fairly heavy artillery."[56] Reilly, who watched Roosevelt whether or not Russian guards were present, was amused to see brutes in lackeys' white coats "busily polishing immaculate glass or dusting dustless furniture."[57] Unconcerned about who his servants were, Roosevelt was disappointed that they either could not or would not talk to him.[58]

The Russian embassy was the center of the world while the Big Three met there. According to one estimate, more than three thousand secret policemen, mostly Russian, guarded it.[59] Within one five-block area, an observer counted seventy-two Russians armed with tommy guns, while armored cars and tanks nosed about the city, and guards with guns at the ready patrolled the streets.[60] One high-ranking British officer, who attempted unsuccessfully to enter the embassy without a pass, was heard to mutter, "This is the most bloody guarded place I've ever seen."[61] Here the Big Three could give their undivided attention to the problems that had brought them together.

4

RAISING THE CURTAIN

We were very worried with the whole situation. We have
not got agreement with the Americans on the main points
for discussion, and it was evident that we were heading
towards chaos.

—Lord Alanbrooke

That the Big Three talks took place in a hectic and disorganized fashion was
partly attributable to the failure to follow a structured agenda. In the early
planning stages, Roosevelt had referred vaguely to subjects that might be
raised "in a tentative way" if a meeting was arranged.[1] He merely suggested
the need to discuss how to invade the continent, when German forces in
France weakened. Churchill was not much more specific. "We must decide
at the earliest moment," he wrote, "the best way of attacking Germany in
Europe with all possible force in 1943," and, on 12 November, suggested
covering the "whole field of the war."[2]

The Russians tried with little success to get a definite agenda. At first,
Stalin defined the purpose of a Big Three summit as simply to establish a
common strategic line, but, by the time of the Anglo-American Quebec
Conference, he was calling for representatives to meet first to draw up an
agenda. Churchill agreed in principle to accept Eden's advice to respond
quickly, but he did nothing more.[3] According to Harriman, the Russians
wanted to make sure that the second front was at the top of the list.[4] Indeed,
on 2 October 1943, Russian *chargé d'affaires* Andrei A. Gromyko gave
Secretary of State Hull a note emphasizing the need to discuss the second
front and calling for the Americans to fix the agenda. But, on 16 November,
when Molotov asked about the agenda, Harriman put him off. The president's conferences with Churchill were informal, said Harriman, and Molotov should not expect a formal agenda at Tehran.[5]

But at the staff level, the Anglo-Americans devoted considerable attention
to the agenda. At Cairo, the American chiefs proposed that their objective
should be to determine an "over-all strategic concept for the prosecution of
the war," with emphasis upon the European-Mediterranean theater.[6] The

British countered that the first priority was to settle Southeast Asian problems, then turn to Overlord and the Mediterranean.

A tentative military agenda emerged from meetings of the combined chiefs of staff. In Marshall's view, the Russians would demand immediate relief on the eastern front, in which case the West would be well-advised to have a plan ready. After discussion, the chiefs accepted a proposed agenda that listed in order of importance subjects to cover with the Russians: coordination of Russian operations with Anglo-American offensives, the prospects and implications of Turkish participation in the war, the need to improve and increase the flow of Lend-Lease, strategic bombing, and Japan. In an addendum, the chiefs proposed to take up shuttle bombing, air transport routes, and weather information. But, they concluded, "Because the military problems to be considered would arise from the political discussions which would be held at the start of the [Big Three] conference," they were therefore relieved of setting the agenda.[7]

On one issue, Roosevelt and Churchill agreed. Both sought to avoid prior commitments on the Polish problem, bound to be a major dispute. In late 1943, Soviet propaganda against the Polish government-in-exile had intensified. On 19 November, Polish Prime Minister Stanislaw Mikolajczyk asked to meet Roosevelt and Churchill prior to Tehran, but neither was willing to grant this request, perhaps because they did not want to run the risk of antagonizing Stalin, or because they wished to postpone dealing with this complicated subject. On 20 November, Mikolajczyk offered to meet Roosevelt anywhere between Washington and Tehran, but Roosevelt refused. Two days later the Polish leader approached Eden, who explained that the Tehran conference "was to be a military one, but I hoped that there might be an opportunity to discuss Polish problems. All I asked was that the Polish Government should not prevent us from raising the question if I got the chance. I would do my best, though the Polish Government should not expect too much from the conference."[8]

When, on the evening of 27 November, Molotov asked for a draft agenda, the Anglo-Americans had none to give him. The Americans steadfastly refused to produce a formal paper, but the British seemed willing to meet the Russian request, and there followed a "lot of argument which was none too civil."[9] Cadogan became angry when Harriman lectured "on how to conduct international conferences, and how they usually developed," since Cadogan believed that he had "forgotten a great deal more about that than [Harriman] ever knew."[10] In turn, Harriman was disgusted with the British, who "caved in on the idea of an agenda and began scurrying around trying to suggest one."[11]

Having no agenda suited Roosevelt perfectly. Despite favorable postwar accounts reputing that he spent long hours studying briefing papers and maps before his first tripartite summit, the president tended to rely upon snap judgment diplomacy.[12] Improvisation, not thorough and detailed preparation, was Roosevelt's trademark. So, "No one was in charge of organizing meetings, setting up schedules, or handling any of the numerous technical preparations."[13] Perhaps the president wanted the Big Three talks to follow a natural course. Yet, because he made, in fact, minimal preparations for the issues that might reasonably be expected to arise, the conference was bound to be "quite informal and somewhat disorganized."[14]

Staff Meetings

On the eve of the conference, British and American military staffs held separate meetings to put their proposals and strategies in final form. Here, they expressed their truest sentiments and convictions. And here they set the goals by which the success of their subsequent diplomacy should be judged. Their staff meetings were crucially important, but, unfortunately, neither memoirs nor minutes have preserved much more than an outline of the subjects covered.

On 28 November, the British chiefs—Brooke (Chair), Portal, Dill, Cunningham, Ismay—and a secretariat of Hollis and Brigadier Harold Redman met at 10:30 A.M. in the British embassy to work out a strategy for reconciling British and American differences. When the chiefs learned that "an undertaking had been given by the president to [Chiang Kai-shek] that Buccaneer would take place," they selected Ismay to address a note to Churchill setting out their objections.[15] They drafted a memorandum to the effect that "on all other points," except Buccaneer, agreement in principle seemed to have been reached.[16] The British could argue that Buccaneer should be dropped because it interfered with Overlord's timetable, or they could offer to accept it in exchange for Mediterranean concessions, but, when the chiefs tried to convince Churchill to adopt the latter strategy, he decided to handle Buccaneer separately.

The meeting, which lasted until lunch, confirmed Brooke's apprehensions. The chiefs might decide whatever they pleased, but the key was how to win over Churchill and then the Americans. At the end, recorded Brooke, "We were very worried with the whole situation. We have not got agreement with the Americans on the main points for discussion, and it was evident that we were heading towards chaos. P.M. has bad throat and has practically lost his voice. He is not fit and consequently not in the best of moods."[17]

Meanwhile, Roosevelt and the American joint chiefs of staff met at 11:30 A.M. in the American legation. The bulk of the meeting was devoted to a discussion of what the Americans expected the Russians and British to demand at the conference table. Some feared that the former would support

British proposals for action in the Mediterranean by appealing for immediate relief on the eastern front, either by intensifying the campaign in Italy or by an Anglo-American invasion of the Balkans. And they expected the British to raise now familiar objections to Overlord.

Roosevelt raised several issues related to the Italian front. The British would probably argue, he said, that the Anglo-American forces in Italy should be committed to reaching the Pisa-Rimini line well to the north of Rome, but this would demand an increased effort to break an existing stalemate. Even assuming a successful campaign, forcing the Germans to retire behind the Alps, what would it cost? The allies could put all their energies into Overlord and ensure a successful landing, or they could concentrate on Italy, but not both. Thus, the "major military question" was to determine whether the British would abide by their commitment to Overlord.[18]

Advancing in Italy, even to the Ancona line (south of Florence), would delay Overlord until the middle of June or even July 1944, but the picture would improve if the allies dropped the British plan to seize Rhodes. Roosevelt suspected the British would "probably say after Rhodes was taken, 'Now we will have to take Greece.'" Next, Americans would be asked to liberate Turkey and so on, until they were hopelessly entangled in the Balkans and far from bringing the Germans to decisive battle. Operations in the eastern Mediterranean, he said, could not be undertaken before February, would be time-consuming, and the "means which would be sucked in" would be considerable.[19]

On the whole, the Americans did not agree with the British argument that the capture of Rhodes would convince Turkey to enter the war, or even that Turkish participation would be an unmixed blessing. Despite the allure of opening another route for delivery of Lend-Lease materiel, the Straits could not be secured as quickly as the British suggested. British emphasis on Turkey was based upon the hopeful assumption that Bulgaria and Rumania would desert the Axis if Turkey declared war. And the British were mesmerized by the prospect of using Turkish air bases to bomb Axis targets in the eastern Mediterranean. Without explanation, Roosevelt said that he did not "have the conscience to urge the Turks to go into the war."[20]

The president asked what could be done if the Russians requested British and American action against the twenty-one German divisions in the Balkans. From the subsequent discussion, there emerged a consensus that the West should support the Partisans, rather than the Chetniks, in Yugoslavia with equipment, but not with manpower. The Americans decided to accept no commitment beyond small-scale commando raids.

What about the Pacific theater? Churchill would undoubtedly use every wile to cut out Buccaneer in favor of Rhodes, but the Americans decided to uphold their Cairo pledge to drive the Japanese out of Burma. Moreover, control of the Andaman Islands would make it possible to isolate Bangkok, said Roosevelt, and, in any event, the allies had given their word. However, landing craft would have to be found somewhere, thus putting further pressure on the already limited resources available for European operations.

The Americans affirmed their commitment to Overlord as the primary operation for 1944. Nothing should be permitted to delay it, and the combined logistical demands of Overlord and Buccaneer would not leave sufficient reserves to carry out Churchill's Mediterranean projects. Marshall suspected that the British would use "committeeism" to diminish the importance of all theaters except the Mediterranean by referring everything objectionable to *ad hoc* committees, where plans, at best, would be delayed and, at worst, shuffled off into oblivion. The Russians, doubtless interested in casting the deciding vote in this debate, definitely wanted something from their allies, and the Americans should "find out what it is," concluded Marshall, who wondered, "what do the Soviets mean by immediate help?"[21]

Roosevelt's Private Meeting with Stalin

On 28 November at 3:00 P.M., shortly after Roosevelt had completed his change of quarters, Stalin, with Molotov, Pavlov, and the omnipresent Russian guards, walked across the grounds of the compound to the embassy sitting room. There, Roosevelt, flanked by pictures of Lenin and Stalin, waited on a small couch. Stalin wore a long slate blue camel's hair military overcoat, a visored cap, and a uniform with broad red stripes down the sides of his trousers; the president wore a gray business suit.

Roosevelt had planned the seating to place Stalin by his "good ear."[22] Greeting Stalin, the president said, "I am glad to see you. I have tried for a long time to bring this about."[23] According to one version, the opening was different, with Stalin welcoming Roosevelt to Soviet territory, thus prompting a cheerful reply: "I protest," laughed Roosevelt. "We firmly agreed to meet on neutral territory. Besides, this is my residence, so it's you who are my guest."[24]

Who was present, besides the Big Two? According to some accounts, Roosevelt met Stalin without his own interpreter, as a gesture of his willingness to trust the Russians.[25] Other witnesses claimed that Bohlen was present on every occasion when Stalin and Roosevelt were together.[26] Reilly could not say one way or the other, because he professed to have spent his time exchanging rude stares with Stalin's security men.[27]

Roosevelt opened the discussion by gently probing into the status of the Russo-German front. Westerners knew that the Russians were advancing gradually on the Germans, but they lacked any specific details. The underlying question seems clear enough: how close were the Russians to beating

Germany? Stalin described the eastern front in somewhat gloomy terms. The Russians had lost the region around Zhitomir, they were about to lose Koresten, and the overall initiative, except in the Ukraine, was uncertain. He blamed unfavorable weather and the German ability to bring a new group of divisions into combat, perhaps a reminder that the Western allies were lax in holding up their share of the fighting. Roosevelt tried to console Stalin by wishing that it were "within his power to bring about the removal of thirty or forty German divisions" from the eastern front.[28] Stalin agreed heartily that this was a good thing if possible, and Roosevelt assured him that it was one of the primary issues to be discussed in the plenary sessions to follow.[29]

Roosevelt changed the subject. The end of the war might well produce a surplus of shipping that could be made available to the Soviet Union, giving the Russians an "opportunity to start developing commercial shipping."[30] Stalin graciously accepted the president's offer and predicted an improvement in Soviet-American relations. In turn, Russia would supply raw materials and become a "big market for the United States after the war."[31]

Turning to the Far East, Roosevelt said that he had enjoyed an interesting discussion with Chiang Kai-shek at Cairo. America was vitally concerned about China and had trained thirty Chinese divisions, with an additional thirty to be armed as time permitted. According to Roosevelt, the Chinese wanted to end British control of Chinese ports and to acquire a Russian guarantee of the Sino-Soviet frontier. Ignoring such issues, Stalin replied that he was deeply concerned about China's participation in the war. Claiming that Chiang's troops were not fighting well, Stalin blamed the leadership. On his part, Roosevelt neglected to tell Stalin about the promise to launch Buccaneer, which would require landing craft and therefore limit what the West might do in Europe.

Following the brief exchange on the Far East, Stalin, to Roosevelt's apparent surprise, inquired about recent events in French-controlled Lebanon, where French refusal of Lebanese demands for immediate independence had led to a revolt, prompting French suppression. The president said that the disturbance had been mishandled, and he blamed General Charles De Gaulle, president of the French Committee of National Liberation, for having exercised poor judgment and squandering force against a friendly nation when the real enemy was Germany.

Admitting that he did not know De Gaulle personally, Stalin nevertheless described the Frenchman as "very unreal in his political activities."[32] De Gaulle, claimed Stalin, was not representative of the majority of Frenchmen, who had submitted without resistance to the humiliation of a German occupation. Roosevelt interrupted to say that Stalin would probably not like De Gaulle much more in person.[33] The French problem, continued Stalin, was that De Gaulle acted "as though he were the head of a great state," when he actually commanded little power.[34] Stalin contrasted what he called the

5

FIRST PLENARY SESSION AND DINNER

And the devil is on my side. Because, of course, everyone knows that the devil is a communist and God, no doubt, is a good conservative.

—Joseph Stalin

The First Plenary Session

The allies met in a seventy-five-by-forty-foot conference room, decorated in white and gold, with a specially made ten-foot oval table with a green baize cover. The shape of the table, without head or foot, forestalled possible arguments about seating.

Roosevelt and Stalin were waiting in the room when Churchill arrived shortly before 4:30 P.M.[1] Saluting the Russian guards, Churchill greeted Stalin; both of them seemed "pleased to meet at what they knew was to be a momentous conference."[2] Moving around the table to Roosevelt's wheelchair, Churchill warmly shook his hand.

Stalin was flanked by his "top general," Voroshilov, and his "top man about foreign affairs," Molotov.[3] And interpreter Pavlov and one secretary, perhaps Berezhkov, completed the Russian party. To the right of the Russians sat Churchill, Eden, Ismay, and Birse. Behind them, in a second semicircular row, were Dill, Brooke, Cunningham, and Portal. To the left of the Russians was the American party with Harriman, Roosevelt, Bohlen, and Hopkins at the table and Leahy, King, Deane, and a secretary, Captain Forrest B. Royal, behind.

Marshall and Arnold missed the first session because they were enjoying an automobile excursion north of Tehran. At the close of the morning meeting of the American staff, Arnold had inquired about the day's schedule. The president told him that a plenary session in the afternoon was not likely. After a late lunch, the two generals left for a trip through the mountains with a vague idea of testing how far Russian territorial power extended around Tehran by driving until they reached a roadblock, and they were sixty miles away when the conference began. King had almost accepted an invitation to join them, but decided at the last minute that he needed to finish some staff work.[4] Consequently, King had to "do the honors" for the American joint chiefs.[5]

The first plenary session was summoned hastily because the Big Three had trouble reaching agreement on when to meet. The British wanted early afternoon, the American preferred the evening, and the Russians hoped to meet late at night. A compromise on 4:30 was not reached until early afternoon, by which time Marshall and Arnold were gone. By accident or design, the two most vocal Overlord advocates were absent. It was a travesty to have traveled so far to reach Tehran, only to miss the conference opening. The mixup revealed, at the least, poor organization within the president's entourage, and, after this embarrassing incident, Harriman met daily with Molotov to make arrangements.

The interpretation process created delays and confusion, which slowed the progress of the conference. Every speech was given twice, translated into either Russian or English. The end result was often boring and called for extraordinary patience.[6] Unconfirmed reports suggested that Stalin knew some English and Churchill some Russian, but neither openly demonstrated such proficiency. King, who carefully watched Stalin, later insisted that the marshal understood several questions in English, but Harriman thought otherwise.[7] Leahy noticed that Churchill did not always wait for the translation and seemed to be getting the gist of Stalin's remarks, but the prime minister frequently stopped puffing his cigar to ask for a whispered summary of what Stalin was saying.[8] As Standley once noted, negotiating through an interpreter was like kissing through a cheesecloth, and even the most eloquent speeches lost their effect—an outcome that most affected Churchill, whose aggravations were increased by his persistent sore throat.[9]

When Roosevelt asked who should preside, Stalin suggested and the others agreed that the president should have the honor. Churchill claimed that he and Stalin had already agreed before the conference that Roosevelt ought to be the chairman, so Roosevelt consented to take the job. Thereafter, he "beamed on all around the table and looked very much like the kind, rich uncle paying a visit to his poorer relations."[10]

Pointing out that he was the youngest of the three, Roosevelt welcomed his elders and asked Stalin to speak first. Stalin replied that he would rather listen. The purpose of the conference, said Roosevelt was to reach common accord and to work together to end the war and establish the peace. He welcomed the Russians to what he called the "family circle."[11] No fixed agenda, he said, had been drawn up, and "everyone could speak as freely as he wished on the basis of friendship. Nothing would be published."[12] He concluded what Brooke called a poor and feeble speech, expressing hope that the three powers would remain in close touch for "generations to come."[13]

Taking the floor, Churchill emphasized allied power. He described the combined strength of the Big Three as the greatest concentration of power that the world had ever seen. The central question facing the allies, he said, was how that power should be used most effectively. Prudent use of their strength would allow the Big Three to shorten the war, win an almost certain victory, and control the "happiness and fortunes of mankind." He prayed that the Big Three might be "worthy of their God-granted opportunity of rendering service to their fellow men."[14]

Stalin, gray and careworn to Birse's eye, followed.[15] Leahy recorded admiringly that Stalin spoke quietly, without gestures, and expressed himself convincingly in remarks that were brief and business-like.[16] Welcoming the representatives of Great Britain and the United States to Iran, Stalin agreed with Churchill that history had given the allies a "great opportunity," and he called for wise use of the power given by their respective peoples. He urged Churchill and Roosevelt to take full advantage of their "fraternal meeting" to begin their work.[17]

The opening speeches, wrote Deane, were "curiously symptomatic" of the different personalities and perspectives of the Big Three. Roosevelt was more interested in the peace than the war; Churchill was concerned about how the war would be won; and Stalin wanted to get down to business.[18]

Roosevelt then began a "general survey of the war as a whole and the needs of the war from the American point of view."[19] He chose to start with an overview of the Pacific war because, he said, the United States was bearing the brunt of the war in that area. A policy of attrition was being used successfully against the Japanese. The West intended to destroy Japanese forces in Indochina by launching land offensives in the north and amphibious operations in South Burma. The purpose of Pacific operations was to open the road to China, keep the Chinese involved in the war, and eventually to use Chinese airfields to bomb Japan.

Roosevelt next turned to the European front, which he called the most important of the war. "The governing object," he said, "should be that the Anglo-American armies should take such action as would draw the greatest weight off the Soviet forces in the splendid fight in which they were engaged."[20] But the difficulties involved in sea transport had made it impossible before the Quebec Conference to set a date for an assault across the English Channel, a "disagreeable body of water."[21] After Churchill interposed that the British had every reason to be thankful that the channel was disagreeable to potential invaders, Roosevelt reaffirmed the Quebec decision to launch Overlord on 1 May 1944.[22]

Turning to the disposition of forces in the Mediterranean, Roosevelt suggested using allied armies in such a way "as to bring maximum aid to the Soviet armies on the eastern front."[23] Possible points of future operations, he said, included Italy, the Adriatic, the Aegean, and Turkey. At this point,

Hopkins scribbled a note to King: "Who's promoting the Adriatic business that the president continually returns to?" and King answered, "As far as I know it is his own idea."[24] While Roosevelt explained that some of the proposals might involve a delay of up to three months for Overlord, he nonetheless stated emphatically that the vital thrust in France should not be delayed by secondary operations. Hopkins breathed easier, recorded Leahy, because Roosevelt's commitment to Overlord remained unshaken.[25] But Brooke described Roosevelt's presentation as a "poor and not very helpful speech," and added, "From then onwards the conference went from bad to worse!"[26]

Stalin followed with his own overview of the war. Congratulating his allies for their successes in the war against Japan, he stated his regret that the Russians were too deeply engaged on the eastern front to participate in the Pacific. Russian forces in Siberia would have to be at least trebled before any offensive could be started, but he promised that the Russians would enter the Pacific war following the defeat of Germany. Hopkins later told Moran that Stalin made this momentous announcement in a casual way without raising his voice and then "went on doodling as if nothing had happened."[27]

Perhaps this was a momentous announcement, but Stalin really promised nothing new. Yet, both the Americans and British pointed to this as a decisive breakthrough, a diplomatic coup, a military godsend. Stalin's pledge seemed to relieve the American fear that the Japanese war would be prolonged, and Roosevelt now had an answer for those who, like King, clamored for a buildup of allied forces in the Pacific. Brooke called it "cheering news," while Churchill later wrote that it was the most important announcement of the conference, because the Americans could no longer justify sacrificing the Mediterranean in favor of the Pacific.[28]

Of course, Stalin was primarily interested in the Russo-German front. The Russians had planned an offensive for the summer months, but the Germans had stolen the march and had attacked first. When the German attack stalled, the Russians launched their offensive and discovered that the Germans were much weaker than expected. Russian success had been surprising, Stalin admitted, but he hastened to add that the enemy strength was formidable even in retreat. Germany, by his calculations, had 260 divisions operating along the eastern front, with six additional divisions as reinforcements and up to 12,000 men in each division. He did not add up the figures, but by this reckoning the Germans had committed over three million soldiers to the struggle with Russia. Now the Russian offensive was grinding to a halt under deteriorating weather, the retreating Germans had destroyed everything, and the 300 Russian divisions that had started the campaign had lost their superiority.[29]

Italian operations came next under Stalin's scrutiny. The great accomplishment of the Italian campaign had been to open the Mediterranean to allied shipping, but Italy was a sideshow. He recalled the unsuccessful Russian attempt during the French Revolution to cross the Swiss Alps from Italy, which was not a suitable springboard for an offensive against the heart of the German Reich. He speculated that the Germans were no doubt secretly pleased to trap many allied troops where no decision could be reached.

The only logical point of attack, if Germany were the target, insisted Stalin, was through "northern or northwestern France and even through southern France." The Germans, he warned, would fight "like devils" to prevent landings in France.[30] But, in spite of the acknowledged difficulties, Overlord offered the best solution and Stalin concluded, "Those are all the remarks I have."[31] His speech was blunt and forceful, and Stimson, upon reading the minutes later, was moved to "thank the Lord that Stalin was there" because he "saved the day" for Overlord.[32]

Churchill, who sat patiently through the preceding speeches, only occasionally rustling the papers before him or passing short notes to his staff, now took over. He ignored the Pacific, except to say that the allies must deal first with Germany before turning to Japan. Insisting that the British and Americans had long agreed to an invasion of France, he said that the earliest possible date was "late spring or early summer of 1944" and that the Anglo-Americans agreed on every point except the ways and means of carrying out the operation.[33] The first landings would include thirty-five divisions, sixteen British and nineteen American, and the West would have one million men on the continent by July. And, in reply to a question by Stalin, Churchill explained that details for an invasion of southern France were incomplete, but the "idea was that it might be done in conformity and simultaneously with Overlord" using troops in Italy.[34]

Churchill acknowledged the secondary status of the Mediterranean theater. The allies had been drawn there because, at the time, it was the only area in which they could actively engage the enemy. When Stalin interjected that he had not meant to belittle the significance of what was taking place there, Churchill replied, "The object was to provide a stepping-stone for the main cross-channel invasion," but the British and Americans "had repeatedly asked themselves" what could be done in the Mediterranean before Overlord to bring the greatest pressure to bear on the Germans.[35]

Arguing that the Mediterranean offered many opportunities to the allies, Churchill listed the reasons for British interest there. The shortage of landing craft, the "great bottle-neck of all allied operations," made it impossible to use British forces except where they were already employed.[36] The Anglo-Americans had the chance to destroy or maul up to fifteen German divisions in Italy, and failure to engage these troops would permit the Germans to move them elsewhere. And, he said, a successful campaign in Italy would enhance the prospects of Overlord when it was finally launched. Once the great airfields in the vicinity of Rome had been captured and the Pisa-Rimini line had been secured, allied forces would be free for other operations, possibly in southern France.

Suggesting an expansion of the Mediterranean theater, Churchill proposed an "enterprise across the Adriatic" to provide help to Yugoslavia, where two rival groups were waging a guerrilla war behind German lines.[37] The support would go to Josip Broz, Tito, the commander of the National Army of Liberation and leader of the Yugoslav Communist party. This would mean cutting support to forces operating under General Draža Mihajlović, representing the Yugoslav government-in-exile. Perhaps Churchill thought that aid to communist forces was more likely to curry Stalin's favor or that Tito's Partisans were putting up a more effective resistance against the Germans. As far as an allied commitment was concerned, commando operations, not a large invading army, would be adequate.

According to Churchill, "one of the largest questions" concerning the Mediterranean was Turkey.[38] Turkish cooperation, he said, together with the use of escort vessels already in the Mediterranean, could open an uninterrupted supply route to Russia through the Black Sea. Stalin intervened to observe that a Lend-Lease convoy had recently arrived by the northern route without loss, and, strangely, neither Roosevelt nor Churchill challenged such a provocative falsehood. Germany's Balkan satellites, already looking for any pretext to leave the war, Churchill continued, would withdraw if Turkey entered the war. Rumania had put out peace feelers, and Bulgaria could easily be convinced to abandon Germany, because, he said, Bulgaria owed a debt of gratitude to Russia for her liberation from Turkish rule. Therefore, he asked:

> Would the objectives in the eastern Mediterranean which he had mentioned be of sufficient interest to the Soviet Government to make them wish us to go ahead, even if it meant a delay of one to two months from the 1st May in launching Overlord? The British and American Governments had deliberately kept their minds open on the subject until they knew what the Soviet Government felt. . . .[39]

Stalin replied that Churchill's proposals for the Mediterranean were wrong for several reasons. First, the liberation of Bulgaria had taken place "a long time ago," and he doubted that Bulgaria was really grateful.[40] Also, he questioned the wisdom of dispersing allied forces in diverse operations, including Turkey, Yugoslavia, and southern France. Russian experience proved that a concentrated effort on no more than two fronts at a time could confuse and demoralize the enemy. In any event, he doubted that Turkey would abandon neutrality when she had nothing to gain.

Moreover, Stalin wanted nothing to compromise Overlord. Would the thirty-five divisions, which he understood were earmarked for the cross-channel invasion, he asked, be weakened in any way by the continuation of operations in Italy? Was it intended that the invasion of France should be carried out by forces now in Italy? What Anglo-American forces would be diverted if Turkey entered the war? Directly confronting Churchill, he asked exactly what effects the Mediterranean war would have on Overlord, and he insisted again that secondary operations should not interfere with the cross-channel invasion.[41]

With the exception of seven divisions withdrawn from Italy, Churchill answered, entirely different divisions were involved in the Mediterranean and Overlord plans. The capture of Rome would release up to twenty-three divisions that could be used where needed. He assured Stalin that the West planned to have fifty or sixty divisions, with total strength of forty thousand men each, on the continent by July. Moreover, Turkey's entrance would require only that two or three British divisions be moved up from Egypt together with twenty squadrons of fighters and several anti-aircraft regiments.[42]

Stalin replied that the allies should employ only the strategies that would complement Overlord. An invasion of southern France was of such value that it ought to be undertaken two months before the cross-channel attempt, even if the West had to quit the campaign to take Rome. He pressed the prime minister to abort unprofitable adventures in the Mediterranean.

Churchill hastened to list the reasons for at least continuing the advance on Rome. Abandoning Rome would be regarded on all sides as a "crashing defeat and the British Parliament would not tolerate the idea for a moment."[43] Here, Stalin explained that he meant abandoning the Roman campaign as the extreme case. The allies, Churchill replied, would be no stronger before the capture than after, and nothing could be gained by trying to move the armies in Italy anywhere else. Also, the allies needed airfields in northern Italy for fighter cover to support Overlord, and no substitutes could be found.

At this point, Roosevelt interrupted the dispute between Churchill and Stalin to observe that the Big Three seemed to be facing a question of "relative timing."[44] Any eastern Mediterranean activity would probably postpone Overlord until June or July, and he opposed "any such delay if it could possibly be avoided."[45] The military chiefs should be instructed, he said, to work out plans for the southern France invasion under the guideline that nothing should delay Overlord.

But Churchill, who had not finished, turned to Stalin and stated that he could "not in any circumstances agree to sacrifice the activities of the armies in the Mediterranean . . . merely in order to keep the exact date of May 1" for Overlord.[46] And, while he "did not disagree in principle with the views expressed by Marshal Stalin," he added that

it would be difficult for him to leave idle the British forces in the eastern Mediterranean . . . merely for the purpose of avoiding any insignificant delay in Overlord. He said that if such was the decision they would, of course, agree, but they could not wholeheartedly agree to postpone operations in the Mediterranean. He added, of course, that if Turkey did not enter the war that was the end of that, but he personally favored some flexibility in the exact date of Overlord. He proposed that the matter be considered overnight and have the staffs examine the various possibilities in the morning.[47]

Stalin replied that the Russians had not expected to discuss technical military problems, and he could only promise that Voroshilov would do his best at a staff meeting.

Directing the discussion back to the Turkish question, Churchill downplayed the need to consider how far the allies "could meet Turkey's requests in the event she agreed to enter the war."[48] But Stalin and Roosevelt disagreed with him. Stalin, as he did consistently throughout the conference, expressed doubt that Turkey would ever abandon the advantages of neutrality to join the allies. Britain was Turkey's ally and America her friend, said Stalin, so they should take responsibility for putting pressure on Turkey. Whereas neutrals tended to regard belligerents as fools, perhaps the West could reverse this and show the Turks that they were foolish not to enter the war.[49]

When Churchill asked if the Russians were not really anxious to get Turkey into the war, Stalin said that he favored taking the Turks "by the scruff of the neck if necessary." The prime minister replied that a Turkish refusal to join the allies would be an act of "supreme unwisdom," and he joked that Christmas was a poor season for turkeys. Unfortunately, Churchill's clever joke was lost on Stalin, who asked for an explanation of Western holiday customs. When he perceived the play on words, Stalin said that he was sorry he was not an Englishman.[50]

Reporting that he planned to meet with President Ismet Inönü of Turkey, Roosevelt promised to court the Turks, but he was not optimistic. If he were Inönü, he would ask for "such a price in planes, tanks, and equipment that to grant the request would indefinitely postpone Overlord."[51] In light of Turkish replies to previous appeals, Stalin did not expect Turkey to declare war. When Churchill suggested that the Turks were crazy, Stalin replied, "Some people apparently prefer to remain crazy."[52]

Why did Stalin consistently argue against Turkey's participation in the war? Coordinated Big Three pressure might have pushed the cautious Turks off the fence, creating a second front in the Balkans. Churchill believed that the problem was "probably as much political as military."[53] Apparently Stalin did not want a front there, and Ismay guessed that he wanted Russian, not British or American, forces to liberate the Balkans.[54]

Although the allies were "all great friends," said Churchill, they should not delude themselves into thinking that they saw eye to eye on all matters.

Time and patience, he said, must come first.[55] On this note, the first plenary session adjourned, with the understanding that the next general meeting would be at 4:00 P.M. the following day. Afterwards, Molotov served Russian tea and cakes.

Some Americans were pleased with the first session, which seemed pleasant, polite, and agreeable to them. The Big Three had stated their views, sounded out each other, and decided that the one important question before them was settlement of a date for the promised second front.[56] Arnold later rejoiced that "Uncle Joe had talked straight from the shoulder about ideas very much in accordance with the Americans."[57]

But the British found great cause for alarm. Brooke concluded that after having confused plans more than they had ever done before, the allies had reached a dangerous point where Stalin's shrewdness, assisted by American shortsightedness, might lead anywhere, because Stalin was "too good a strategist not to see the weakness in the American plan."[58] Others worried that old American and British suspicions had "popped their ugly heads from beneath the table."[59] Moran found Churchill so dispirited that he asked what was wrong. "A bloody lot has gone wrong," fumed Churchill, who refused to talk and remained in bad humor through the evening.[60]

Roosevelt's Dinner

Shortly after 8:00 P.M., the Big Three, together with Molotov, Eden, Hopkins, Clark-Kerr, Harriman, and the interpreters, met at Roosevelt's quarters. The president mixed cocktails, handed one to Stalin, watched him drink it, and asked how he liked it. "Well, all right," Stalin replied, "but it is cold on the stomach."[61] After cocktails, Roosevelt hosted a steak and baked potato dinner. Eden noted that the atmosphere was most cordial and filled with real hope.[62] Apparently willing to put aside the disappointments of earlier in the day, Churchill found few things that could not be said and received in good humor at the table.[63]

Part of the conversation was serious. Stalin and Roosevelt repeated, for Churchill's benefit, the substance of the remarks in their private conversation. The tenor of their comments was that France should be punished for her collaboration with the Germans. Churchill interjected that the threat of German revival was more serious than punishment of France, and the allies might assure peace by controlling strategic enemy bases. But Stalin would have none of that.

Shifting to Germany, Roosevelt suggested that the concept of the "Reich should be stricken from the German mind and language."[64] Stalin proposed that the Germans be subjected to the harshest possible controls, and he argued with such ardor that Bohlen speculated that he was deliberately overstating the case to see how his allies would react.[65] Insisting that Germany must pay for her crimes, Stalin proposed that the Germans lose their holdings to the east of the Oder River, which should mark the border between Poland and Germany. Neither Roosevelt nor Churchill seems to have objected.

Stalin told a story to illustrate the German need for authority. When he visited Leipzig in 1907, 200 German workers had failed to show up for an important rally because no one had been on duty to punch their tickets when they had arrived at the train station. They had patiently waited for someone to tell them what to do, rather than act on their own. He concluded that the Germans were clearly unfit to govern themselves, much less to manage the territory of others.[66]

Stalin described Hitler as a "very able man but not basically intelligent, lacking in culture and with a primitive approach to political and other problems."[67] When Roosevelt suggested that the German leader was mentally unbalanced, Stalin disagreed, insisting that only a capable man could have united the German people. At the same time, said Stalin, Hitler "through his stupidity in attacking the Soviet Union, had thrown away all the fruits of his previous victories."[68]

Concerning territorial issues, Roosevelt suggested a trusteeship system. The allies could jointly control enemy territories through a United Nations organization. The type of institution that he had in mind was, by his reckoning, a "concept which had never been developed in past history."[69] As an example, he proposed that the Baltic Sea could be internationalized, particularly the area near the Kiel Canal. Stalin took exception, apparently mistaking the example as a reference to the Baltic states of Estonia, Latvia, and Lithuania, which had been absorbed by the Soviet Union in 1939, lost to the Germans in 1941, and regained in 1943. Roosevelt explained hastily that his trusteeship plan did not include the Baltic states. Thereupon, Stalin seemed to accept the idea of ensuring "free navigation to and from the Baltic Sea."[70]

Throughout the conversation, Eden had detected that the president was "below par," and he overheard Hopkins whisper that Roosevelt looked like he might faint at any moment.[71] Shortly afterwards, Roosevelt suddenly turned color, great drops of sweat began to bead off his face, and he put a shaky hand to his forehead. He was wheeled into an adjoining room and hurriedly examined by McIntire, who returned to say that Roosevelt had not been poisoned, as some in the American party had at first suspected.[72] Indigestion was the culprit. According to McIntire, Stalin got up from the table, looked at Churchill, and dryly remarked, "Well, I'm glad that there is somebody here who knows when it is time to go home."[73]

Following Roosevelt's departure, the prime minister, who wanted, he said, an opportunity to give his views to Stalin, guided the Russians to a sofa and suggested that they talk about what would happen after the war. Postwar Germany should have neither aviation nor a general staff, said Churchill, and German industry should be placed under constant supervision. Dismembering Germany would make the world safe "for at least fifty years."[74] Stalin asked if Churchill would "forbid the existence of watchmakers and furniture factories for making parts of shells" or prevent the Germans from manufacturing "toy rifles which were used for teaching hundreds of thousands of men how to shoot."[75] Nothing was final, replied Churchill, and the world would roll on, but it could be safe for at least fifty years. But Stalin predicted that German nationalism could recover and cause a new war within fifteen to twenty years. When Stalin pointed out that controls after the last war had failed to work, Churchill admitted that the powers were inexperienced then, the last war was not to the same extent a national war, and Russia was not a party at the peace conference, but he insisted that Russian armies, British navies, and American air forces could keep the peace for a century.[76]

Arguing against the unconditional surrender policy, Stalin said that unclarified terms merely served to unite the German people. Specific terms, no matter how harsh, would hasten surrender. Harriman, who was listening, was pleased to hear Stalin's statement, because he regarded the surrender policy as a mistake.[77] But Churchill evaded this issue and said that he was "not against toilers in Germany but only against the leaders and against dangerous combinations."[78] Stalin replied that when German prisoners from the laboring classes insisted that they were only following orders when they fought for Hitler, he had them shot. According to the British minutes, Churchill anticipated "more than merely keeping the peace. The three Powers should guide the future of the world."[79]

When Stalin's mood mellowed, Churchill asked him to state what was necessary for the defense of Russia's western frontier. At first Stalin was evasive, replying that he did "not feel the need to ask himself how to act," because "so far his heart did not feel stimulated."[80] Eden reminded Stalin that he had earlier suggested the Oder River as the Polish border. Did the British think he was going to swallow Poland up? asked Stalin. The British, said Eden, did not know how much the Russians were going to eat or how much would be left undigested.[81] Stalin answered that the Russians did "not want anything belonging to other people, although they might have a bite at Germany."[82] The Russians, he added, would help the Poles gain the Oder.

Churchill pushed the discussion further. Russian security was critical, but Britain would support a strong and independent Poland, which was, he said, an instrument necessary in the orchestra of Europe. Stalin replied that Polish culture and language must, of course, exist. When the prime minister asked if the allies should draw frontier lines, Stalin agreed. Using three match sticks to represent the boundaries of Germany, Poland, and Russia, Churchill proposed to move the borders two steps toward the west like soldiers performing a precision drill, and he moved the matches to show how it could be done. If Poland trod on some German toes, he said, that could not be helped, but Poland must be strong. Further, the "three heads might see if some sort of policy might be pressed on the Poles." Stalin replied, "We could have a look," and Churchill added, "We should be lucky if we could."[83]

Near the end of the conversation, civility began to wear thin. Churchill waved his finger at Stalin and burst out loudly and angrily, "But you won't let me get up to your front and I want to get there." Whereupon, Stalin grinned and replied, "Maybe it can be arranged sometime, Mr. Prime Minister. Perhaps when you have a front that I can visit too."[84] Churchill said that he wanted to see the Russian front because he was getting old, being in his seventieth year, to which Stalin replied that Churchill had "no need to boast," because only four years separated them.[85]

As the British and Russians sat in a circle with coffee and cigars, Churchill remarked: "I believe that God is on our side. At least I have done my best to make Him a faithful ally." Stalin responded to the translation with a grin, saying, "And the devil is on my side. Because, of course, everyone knows that the devil is a communist and God, no doubt, is a good conservative."[86]

Reflecting on the progress of the conference shortly before he retired, Roosevelt was "greatly set up over the day's events, felt a *great* deal had been accomplished, and was thoroughly satisfied in every way."[87] He would later tell his son Elliott that he was sure he would "get along very well indeed" with Stalin.[88] Churchill, perhaps expecting the worst after Russian bluntness during the earlier plenary session, later wrote that the day ended with Stalin in a good mood.[89] But the end of the first day was the lull before the storm. Those familiar with Russian negotiations knew that the first meetings were always wonderful, that one left feeling the Russians would agree to anything and wondering how anyone could ever say bad things about them. But the next day was inevitably a maelstrom resembling a "pack of caterwauling cats."[90]

6

SECOND-DAY WARM-UP TALKS

If you think about it, you will do it.
—Kliment E. Voroshilov

Military Experts Meeting

Neither the Americans nor the Russians greeted the prospects of a staff meeting with enthusiasm. Some of the former suspected that the British wanted to block Russo-American agreement on invading northwestern Europe by referring the matter to the military chiefs, who were no more likely to reach consensus than the Big Three. Following stalemate at the first plenary session, Stalin had only reluctantly agreed to have the staffs meet.

The military chiefs met at 10:30 A.M. on 29 November in the conference room of the Russian embassy. Representing the United States were Marshall, Leahy, Deputy Secretary Colonel Andrew J. McFarland, and interpreter Henry H. Ware. The British delegates were Brooke, Portal, Secretary Redman, and interpreter Hugh A. Lunghi. According to Cunningham, he and Dill stayed away so that the delegations would be closer in size.[1] The streamlined Russian party consisted of Voroshilov and an interpreter, either Pavlov or Berezhkov.[2]

According to King, absent because the Pacific war was not likely to come up for discussion, the purpose of the staff meeting was threefold. The main problem was keeping enemy divisions in the west engaged and preventing them from moving to the eastern front before Overlord began. Second, the allies needed to determine how best to use their large forces in the Mediterranean as support for Overlord. A less important task was reaching agreement about the value of Turkey's entering the war.[3]

Brooke, delivering the opening speech, said that the first order of business was selecting strategies designed to put pressure on Germany, and he admitted that the cross-channel invasion would conform to this cardinal principle by diverting a large number of German troops from the Russian front. But the "very earliest date" for Overlord was 1 May 1944, and the allies must devise some means of keeping Mediterranean forces occupied during the six months before Overlord.[4] Besides, twenty-three enemy divisions in Italy should not be free to move elsewhere.[5] Curiously, the Americans do not seem to have questioned Brooke's figures, which conflicted with a report listing twenty-five divisions.[6] The allies' supporting Tito in Yugoslavia, Brooke predicted, would tie down an additional twenty-one German and eight Bulgarian divisions.

Voroshilov, who had shown little interest in Brooke's remarks up to this point, interrupted. He insisted that the British had grossly exaggerated the German forces in the Balkans, and the enemy was not nearly as powerful there as Brooke imagined. In reply, Brooke suggested that intelligence staffs should get together and arrive at an agreed figure, and, he promised, the British staff would check the accuracy of his report, but neither proposal seems to have been carried out.[7]

Turning to the eastern Mediterranean theater, Brooke described the advantages of bringing about Turkish participation in the war. Opening the Dardanelles would permit the allies to establish a supply route to Russia through the Black Sea, and the presence of allied forces in the region might well embolden both the Rumanians and Bulgarians to desert the enemy camp. Further, the allies could use Turkish air bases to bomb enemy targets and more quickly force Germany to abandon the Balkans.

Brooke admitted that success in the Mediterranean could not be purchased cheaply. The cross-channel invasion would need to be delayed temporarily to provide necessary landing craft for amphibious operations in Italy, Turkey, and the Aegean Islands. But, in exchange, the allies would be able to "hold and destroy the German forces now in the Mediterranean area while awaiting the date for Overlord."[8] His failure to state exactly how much delay would occur, however, could hardly have reassured the increasingly distrustful Americans, who were "embittered by the pent-up impatience and frustration growing out of a drift of events in the European war that seemed somehow usually to have acceded to British aims and perhaps even responded to British manipulation."[9]

When Voroshilov suggested going on the defensive in the Mediterranean in order to concentrate all energies on northwestern Europe, Brooke contended that the allies would be ill-advised to turn from offensives that promised at least some success, to a defensive posture that would give the initiative to the enemy. Taking the defensive in Italy would still require strong forces to contain the Germans and thus free "only very limited forces" to reinforce other fronts.[10] And closing operations in the Mediterranean would encourage the Germans to move their troops to another, undoubtedly the eastern, front.[11]

While Stalin was right to want pincer attacks on Germany from more than one direction, land warfare tactics were not always possible in naval operations. With this in mind, suggested Brooke, the allies should abandon the proposed invasion of southern France. Only three or four divisions would be available for an operation that would require an inordinate number of landing craft. Increasing the commitment in Italy and undertaking new operations in the eastern Mediterranean would, in Brooke's view, best support Overlord.[12] Brooke then offered to give the floor to Portal for a review of air operations against Germany, but Voroshilov, uninterested in the air war, interrupted to say that he preferred to "hear the American report on land operations."[13]

In line with the Russian request, Marshall presented what he called the "purely American point of view."[14] Unlike Brooke, Marshall was cautious in appraising what the allies could do militarily. The necessity of waging war simultaneously in the Pacific and Atlantic had created a serious dilemma for the United States. The acute shortage of shipping and landing craft almost forced the Americans to ignore strategy in order to advance communications. The "necessity for improving the arrangements for communications and for the transportation of troops came first and strategy second," said Marshall, who also observed that the allies were hamstrung by logistical problems unique in warfare.[15]

The Western allies faced no shortages of men or of supplies. As soon as training was completed, air forces could be sent to front areas, delivering both trained personnel and new aircraft, but infantry and armored units could not transport themselves. American planners were concerned about the length of voyages, the time required in ports, and the time needed to complete a round trip from the United States to the various fronts around the world. On the basis of these vital criteria, Marshall said, the Americans had favored Overlord "from the start," because it involved the shortest transport route.[16]

Concerning the Mediterranean, Marshall insisted that all decisions were tentative pending the results of the present conference, and he agreed with Brooke that the allies should decide how to employ armies in the six months before Overlord was scheduled. The specific question now to be resolved was "what should be done during the next three months and during the next six months, the latter, of course, being dependent on the former."[17] Also, he agreed, the allies should give up launching Anvil, the code name for the invasion of southern France, much in advance of Overlord. But, unlike the British, he opposed scrapping Anvil altogether and suggested that it might be successful if launched only "two or three weeks" before Overlord.[18]

Another American concern was securing the necessary ports to unload heavy equipment and ammunition after the first stages of an amphibious landing. In the past, the enemy had gone to great lengths to destroy ports when the allies used amphibious craft to establish a beachhead. American engineers had accomplished nothing short of marvels in restoring damaged ports, but a dangerous delay always followed an amphibious landing. Marshall cited the comparatively small landings at Salerno where, even with adequate air cover and good weather, it had taken eighteen days to open the port.[19]

Marshall's comments on the air war opened the door for Portal. During the Salerno campaign, claimed Marshall, fighters could manage only fifteen to twenty minutes of flying time over the target area. The prospects for Overlord were much better, and the limit would be about thirty minutes.[20] In the interval, Portal reported, Anglo-American bombers were successfully destroying the enemy's industry and communications, while luring enemy planes into open battle. Although forced to keep as many as 1,700 fighter planes in western and southern Germany, and while maintaining only 750 planes on all other fronts combined, Germany was unable to prevent the West from dropping 20,000 tons of bombs monthly on German targets.[21]

When Voroshilov praised the Anglo-American bombing efforts, Portal challenged the Russian air force to set aside planes to bomb areas normally beyond the range of Western flights, thus increasing pressure on Germany and relieving Western forces from carrying the entire burden of the air war. Voroshilov promised that, "when there should be any respite it would be used by the Russian Air Force for attacking targets in eastern Germany, but it was unlikely that much would be possible."[22]

Changing the subject, Voroshilov said that he knew Overlord was being prepared for a target date "about May 1," but he wanted to know what measures were being taken to solve the shipping and landing craft shortages to launch the operation on time.[23] He understood that the United States considered Overlord of the first importance, and he wondered if the British shared this conviction. Turning to Brooke, he asked if the British believed that Overlord "could be replaced by another operation in the Mediterranean or elsewhere."[24]

Marshall responded first, saying that everything possible was being done to resolve the transport difficulties. Both the Americans and British were concentrating on the construction of landing craft and landing barges capable of carrying forty tanks each, and this program was well in hand. Also, allied planners had been experimenting with various ways of building temporary ports, thereby to deny the enemy the advantage of knowing where to expect landings.

Brooke told Voroshilov that Overlord had always been reckoned a vital part of the war, but, as Churchill had said, it "must be mounted at a time when it would have the best chances of success."[25] To keep the 1 May target date would force current operations in Italy to a standstill. German fortifications in France were formidable and linked by an excellent communications network, and Overlord could lead to a decisive allied defeat. But favorable conditions for a successful landing, Brooke mused, might develop in 1944.[26]

Evidently displeased, Voroshilov turned to the British delegation and, apologizing for his failure to understand exactly what Brooke meant, asked Brooke "if he could say a little more precisely whether he regarded Overlord as the most important operation."[27] The Americans seemed to give Overlord top priority, and, "from the Russian point of view, it was an operation of vital importance."[28] In reply, Brooke endorsed the cross-channel operation as a major plan, with the single reservation that it should not be permitted to fail, which would occur, he insisted, unless the allies carried out auxiliary operations in the Mediterranean.[29]

Voroshilov argued that the cross-channel assault must be given top priority, with the clear understanding that Mediterranean operations were of secondary importance. An invasion of southern France was indispensable to the success of the main invasion and it should be attempted as many as three months before, shortly before, or even simultaneously with Overlord. Surely the West could solve the logistics problem: "If you think about it, you will do it."[30] With the "will to do it," suggested Voroshilov, the British and Americans would find that Overlord could succeed in similar fashion to the successful Russian crossings of enemy-held rivers.[31] During recent operations, for example, the Russians had crossed several large rivers, defended in each case by the enemy, who had held the higher west bank.

Voroshilov's tactless comparison of the English Channel to a river provoked both the British and the Americans. Brooke expounded on the unique difficulties of crossing the channel, not to be compared to the Russian river crossings, although the latter operations "had been studied with the greatest interest and admiration and marvels in the way of technical feats had been performed."[32] Supporting Brooke, Marshall said that defeat in a river crossing might be a mere setback, but defeat in a landing across the ocean would be disastrous, because it would mean the complete destruction of the landing craft and troops. Voroshilov "said quite frankly that he did not agree," prompting Marshall to reply that he "would be equally frank," and to insist that artillery support from the sea was more complicated than from the opposite bank of a river.[33] Apparently the Russians could not understand, wrote King later, "what a great job it was to go across the English Channel."[34]

The lateness of the hour and, perhaps, the absence of consensus prompted Leahy to suggest adjournment. But Voroshilov insisted that they must reach agreement before adjourning. At this point, Brooke suggested postponing a decision until after a second meeting, which he proposed for the following morning at 10:30 A.M. Brooke's suggestion won American support, and the meeting adjourned.

Reading into the minutes of the meeting an agreement that was not there, one observer concluded that the military chiefs decided to start Anvil either two or three weeks preceding or simultaneously with Overlord.[35] Leahy, not so hopeful, recorded in his diary for 29 November that the staffs made little progress toward agreement because of the British desire to postpone Overlord.[36] Brooke was disgusted: "Our friend Voroshilov refused to see any of our arguments," having evidently been briefed by Stalin, "who no doubt had also been prompted by Harriman!"[37] Although the chiefs were not successful, their meeting was significant because it marked a decided shift in atmosphere. In contrast to the first day, Russian questions were now less general, more strident, and sometimes embarrassingly blunt. This was the pattern of things to come.

Roosevelt's Second Meeting with Stalin

Anxious to meet privately with Roosevelt, Churchill proposed that the two dine together at noon. The president, however, sent Harriman to explain that he preferred to have a quiet meal with his son Elliott, who had flown to Tehran during the morning. Churchill replied huffily that the Big Three should treat each other with equal confidence and was "plainly put out" by Roosevelt's continued refusal to meet privately with him.[38]

If Roosevelt's door was closed to Churchill, the same could not be said for the Russians. At 2:45 P.M., Stalin, Molotov, and Pavlov arrived at Roosevelt's quarters for a second private meeting. Stalin offered Russian cigarettes, which consisted of two or three puffs of strong black tobacco at the end of a two-inch cardboard holder.[39] Roosevelt seems to have sincerely believed that he could arrive at a meeting of minds with Stalin, if they shared experiences and talked often enough.[40] The president's purpose in this session was to discuss allied cooperation in military operations and to move beyond agreement in principle on several issues.

As in their earlier meeting, Roosevelt took the lead and handed Stalin a series of reports. Predicting that cold, hungry, and inadequately armed men would "surely remember from whence aid came when they were fighting for their very existence," one report recommended giving aid to Tito's Partisans.[41] Another paper called for the Russians to permit Western planes to use Russian bases to shuttle bomb Germany, a proposal accepted in principle at the Moscow conference of foreign ministers. But the Russians continued to drag their feet, later prompting Arnold to try offering "some 300 or 400 of our B-24's, which the Russians could use against the Germans."[42] And, while Roosevelt expressed his delight at having heard with his own ears the Russian promise to fight Japan, the allies needed to "do some advance planning" and make arrangements for joint air and naval operations.[43] If the president was seeking concrete results, he must have been disappointed when Stalin put off making comments, alleging that he needed time to review the papers.[44]

According to Roosevelt, the reports were important, but minor, compared to deciding the nature of the peace. He told Stalin that he would like to discuss informally a "great many other matters relating to the future of the world," in exchange promising to discuss "any subject military or political which the marshal desired."[45] Stalin replied amiably that he could think of nothing that would prevent the two leaders from discussing whatever they wished.[46]

The question of a postwar organization to preserve peace, said Roosevelt, had not been explored sufficiently. He wanted to discuss the possibilities of an organization based on the United Nations, the allied nations at war with Germany and Japan. His plan had three parts. Sometime during the conference, Roosevelt drew three circles to represent the individual elements of his scheme. The sketch was dated 20 November but was likely drawn for Stalin's benefit at this meeting.[47]

The first part of the plan concerned membership. Roosevelt proposed to create an international structure, composed of "some thirty-five members of the United Nations," that is, the Big Three powers and their junior partners.[48] None of the Axis powers would be admitted, at least at first. United Nations representatives could meet periodically to discuss matters that were worldwide in range and scope, and their meeting place might be moved from time to time.

Concerning the administrative system of the United Nations, Roosevelt proposed an executive committee controlled by Russia, the United States, Britain, China, two additional European states, and one nation each from South America, the Far East, the Near East, and the British Dominions. He joked that Churchill opposed this plan because the British "would have only two votes, that of Great Britain and one of the Dominions."[49] The ten-member committee, added Roosevelt, would deal with "all non-military questions such as agriculture, food, health, and economic questions, as well as with the setting up of an International Committee."[50]

Stalin interrupted to ask if the decisions of Roosevelt's executive committee were supposed to be binding or merely suggestions. Roosevelt answered "yes and no," explaining that the committee would make its recommendations for settling all disputes with the "hope that the nations concerned would be guided thereby."[51] He admitted that most decisions would involve voluntary compliance, because the American Congress, for example, would hardly accept dictation from any international body.

The third element of Roosevelt's international organization was what he called the "Four Policemen." Composed of the Soviet Union, America, Britain, and China, the "Four Policemen" would keep the peace by collective security procedures and by dealing immediately with any threat to the peace. Italy's attack on Ethiopia in 1935 could have been prevented by closing the Suez Canal. This was the sort of thing he had in mind.[52]

Stalin expressed doubt that Roosevelt's plan was practical. Small nations might well resent intrusions by the four big nations. Also, he doubted that any Chinese interference in the affairs of a European state could ever be considered appropriate, and he asked how China could police the rest of the world when she could not even keep her own house in order. As an alternative, he proposed creating European and Far Eastern committees as separate bodies, or creating a European committee that would be separate from a worldwide organization.[53]

Roosevelt replied that Stalin's suggestion was similar to a British plan to establish regional committees. The difference was that Churchill proposed one committee for Europe, one for the Far East, and one for the Americas. The Russian plan called for the United States to join Russia, Britain, and "possibly one other European state" in the European committee.[54] Roosevelt claimed that Churchill's plan would not work, because Congress would never accept membership in an exclusively European organization in light of the entangling interests that would inevitably result. He feared American troops might have to be sent to Europe if the British plan were adopted and some future threat to the peace called for a military response.

Stalin, understandably puzzled by Roosevelt's remarks, asked the president if the "Four Policemen" idea might not also require American involvement in European affairs.[55] In reply, Roosevelt foresaw sending materiel, but not troops, to Europe if needed. Any threat to the peace, at least in Europe, would have to be handled by the British and Russians, and he explained that Americans might not have become involved in the present war had it not been for Pearl Harbor. Stalin was silent.

Alternative means for dealing with threats to the peace might make the use of troops unnecessary. The allies could impose a quarantine or embargo in order to deal with any disturbances "arising out of a revolution or of developments in a small country."[56] If a quarantine or embargo did not have the desired effect, the "Four Policemen" could issue ultimatums to be followed, if necessary, by bombardment and invasion. Naturally, Roosevelt did not mention dealing with a threat to the peace from one or more of the policemen.

Stalin insisted that any threat to future peace would undoubtedly arise in Germany. His conversation with Churchill the previous evening led him to believe, he said, that the British were more optimistic about the German situation than seemed reasonable. German recovery and rearmament seemed to follow a cyclical pattern and, after each war, the Germans rebuilt more quickly than before. The first modern German aggression, in 1870, was followed some forty-two years later by the First World War, after which Germany had been able to recover and wage war again in just twenty-one years. He predicted that Germany would threaten the peace fifteen to twenty years after the Second World War.[57]

Therefore, Stalin insisted that something "more serious" than the organizations proposed by either Roosevelt or Churchill was needed.[58] Allied possession and control of strong points within Germany, along her borders, or even farther away would help prevent aggression and ensure good behavior. He mentioned Dakar, previously a French base, as an example of a suitable allied strong point. What was good for Europe, he added, was good for the Pacific as well, and he urged that any organization to preserve the peace should include the maintenance of strong points around the world. Roosevelt replied that he agreed 100 percent. He wanted Stalin to know that he could be as firm as needed.[59] In that case, said Stalin, everything was settled.[60]

Stalin again expressed grave misgivings about China being numbered with the Big Three. Didn't Roosevelt know that China was impotent? The president admitted that China's present weakness was well known, but he predicted a different China in the future, and, in any event, four hundred million people should be friends and not potential enemies.[61]

And so the second private meeting between Roosevelt and Stalin ended on a different note than the first. And, if one private meeting agitated the British, the second did little to calm their fears that the Russians and Americans were finding common ground.[62] Based upon Stalin's behavior in the second round of talks with Roosevelt, however, the British had less to dread than they imagined. Stalin raised questions, disagreed with the president's ideas, and, on the whole, appeared much less cooperative than he had the previous day. So far, the Russians were running true to form, but Roosevelt did not seem to be concerned.

7

SECOND-DAY MEETINGS OF THE BIG THREE

What a waste of time this is.
—Andrew B. Cunningham

Sword of Stalingrad Ceremony

An interesting sidelight of the conference took place on 29 November when the British presented a ceremonial sword to the Russians in memory of their February 1943 victory at Stalingrad. In any other context, the presentation would have seemed a genuine display of camaraderie. Actually, the ceremony was marred from the start by the British failure to show up on time. They changed the time from noon to 2:00 P.M. to permit the prime minister to take a nap.[1] Churchill supposedly took to his bed in bad temper over Roosevelt's second private meeting with Stalin, and no one dared rouse him until his daughter at last risked his ire to wake him after two o'clock.[2]

A more likely explanation for the delay was that the British chiefs held a planning session in the early afternoon. Responding to a Marshall draft memorandum on Anvil, they rejected a proposal to strip Italy of all but four divisions. Unmindful of the time and deeply concerned about the Russian and American reaction to their Mediterranean proposals, they continued to talk past three o'clock.[3] Not until 3:30 did the British, Russian, and American delegations gather in the conference room of the Russian embassy.

Stalin vetoed a plan to hold the ceremony outside to permit pictures to be taken in natural light. Perhaps concerned about security, Stalin preferred to use the conference room where protective measures, as Hollis remembered, were staggering.[4] British and Russian honor guards were drawn up on either side of the room. Arnold and King were much impressed by the tall, youthful, and heavily armed Russians who stood ramrod stiff during the ceremony.[5] Not to be outdone, the British guards were "less impressive in stature but were smart."[6] After the scene was set, Churchill, attired in the "natty blue" uniform of a commodore of the Royal Air Force entered; Stalin in a suntan-colored uniform solemnly took his place; and then Roosevelt was wheeled into the room.[7] A Russian band struck up the "Third International" and "God Save the King."

Churchill took the two-handed, four-foot sword from a British lieutenant, turned to Stalin, and said that he had been commanded to present "this sword of honor" bearing the inscription, "To the steel hearted citizens of Stalingrad, a gift from King George VI as a token of the homage of the British people."[8] Unlike most of Churchill's speeches, judged Admiral King, this one was short.[9] Receiving the sword "with grace," Stalin seemed to have a lump in his throat and was obviously moved deeply.[10] Raising the sword to his lips, he kissed the scabbard covered in red Morocco leather and almost inaudibly thanked the British.[11] He then offered the sword for inspection to Roosevelt who had also been stirred by the ceremony. With the prime minister holding the scabbard, Roosevelt drew the sword, admired the gleaming glade, and exclaimed, "Truly they had hearts of steel."[12]

At the end, Stalin handed the trophy to Voroshilov, who, evidently taken by surprise, fumbled the sword, which headed for the floor. Some observers recalled that the sword thumped Voroshilov on the foot or clattered on the floor.[13] But he may have caught it before it struck the floor and returned it to its scabbard by a "clever conjuring trick."[14] The honor guard made the "usual salutes to the sword ending with the Russian 'Hurrah' to Stalin" and then carried the precious burden from the room.[15]

From one standpoint, the sword ceremony was a rousing success. In a simple but impressive moment, the allies set their quarrels aside, and, since the Overlord debate was beginning to heat up, the respite was welcome. Perhaps Moran was exaggerating when he detected "genuine friendship," but the presentation was useful in forwarding propaganda about allied harmony.[16]

Nevertheless, the Tehran Conference was not the proper setting to pay homage to the Stalingrad epic, which was truly deserving of recognition otherwise. The effect was to add weight to Stalin's claims that Russia, not her allies, was absorbing most the war's costs, especially in manpower. Besides, the ceremony made it awkward for Churchill to take a hard line with Stalin in subsequent negotiations.

Following the sword presentation, the Big Three retired to the portico of the Russian embassy for group pictures. At the top of the stone steps between two white pillars, three chairs were placed directly beneath the hammer and sickle insignia. Roosevelt sat in the center, Churchill on the left, and Stalin on the right. For fifteen minutes, shutters clicked and movie cameras shot away in a "photographic orgy" of allies putting on a show of unity.[17] After the official photographs were taken, Roosevelt asked that his picture be taken with Elliot, John Boettiger, and Sarah Churchill. When Sarah approached, Stalin quickly rose to his feet, bowed from the waist, took her hand, and kissed it in the old-fashioned elegant European manner, which, Roosevelt later confessed, gave Stalin the best of that moment.[18]

Second Plenary Meeting

At 4:00 P.M., the allied delegations moved into the conference room for the second plenary meeting. The Americans present were Roosevelt, Hopkins, Harriman, Leahy, Marshall, King, Arnold, Deane, Bohlen, and Ware. The British participants were Churchill, Eden, Dill, Brooke, Cunningham, Portal, Ismay, Martel, Hollis, Clark-Kerr, and Birse. The Russians were Stalin, Molotov, Voroshilov, Pavlov, and Berezhkov.[19]

Not having met Stalin the day before, Arnold asked Molotov to introduce him. This caused several minutes of animated discussion among the Russians, and Arnold speculated that his request, when translated, perhaps challenged Stalin to a duel or worse. Turning to Molotov, Arnold explained, "Listen, all I want to do is say 'How do you do' to Marshall Stalin, to meet him, that's all." Apparently reassured, Molotov did as requested and "everything was OK."[20]

But the immediate prospects of the meeting were not promising. If Overlord was the Gordian knot of allied diplomacy, the Big Three needed more than a ceremonial sword to cut the tangles. The British were presumably unhappy because the Americans and Russians were in "practically complete agreement"; the Americans were upset because the British would not drop their Mediterranean schemes; and the Russians were angry because the West seemed reluctant to accept definite commitments on the second front.[21] With this backdrop, Roosevelt called for a report on the military staff meeting and professed not to know what had been discussed, but he actually had met earlier with the American chiefs to go over that very session.[22]

Brooke reported that the military committee could not yet announce definite recommendations. They had "taken into account the fact that, unless active operations of some kind were undertaken in the Mediterranean in the interval that must elapse between the present time and the launching of Overlord, the Germans would be able either to withdraw forces to Russia or to strengthen the defences of France in anticipation of Overlord."[23] Marshall added that landing craft shortages threatened all allied planning. And Voroshilov, "active and very agreeable in his manner of speech," said that his questions had related to the technical aspects of Overlord.[24] As for detailed planning, the chiefs had generated more questions than answers concerning the cross-channel invasion, and discussion about Turkey and Yugoslavia was incomplete. In short, the military staffs had not accomplished very much.

Inquiring further about Overlord, Stalin got the session "started off on the wrong foot."[25] He wanted to know the name of the commander selected to direct Overlord. When Roosevelt replied that he had not yet decided, Stalin observed that nothing would come of the operation unless one man was made "responsible not only for the preparation but for the execution of the operation."[26] Actually, Lieutenant General Frederick E. Morgan, a British officer, was responsible for laying the foundations, but he would not assume field command. Although the invasion was to be launched from British soil, explained Churchill, the bulk of the troops would be American and should be commanded by an American, while a British general should command the Mediterranean forces. Choosing the actual commander, Churchill suggested, was "more appropriate for discussion by the three heads of government rather than in a somewhat large conference."[27] Roosevelt insisted that the decision should follow the Big Three talks. The Russians, said Stalin, had no desire to influence the decision to name a particular officer; they merely wanted to know who he was.

Roosevelt's apparent reluctance to name a commander was curious in light of the constant American insistence that Overlord must be the major 1944 campaign. Turning to Leahy, Roosevelt whispered, "That old Bolshevik [Stalin] is trying to force me to give him the name of our supreme commander."[28] Here was the weakness of the American position. Espousing the firmest commitment to Overlord, Roosevelt was dragging his feet on settling the command responsibilities. Churchill must have enjoyed the spectacle of someone else on the Overlord hotseat. Perhaps the commander could be announced within the fortnight, suggested Churchill. Roosevelt did not respond.

Saying that he "hoped that it would be convenient if he deployed the British case," Churchill switched the conversation to his favorite subject, the Mediterranean theater.[29] He and the British staff were most anxious to keep British armies busy and not have them "stripped of essential elements."[30] Landing craft could be used for six months in the Mediterranean and then employed in support of Overlord. His idea was to take Rhodes, to bring Turkey into the war, and then to conduct Anvil five or six months later. This would mean delaying Overlord six to eight weeks or recalling landing craft from the Pacific. The allies were thus on the horns of a dilemma, but just two divisions borrowed from Overlord for six months would make a significant difference.

Abandoning proposed Mediterranean operations, Churchill warned, would enable the Germans to move forces from the Balkans. While the British had no interest "of an exceptional or ambitious kind" in the Balkans, he added, all he wanted was to nail down thirty hostile divisions.[31] According to American minutes, he counted twenty-one German and twenty-one Bulgarian divisions there. These he described as "easy prey."[32] Stalin disagreed, accusing Churchill of overstating the case. By Russian reckoning, the Germans had eight divisions in Yugoslavia, three or four in Bulgaria, nine in Italy, and twenty-five in France.[33]

But Churchill had another card to play. Turkey was his trump. If Turkey chose to be uncooperative, he said, "we should lose interest in her territorial rights, particularly the Dardanelles and the Bosphorus."[34] But the overall objective was to keep the Germans tied down in the Balkans, and Turkey could add significant weight to the allied cause. The time had come to reap the harvest, if the allies would pay the "small price."[35] Of course, Turkey might provoke Bulgarian interference. In that case, promised Stalin, the Russians would consider themselves at war with Bulgaria, and Churchill could so inform the Turks. This was more than a bit awkward. The advantages of a front in the Balkans were considerably lessened if the Russians ended up having to bail out Turkey, which, in turn, was bound to be uneasy about any prospects of Russian activity near the Straits.

More so than in the first plenary session, Stalin did not accept Churchill's views unchallenged. Now he insisted that none of the issues involving Turkey, Yugoslavia, or even the conquest of Rome was really important. Turkey would not enter the war as Churchill imagined. While the allies might lend limited support to the war in Yugoslavia, all other operations in the Mediterranean were sideshows. The most important operation, he said, was Overlord, and nothing should be done to detract from the earliest possible invasion of France "sometime in May and no later."[36] If Roosevelt and Churchill were as serious about Overlord as they claimed, they should launch it without delay, plan Anvil "in conformity with the desires of the Russians," and appoint the commander before the end of the conference or, at the latest, within a week. He challenged his allies by concluding, "It would be best to settle these matters during our stay here, and I see no reason why this cannot be done."[37]

Reasons were soon forthcoming. Roosevelt, expressing interest in hearing the various views on military planning, insisted that the central issue was determining the date for Overlord. He attached great importance to dates and said that the West should meet the target date of 1 May 1944 in keeping with the Quebec decision. Here was ambivalence and evasiveness combined. The May date was presumably a moot point, having already been promised. Was Roosevelt leaving the door open for the West to break the latest in a long series of pledges? Why did he ignore both the commander issue and Anvil?

The conference "proceeded with much acerbity."[38] Stalin said that he would not insist on beginning a cross-channel invasion the first, fifteenth, or twentieth day of the month, so long as a definite date was chosen. But Churchill refused to accept any obligatory date because, he contended, flexibility should be the guiding rule. He added that the various views were not as far apart as they seemed, but actually coincided more or less.[39] Of course, less was closer to the mark.

Churchill reminded Stalin that Overlord's success depended upon restricting German forces in France to no more than twelve mobile divisions behind the coastal fortifications and to no more than fifteen divisions as reinforcements within sixty days after the first landings. But, when Stalin asked if thirteen or fourteen divisions would rule out Overlord, Churchill replied, "Certainly not."[40] As to what might constitute the upper limits, Churchill said no more. The reason is that he continued to view Overlord from a Mediterranean perspective. "I was willing," he later wrote, "to do every-thing in the power of His Majesty's Government to begin Overlord at the earliest possible moment, but I did not consider that the very great pos-sibilities in the Mediterranean should be ruthlessly sacrificed and cast aside as if they were of no value, merely to save a month or so in the launching of Overlord."[41]

Stalin, evidently put out at the lack of decision, asked how long Churchill and Roosevelt intended to stay in Tehran. Perhaps he was suggesting that his allies should either get down to business or go home. When Churchill responded that he was personally prepared to stop eating until agreement was reached, Stalin explained that what he had meant to ask was when the conference should end. For his own part, he said, he could not extend his visit beyond 1 December or, at the latest, the second. Roosevelt offered to stay until the conference was finished, and Churchill "said he would stay here forever if necessary."[42]

Perhaps to relieve the tension, Roosevelt proposed to delegate some prac-tical matters to the military staffs. He suggested that the Big Three instruct the combined chiefs to accept Overlord as the major operation and to discuss Mediterranean projects in relation to their potential effects upon Overlord. Churchill agreed and said that the staffs could work to determine the dates of Overlord as well. Why should the staffs trouble themselves with matters properly in the domain of the Big Three? asked Stalin, who slyly suggested that the Soviet Union had tried the committee system and had found that it did not work.[43] Saying that he wished to raise an "indiscreet question," he turned to Churchill and asked, "Do the British really believe in Overlord or are they only saying so to reassure the Russians?"[44]

Churchill was certainly irked to hear such a blunt query; a thinly veiled accusation that he, not so much the Americans, was being less than honest. According to one report, he got so mad that he "stood up and told Stalin that he couldn't talk to him and anybody in Britain like that" and continued to sound off until Eden calmed him down.[45] When he regained his composure, he answered Stalin's question: "Provided the conditions previously stated were established when the time comes," his countrymen would have the duty of hurling "every scrap of strength across the channel."[46]

Over Stalin's objections, the military staffs were instructed to meet the next morning. Stalin having yielded, Roosevelt and Churchill offered dif-ferent instructions. The president wanted Overlord to be considered the dominant operation in 1944, whereas Churchill wanted the chiefs to "con-sider the timing of the supreme operation Overlord having regard to any subsidiary operations which may be undertaken in order to produce the conditions necessary for the success of Overlord and to keep as much weight off Russia as possible in the interim."[47]

At the end, the prevailing impression of what had been accomplished was mostly negative. Brooke, who later said that he felt like entering a lunatic asylum or nursing home, vented his frustration in his diary: "I am *absolutely* disgusted with the politicians' methods of waging a war!! Why will they imagine they are experts at a job they know nothing about! It is lamentable to listen to them!"[48] And Stalin was probably peeved at having the crucial Overlord decisions shunted off to a committee. Only Roosevelt was happy; Churchill was bearing the brunt of Stalin's questions.

Stalin's Dinner

The strained atmosphere carried over into a "stormy private dinner" hosted by Stalin in the evening.[49] Superficially, the allies tried to soothe each other with complimentary toasts. For example, Churchill toasted "Stalin the Mighty," but not even an endless litany of toasts could disguise the disagreements.[50] The dinner party—the Big Three, Hopkins, Eden, Molotov, Harriman, Clark-Kerr, and the interpreters—was treated to a lavish table heavily laden with cold hors d'oeuvres, hot borscht, fish, meat of various kinds, salads, fruits, vodka, and wines.[51]

Throughout the evening, Stalin needled Churchill, to an extent that made some observers wonder whether the teasing was either intended or accepted as good-humored raillery.[52] Stalin "pulled Winston's leg" and the latter rose "to every fly."[53] At one point, remarking that Churchill nursed some secret affection for the Germans, Stalin chided Churchill for wanting a soft peace. The prime minister bore everything patiently, until Stalin, in a deceptively gentle manner, suggested that the 50,000 officers of the German Commanding Staff be liquidated at the war's end without trial.[54] Churchill responded that the British people would never tolerate mass executions in cold blood. Stalin pursued the subject until Churchill exclaimed angrily that he would rather be taken out into the garden and shot himself than to sully his own or his country's honor "by such infamy."[55] Instead of getting honestly indignant or passing the whole thing off as a joke, judged Bohlen, Churchill adopted a plaintive tone that conveyed a sense of guilt, making the performance less than his best.[56]

In what was, at best, a heavy-handed effort to change the mood, the president proposed what he called a compromise. The allies, he said, should execute only forty-nine thousand Germans.[57] Churchill, who may have been as shocked by Roosevelt's apparently flippant manner as by Stalin's barbarous suggestion, was not amused. Was he the victim of a cruel joke, followed by one in bad taste?

Elliott Roosevelt, who had not originally been invited to the dinner, sat in an adjoining room listening through the open door. Stalin had learned of his presence and summoned him to the table. Following his father's compromise suggestion, Elliott stood to propose a toast to the allied soldiers, who would solve the problem, he said, by killing the Germans in battle. Stalin thereupon leaped to his feet, embraced Elliott, and clinked glasses with him. But the prime minister, furious, said, "Much as I love you, Elliott, I cannot forgive you for making such a dastardly statement," and stumped from the room.[58]

Some observers have blamed Churchill's outburst on too much brandy. But, in Reilly's estimation, the world did not contain enough alcohol to affect the prime minister.[59] At the time, Churchill seems to have been "shocked, very definite that he would have no part of Stalin's suggestion, and very sober about the whole thing."[60]

Stalin followed Churchill from the room, clapped his hands on the prime minister's shoulders from behind, grinned broadly, and declared that he was only playing and that nothing of a serious character had entered his head. At this, Churchill agreed to return to the table, but he wrote afterwards that Stalin was in earnest when he proposed to kill the German officers.[61] Stalin may have demonstrated a murderous streak or, more rationally, he may have offered the suggestion as a trial balloon, to gauge Western feelings. The other explanation, of course, is that Stalin was indeed only joking. The translation, claimed Bohlen, came out stilted, whereas Stalin made the remark in a quasi-jocular fashion with a sardonic smile and wave of the hand, meaning this as a gibe at Churchill.[62] And even Churchill was occasionally disposed to interpret the incident as a simple case of gallows humor, because Stalin "had been trying to get a rise and had winked at Anthony [Eden]."[63]

Churchill found another cause for displeasure when Stalin raised the subject of colonialism. The prime minister angrily refused the suggestion that all colonial areas be given independence at war's end. He declared that Britain would never relinquish Singapore or Hong Kong unless stripped of them by war. Some British colonies might be granted eventual independence, he argued, but only in accordance with British timing and discretion. He rejected the notion that Britain would release colonial areas merely because that policy found favor among the Russians and Americans.

Perhaps to mollify Churchill, Stalin said that he favored an "increase in the British Empire, particularly around Gibraltar."[64] With the issue of territorial changes now before them, Churchill asked what areas the Russians would demand for their share of the spoils. But Stalin cagily refused to give a direct answer and said only, "There is no need to speak at the present time about any Soviet desires, but when the time comes, we will speak."[65]

Throughout the dinner, Churchill and Stalin were thus often at odds. With an expression of great contempt, Stalin said "that one thing he was glad of was that Churchill had never been a liberal." When Churchill noted that the

1938 Munich agreement had been stupid and shameful, Stalin replied that the Russians had never believed the Czechs would fight. Later, in reply to Churchill's confession that, after the last war, he had done everything in his power to stop the spread of Bolshevism, Stalin said that the British need not have worried quite so much.[66]

But, if they exchanged words in anger, Churchill and Stalin at least parted on friendly terms. They stood with their hands on each other's shoulders, looked into each other's eyes, and ended their conversation with a convivial embrace. It was a pity, Clark-Kerr later regretted, that their words were not recorded, "that people might know what piffle great men sometimes talk."[67]

Assessing the results of the conference thus far, many of the British were disappointed. For one thing, Hopkins apparently told Churchill that the British were fighting a losing battle in trying to delay Overlord.[68] Cadogan gathered that the "Great Ones had the usual woolly and bibulous evening."[69] Cunningham exclaimed, "What a waste of time this is," and Portal suggested returning to Cairo since "no useful purpose is served by our being here."[70] And, at midnight, the prime minister closed his eyes and with a tired, slow voice told Moran, Clark-Kerr, and Eden, "There might be a more bloody war. I shall not be there. I shall be asleep. I want to sleep for billions of years."[71]

8

THIRD-DAY STAFF AND PRIVATE MEETINGS

Detailed application of what had been decided could still be
left to the arbitrament of circumstances.

—Lord Alanbrooke

Meeting of the Combined Chiefs

When Brooke arose on the morning of 30 November, he feared that the
British faced an unpleasant day.[1] Realizing that their plans were being
jeopardized by the growing Russo-American opposition, the British chiefs
met at 8:45 A.M. to review the impasse that confronted them. They wanted
to strengthen their proposals and iron out some of the trouble spots that
seemed to hinder acceptance of their plans.

After reading Eisenhower's comments about the problems of invading
southern France, the British decided to recommend postponing Anvil until
"maybe after Overlord."[2] Also, the allies must advance to the Pisa-Rimini
line in Italy, provide commando support to Tito, and retain landing craft in
the Mediterranean until 15 January 1944—all of which meant that the
earliest possible date that they would accept for Overlord was 1 June 1944.[3]
Aegean operations, they concluded, were entirely dependent upon Turkey's
decision about entering the war. And Stalin's promise to enter the war
against Japan encouraged them to insist that Buccaneer be scrapped.

When the Americans arrived at the British embassy for the 9:30 A.M.
meeting, the British were primed to put up a stiff debate. The Russians
stayed out to let the British and Americans resolve their differences. Leahy
expected the session to lead to agreement, because, he wrote, the British
could not fail to see the advantages of Overlord. But such optimism was
misplaced. The British staff was not, as he erroneously believed, secretly in
agreement with the Americans, although forced to follow Churchill's lead.[4]
Rather, they defended their Mediterranean plans with tenacious energy.

The basic problem, said Brooke, was to form an "agreed basis for discussion with the Soviets."[5] The solution was simple: Americans should yield

the floor to British strategy. Allied forces should continue to advance in Italy and, after taking Rome, should not stop short of the Pisa-Rimini line, even if the Overlord date was thereby altered. All possible aid should be sent to Tito. In short, what was the preferred sequence of campaigns? Italy was the top priority; followed by Rhodes, if Turkey entered the war; and then Anvil, which was "important but not vital."[6] Landing craft used to seize Rhodes could be returned for Anvil, although the date of the latter campaign would necessarily be delayed.

The Americans disagreed. Brooke seemed to have overlooked Overlord, the sole point of contention being the exact date, and other operations, not it, should be delayed or aborted. Leahy threatened that if the West could not launch the main invasion by 1 May 1944, as originally decided at Quebec, then neither could they undertake any of the British-favored operations in the eastern Mediterranean.[7] Urging that the allies make every effort to fix the invasion date, Marshall named 15 May.[8] This shift from the previous American insistence on 1 May apparently passed without comment. Marshall insisted that Anvil would have to be undertaken, that launching two separate invasions of the French coastline would stretch allied resources to the limit, and that the Italian campaign would have to make some sacrifices. Lacking sufficient landing craft, the West could not invade Rhodes and southern France simultaneously.

So, the crux of the matter was that the allies had to solve the landing craft dilemma. Brooke argued that repair and training schedules made it necessary to move shipping from Italy no later than 15 December 1943, if the allies hoped to invade Rhodes first and then use the same ships to invade southern France. Dropping the Rhodes campaign, rebutted Leahy, would permit retention until 15 January. But Rhodes could be pursued, Brooke shot back, if the Americans would drop Buccaneer.[9]

One problem was that the chiefs could not reasonably estimate what damages might be sustained by landing craft in actual operations and, therefore, the time that would be needed between operations for repairs and training replacement crews. By American calculations, landing craft would have to be released from the Mediterranean two-and-a-half months before Overlord. British records indicate that the Americans proposed 1 March as the latest date for transferring the necessary ships, based upon the premise that Overlord would take place on 15 May.[10] But, if no more than one hundred days were an adequate turn-around time and if all diversions were set aside, King set 1 February as the limit. Cunningham disagreed, insisting that 15 February was better, the difference being that he was counting both on operations in the eastern Mediterranean and on Overlord taking place at the end of May.[11] Significantly, the Americans had now clearly abandoned the Quebec decision.

From the plenary sessions and earlier staff meetings, it was evident that

Overlord was not enough to suit the Russians, who also called for landings in southern France. If the allies could capture Rome by the end of January 1944 and if the Rhodes campaign, underway about 21 March, required no more than one month to complete, the earliest possible date for Anvil, Marshall surmised, would be 15 July. When Portal cautioned the military chiefs to avoid the temptation to be overly conservative, Marshall explained that his estimate, using a force barely sufficient and not counting losses, was the best case; the worst was leaving all landing craft in the Mediterranean, thereby setting back the invasion of France by three months.

King asked if he understood correctly that landing craft could not be made available for Overlord to take place on 1 May, even if all other operations were cancelled. Overlord could be launched during May, he argued, if the allies did not squander landing craft in the Mediterranean.[12] The British, on the other hand, pointed out that delay in Overlord was inevitable, so Mediterranean opportunities should not be wasted. Brooke insisted that if landing craft were removed from the Mediterranean on 15 January, the earliest date mentioned by the Americans, Overlord still could not be undertaken before 1 June.[13] But the Americans held out for 15 May as the target for Overlord.

Setting the date for Anvil was solved more easily. This operation, said Marshall, should not be carried out more than two or three weeks before Overlord, and he preferred simultaneous landings. Having both invasions on the same date, added King, would provide a "much better basis for planning."[14] Overall agreement followed, in spite of Portal's warning about the inadequacy of fighter cover. He had apparently forgotten his speech about the evils of overestimating the enemy.

But the chiefs still could not agree on when to set Overlord in motion. If the allies could not fix a firm date, Brooke warned, there was no point in proceeding with the conference, yet both he and Portal called for further postponements on the grounds that more landing craft would be available the longer they waited. Overlord could be planned for 1 June, or even earlier in May, said Brooke, if the allies dropped all other operations, including Anvil.[15] King objected that moving the date from 1 May would mean up to two-and-a-half months of inactivity for Overlord's thirty-five divisions. 1 June, insisted Cunningham, was the earliest possible date for Overlord.[16]

The Americans expressed surprise at the British proposal of a June date. Although the Americans themselves seemed to want a later date, King and Leahy asked if the British had not previously accepted 1 May. Brooke replied that the May date had been a compromise and was therefore not strictly binding.[17] Also, the Russians had promised a general offensive along the eastern front to coincide with Overlord; and, never before, said Brooke, had the Russians started an attack in May. Ismay added that even if they had told the Russians to expect Overlord in May, they had not bound themselves to 1 May.[18]

Leahy asked Brooke if he foresaw any conditions favorable to the success of Overlord, short of total German military collapse.[19] Brooke, who might well have wondered if Voroshilov or Stalin had come to the meeting in disguise, replied that Overlord had a good chance of succeeding if it was scheduled for no later than 1 June and if the Russians cooperated by attacking the Germans at the same time.[20]

Whereas Cunningham suggested that the Anglo-Americans could keep a 1 June deadline, Portal proposed giving Overlord two alternative dates, depending upon what Turkey did. Turkish intentions would probably be known by mid-February 1944, he said, and a Turkish decision to enter the war would force a postponement of Overlord.[21] King's rebuttal was that neither Anvil nor Italian operations was contingent upon what happened with Turkey, and, by inference, the same standard should apply to Overlord. And Marshall responded that landing craft withdrawn for Turkey's benefit might never be used, thus proving wasteful all around.[22]

But the British began to wear down American resistance. Brooke offered to accept 1 May as a Rankin date—that is, an emergency invasion in case of imminent German or Russian collapse—while reminding the Americans that 1 May had "not been based on any particular strategic consideration."[23] From the air war perspective, chipped in Portal, a date in June or July would be better. Leahy then agreed that the Russians would not refuse 1 June if the West was firm.[24]

After an hour-and-a-half of haggling, the chiefs approached agreement.[25] To reach the Pisa-Rimini line in Italy, sixty-eight Landing Ship Tanks, scheduled for use in Overlord, would be retained in the Mediterranean until 15 January. This, wrote Ismay, meant that Overlord could not be launched until 1 June.[26] But the chiefs proposed to tell the Russians that the cross-channel invasion would take place "during May," with a supporting operation against southern France on the largest scale possible.[27] Afterwards, Leahy assumed that the Americans had finally succeeded in wresting a definite commitment from the British on Overlord. However, Brooke later wrote that even the 1 June date was understood to be approximate.[28]

The British were divided in opinion on the nature of their agreement with the Americans. Ismay sadly compared the British position to that of a man who has signed a formal agreement to purchase property "at some future date without knowing how much it is going to cost, or whether he will have the money to pay for it when the time comes," with the contract forbidding the purchase of a more desirable property that may have subsequently come on the market.[29] But Brooke, much closer to the mark, noted privately that the "detailed application of what had been decided could still be left to the arbitrament of circumstances."[30]

The chiefs were unable to reach agreement on Aegean operations, deferring this question to the Big Three, and they postponed their debate on Buccaneer. Although some commentators later described this meeting as a

British surrender to the Americans on Overlord, the reverse seems to have occurred. The Quebec decision on Overlord was lost in the shuffle, but the debate was not yet over. Now the question was whether Overlord would be targeted for launch on 15 May or 1 June 1944. The Russians, of course, would not be so informed.

Churchill-Stalin Meeting

Alarmed because Roosevelt had already twice met privately with Stalin but had refused to meet with the British "in spite of their hitherto intimate relations and the way in which their vital affairs were interwoven," Churchill sought a private meeting with Stalin.[31] The most important reason, wrote Churchill later, was because he feared Stalin had formed the false idea that the British meant to stop Overlord. He may also have wanted to soften the increasing Russian and American opposition to his Mediterranean projects.

At 12:40 A.M., Churchill walked to the Russian embassy where Stalin was waiting in a small room. Birse was the only interpreter present, and he translated both ways. The prime minister explained that he held a great affection for the American people, partly because his mother was American, so "what he was going to say was not to be understood as anything disparaging of the Americans, and he would be perfectly loyal towards them."[32] But there were things, he added, better said outright between two persons. If the British gave the impression of being interested only in the Mediterranean, that was because they dominated that theater. British strength there was three or four times greater than American forces. For example, of thirteen to fourteen divisions in Italy, nine or ten were British, and he was understandably anxious that "troops should not be hamstrung if it could be avoided, and he wanted to use them all the time."[33] Churchill was, to be sure, always concerned that there should never be grounds for accusations that the British were not pulling their fair share of the load.[34] The Americans, said Churchill, were committed to Overlord, regardless of the possible effects on other theaters.

The central issue, Churchill told Stalin, was not to choose between Mediterranean operations and an early date for Overlord. Rather, the real choice was between European operations and the proposed offensives in the Bay of Bengal. Churchill was "not keen" about Buccaneer, because its cancellation would free enough landing craft for operations in the Mediterranean.[35] Following Stalin's "momentous announcement" about Russia joining the war against Japan, added Churchill, he had immediately suggested to the Americans that landing craft might be diverted from the Indian Ocean or the Pacific. While this proposal was reasonable, Churchill explained, the Americans were "very touchy about the Pacific."[36]

Although it would be launched from British bases, Overlord was essentially an American operation, and American forces would outnumber the British. The numerical imbalance would increase as American reinforcements were used after the first landings. At Quebec, Roosevelt had asked Churchill to accept an American commander, and he had agreed, so the delay in appointing a commander could not be blamed on the British.[37] Suggesting that Roosevelt's reluctance stemmed from the political effects of appointing an officer to high command, Churchill assured Stalin that he had personally urged the president to make his choice before the end of the conference. In reply, Stalin said, "That is good."[38]

Turning to Overlord's date, Churchill insisted that the British would be "ready for the date that is fixed."[39] Without revealing the extent of the debate among the British and Americans, Churchill hinted that a firm date could be reached before the Big Three parted.[40] The British, Churchill promised, would be in fighting trim "by the date fixed in May or June," with sixteen divisions at the start, reinforced to nearly half a million men by June 1944, and this commitment belied the accusation that the British wished to obstruct the cross-channel invasion.[41]

Insisting that the difference between himself and the president was "in fact a very narrow one," Churchill said that he wanted to get what he needed for the Mediterranean and, at the same time, keep the date of Overlord.[42] This had been his purpose at Cairo, but, unfortunately, Chinese affairs had taken up almost all of the time. He hoped that enough landing craft could be found for all operations. He blamed American efforts to build up Overlord forces for denuding the Mediterranean and thus making it impossible for the allies to take full advantage of the Italian surrender. But a great battle, perhaps a miniature Stalingrad, was impending in Italy. The British intended to push on with amphibious landings near the Tiber and expected to hold the narrow leg rather than expand into the wide part of Italy. Meanwhile, Churchill took a "favorable view" of a landing in southern France when the time came for Overlord, "or somewhat earlier or later," using as many of the divisions in Italy as possible.[43]

Churchill listed the preconditions for Overlord. The Germans should not be allowed to shift troops from the eastern front to France, because thirty to forty divisions there would ruin Overlord. And he feared that the enemy might destroy the invasion thirty or forty days after the first landings. But, if the Red Army engaged the enemy, if the Germans were held in Italy, if Turkey entered the war, if Buccaneer were cancelled, and if the southern France invasion could be scheduled properly, Overlord might work.[44]

The Russians, replied Stalin, were counting on Overlord, and they expected it to be launched in May. If May passed with no invasion, Overlord would probably not occur at all in 1944, and that, he warned, would cause severe disappointment and bad feelings in Russia. He wanted to know beforehand if Overlord was not going to materialize in order to forestall feelings of resentment that might be aroused among his countrymen. A Russian offensive could be planned, he hinted, if he knew with certainty when the Anglo-American assault would occur. Spring was the best time for an attack, since the Germans feared a Russian advance at that time. So, he asked, when would Overlord begin?[45]

Wondering if he would be the "only outsider to know the fateful date," Birse listened, he later wrote, breathlessly for Churchill's reply.[46] But Churchill neatly sidestepped the question on the ground that he could not disclose the date without Roosevelt's approval. The answer, he promised, would be given at lunch, and he "thought that the marshal would be satisfied."[47]

Showing little interest in the Mediterranean, even when Churchill handed him a map of Yugoslavia to compare with his own, Stalin threw his support behind Overlord. Afterward, Churchill told Moran that Stalin apparently wanted the invasion in May because the Red Army was war weary.[48] The prime minister must have been disappointed to find Stalin so adamant about Overlord, so inflexible about the date, and so unwilling to lend support in persuading the Americans to trade the Pacific theater for the Mediterranean.

Little Three Luncheon

Another important meeting of the day brought together the foreign ministers of Britain and Russia, Eden and Molotov, with Harry Hopkins, who assumed the role of the American secretary of state, at a noon luncheon in the British embassy. Among the subjects they discussed was a proposal to seize and retain control of certain, as yet unspecified, strategic military bases, to prevent German and Japanese aggression after the war. They agreed that something must be done to forestall the enemy's recovery, but they differed on a program of control. Molotov suggested, for example, that France be punished for her collaboration with Germany by being stripped of Bizerte and Dakar. The Russians, he said, would have no objection to placing French bases under American or British administration, but France must be treated as a defeated power. Eden "objected mildly."[49] France, he insisted, should not be punished. British experience with France suggested that the allies would be well advised to treat her with lenience. His countrymen did not want any more territory, added Eden, but "he considered that strategic points in enemy territory should pass under the control of the United Nations."[50] If Molotov insisted, perhaps the French would voluntarily give these bases over to United Nations' control.

Molotov continued to call for the punishment of France until he discovered that Hopkins sided with Eden. Strongpoints, said Hopkins, should be worked out with a view to potential enemies, and he listed Germany and Japan, not France, in that category. Offering to leave the question of any strong points in Europe to Russian and British discretion, he observed that the United States was not particularly worried about any postwar threat from Germany. But Americans were concerned about strongpoints in the Pacific and intended to maintain bases in the Philippines even after granting that country its independence. The Americans would establish bases on Formosa, if it returned to China after the war. The size, character, and duties of occupying forces on such bases would have to be worked out in detail, but, he insisted, his country must have freedom of action.[51] When Molotov asked about the disposition of the Dutch islands, Hopkins turned evasive. This, replied Hopkins, was a difficult question, but "he was referring mainly to the enforcement of peace against Germany."[52] He did not explain the connection between Germany and strong points in the Pacific.

Would it be possible, Hopkins asked, to establish allied bases in Belgium? Eden replied that complications arising from Belgium's sovereignty and status as a friendly nation could be resolved by following the pattern of British leases to America in the West Indies, where bases had been exchanged for military equipment. Mention of the West Indies set off a testy exchange between Eden, who insisted that Britain wanted American presence in the region, and Hopkins, who retorted that the deal was nothing more than a cold-hearted swap, producing mutual benefits.

The Little Three barely scratched the surface of the strong points issue, although they agreed it was "one of the most important postwar problems."[53] Saying that Churchill and Stalin had already discussed the problem, Hopkins tried to shift the responsibility for making decisions on this question to the Big Three. Molotov observed that the foreign ministers could do little more than clarify the subject, and Eden added that their exchange of views had fulfilled their obligation.

With the same disharmony that plagued the Big Three, the Little Three discussed the prospects of Turkey's participation in the war. Although agreeing in principle that Turkish help was desirable, they acknowledged that the likelihood of a favorable decision by Turkey was remote, and they could not decide on how to change this. When Eden proposed to give Turkey a joint summons to enter the war, Molotov asked if Eden, in earlier conversations with the Turks, had not already spoken "in the name of all three United Nations," to which Eden replied that he had "felt authorised to do so."[54] Inönü should be invited to Cairo, where combined pressure might be brought to bear on him, especially if the Russians would add their weight. If Inönü refused to come, Eden proposed sending an ambassador or special messenger to Turkey, and he asked if his companions could suggest someone who could be entrusted with such a matter.

Molotov, ignoring Eden's clumsy attempt to have himself named the special messenger, went on to other matters. While the Russians favored bringing Turkey into the war before the end of the year, no one thought this likely.[55] Russia, he promised, would break diplomatic relations with Bulgaria in the even more unlikely event that a Turkish decision to enter the war provoked Bulgarian hostility. He asked Eden to explain Churchill's statement that a Turkish refusal to join the allies would affect the Straits. In reply, Eden said "that Mr. Churchill meant by this that it would alter the whole basis of friendship between Great Britain and Turkey," and "he did not think that he had meant more."[56]

Here was a familiar and consistent pattern illustrating agreement in principle at work. Promises about military operations or territorial changes might be proliferated with reckless abandon. But, when called to task, the benefactor would begin backpedaling. Had Churchill implied that Russia would benefit from the Turkish issue?—Yes. Did he really intend that Russia would gain easy access to the Straits?—Probably not.

Hopkins predicted that a Turkish decision to enter the war would lead to allied involvement in the eastern Mediterranean in large operations such as those proposed for Rhodes. Turkish campaigns, he deduced, would undoubtedly delay Overlord. The only justification for a postponement would be to bring about Finland's withdrawal from the war, at best a slim chance. He concluded that the urgent needs were to decide on a definite place and time for Overlord, to name a commander, and to determine the nature of a supporting invasion of southern France. When Molotov insisted that the Russians opposed any delay in Overlord, Hopkins observed that the chiefs of staff "considered that Turkey would not declare war unless we seized the Dodecanese," and that, in effect, would postpone the cross-channel invasion.[57]

Eden asked if the Russians wanted to send a mission to confer with Tito. Molotov, rather unenthusiastically, replied that the Russians would make definite plans about that upon their return to Moscow, but he asked why the mission should go to Tito, rather than to Mihajlović, the nominal head of Yugoslav resistance. Eden, who was not sure whether sending a mission to both was physically possible, owing to intervening German forces, replied that Mihajlović was "no good to deal with," but the Russians could send a separate mission if they insisted.[58]

Perhaps to garner support for increased operations in the eastern Mediterranean, Eden proposed to give the Russians an air base in northern Africa and asked Molotov to name a suitable site. Molotov thanked Eden, but he apparently was unprepared to blurt out the name of a choice location, because he never answered the question. When Eden pointed out that the British had a base in Cairo and offered to let the Russians have one there as well, Molotov still did not rise to the bait. Although Cairo was fine, said Molotov, the British could make the final choice.

Finally, Eden asked for an explanation of the indiscreet conversation of 28 November between Churchill and Stalin on the settlement of Poland's frontiers. "If the question could be resolved by an agreement to which all could subscribe that Poland should take two steps to the left," said Eden, the allies could examine the size of these steps.[59] The president, interrupted Hopkins, would say all that was on his mind about Poland to Stalin, and he presumed that the same could be said about Churchill. Hopkins suggested that the subject properly rested in other hands, and the discussion on the Polish issue was shelved.

At the close, Hopkins and Eden talked about the prospects of the upcoming American elections. The results, speculated Molotov, who asked what they were discussing, would be "satisfactory as showing that the union of the three great powers was strong" and people "like strength and friendliness."[60] In much the same congenial manner, Hopkins observed that the Moscow Conference had produced great effects in America. When Eden suggested another meeting for the following day, Molotov offered to serve as host. But what had the Little Three actually accomplished in their first meeting? With the exception of the strong points discussion, which was inconclusive, they covered no new ground and merely tracked the same old ruts.

9

THIRD-DAY MEETINGS OF THE BIG THREE

In war-time, truth is so precious that she should always be attended by a bodyguard of lies.
—Winston S. Churchill

Big Three Luncheon

The Big Three reassembled at 1:30 P.M. on 30 November in Roosevelt's quarters for lunch in an atmosphere far more cordial than that of the previous day. Before the meal, Roosevelt read to Stalin the recommendations of the military staffs. Overlord, Roosevelt read, would be launched during May 1944. Stalin showed great pleasure and said he was satisfied.[1] Relieved to have outlived what he called the "long and tiresome campaign" for the second front, Birse believed that the allies had finally resolved the cross-channel debate.[2]

But Churchill hastened to reiterate the conditions that had first to be met, and he painted such a gloomy picture as to suggest that only a German collapse prior to the cross-channel invasion would ensure its success. The exact date, he said, depended on the phases of the moon. He ignored Roosevelt's suggestion that the most suitable time appeared to lie between 15 and 20 May.[3] Churchill, obviously still reluctant to make an irrevocable pledge, did not comment upon Roosevelt's further announcement that Anvil and Overlord would occur simultaneously.

Acknowledging that the cross-channel invasion would naturally require one or two weeks in May, Stalin said that he was not seeking to be told the exact date, but he did ask again about the selection of a commander. According to one report, Stalin had been told that Marshall was the unofficial appointee, but this information had not come from Roosevelt.[4] As Stalin had said earlier, so long as Overlord had no commander, planning must inevitably remain tentative.

Replying that he would have to consult with his staff on the question, Roosevelt promised a decision within three or four days. The choice, he said, was complicated by having to determine whether the officer would operate from England, whether a separate commander would be named for the Mediterranean, and whether command of Anvil would fall under Overlord or under the Mediterranean command. Such issues, of course, involved the British. Operations against southern France, emphasized Churchill, should fall under the Overlord command, while the British would handle the Italian theater. Moreover, an American should command Overlord, and a British general should command the Mediterranean. Stalin agreed with what he called "sound military doctrine."[5]

By asking Stalin if he had read the Cairo communiqué on the Far East, Churchill raised a discussion on a whole range of colonial issues. It was a good communiqué, replied Stalin, but he had nothing to say except that Russia "would have something to add when she herself was active in that part of the world."[6] Nevertheless, he endorsed Korean independence. And he thought it proper that Manchuria, Formosa, and the Pescadores Islands be returned to China, but added that the Chinese would certainly be more deserving if they could resist the Japanese more effectively than they had in the past.

When the talk turned to the great size of the Russian land mass, Churchill described the Big Three conference as having passed from weighty military matters to "lighter subjects."[7] Calling Russia's terrain a valuable ally, Stalin explained that the Germans might have won the war had they not miscalculated the costs of conquering such a vast land. Thereupon Churchill observed that such a land mass deserved access to warm water ports, and he said that the question should be part of the peace settlement. Specific details could be handled "agreeably and as between friends."[8]

Following Churchill's suggestion, Stalin asked about removing restrictions on Russia's access to the Turkish Straits. The Big Three, he proposed, should revise the 1920 Treaty of Sèvres. This agreement had demilitarized the Straits, a decision upheld until the 1936 Treaty of Montreux had granted Turkey the right to fortify the region. As a result, complained Stalin, Russia had no outlet. Replying that he had no objection in principle, Churchill pointed out that he wanted to get Turkey into the war, and this was an awkward moment to raise the question. The time would come later, said Stalin, who added that he was in no hurry to go beyond a general discussion.[9] Churchill looked forward to seeing Russian fleets, both naval and merchant, on all the world's seas following the war, to which Stalin replied that this seemed contrary to British attitudes in the past. Churchill admitted that Russia and Britain had not seen eye to eye on this question in earlier days, and Stalin agreed that Russia had been quite different then.

Saying that direct action should be taken to open the seas of the world to the Russians, Roosevelt turned to applying this principle to the Baltic Sea. He liked the idea of combining the former Hanseatic cities of Bremen,

Hamburg, and Lübeck into some type of free trade zone. Also, he proposed that the Kiel Canal be placed under international "control and guaranty," to ensure freedom of passage.[10]

Stalin then asked what could be done for Russia in the Far East. When Churchill pointed out that Russia already had Vladivostok, Stalin rebutted that this port was "closed and depended on the Straits of Tsushima," which was only partly ice free and was situated near Japan.[11] Petropavlovsk and perhaps Kamchatka were better, even though both were handicapped by poor railroad service. He concluded that the Russians had only one warm water port, Murmansk, and its difficulties were well known in the West.

Roosevelt offered a solution. Why not, he asked, make Dairen a free port? When Stalin replied that the Chinese might object to losing it, Roosevelt predicted that they would appreciate the advantages of having the city under international control. The president said that he had discussed this very idea with Chiang Kai-shek, who was not opposed to setting up a free port. However, according to the Sextant (First Cairo Conference) minutes, Roosevelt actually promised Chiang that Dairen would return to Chinese control.[12]

Churchill observed that he "wished to meet the Russian grievance because the government of the world must be entrusted to satisfied nations who wished nothing more for themselves than what they had."[13] There would always be danger if governments were in the "hands of hungry nations," he warned, but "none of us had any reason to seek for anything more."[14] They would keep the peace because their power placed them above the rest, and they were "like rich men dwelling at peace within their habitations."[15] Churchill may have been drawing Stalin out to learn what specific territories the Russians wanted. Fixing the cost of Russian participation would avoid a blank check arrangement. Whatever his intentions, Churchill again asked Stalin to spell out Russian demands. He told Stalin that one reason he had raised the Cairo communiqué was to discuss warm water ports in the Far East. But Stalin hedged, claiming that "it would perhaps be better to await the time when the Russians would be taking an active representation in the Far Eastern war."[16]

Third Plenary Session

At 4:00 P.M. on 30 November, the Big Three, with the same aides as on the previous day, met in the conference room.[17] The meeting was short, because, as Leahy observed, the "military part of the conference was over."[18] The major purpose of this session was to formalize the agreements reached by the Anglo-American combined chiefs in their morning talks. Saying that he was personally happy that the decisions were ready, Roosevelt asked Brooke to read them.

Taking the floor, Brooke said that the combined chiefs had agreed to recommend that Overlord take place in May 1944, but he did not name an exact day. Also, the chiefs recommended a supporting operation in southern France, "on as large a scale as possible, depending on the number of landing craft available."[19] That was all—Brooke's anticlimactic and threadbare announcement included no reference to the Italian theater and its connection to Overlord's date and no references to the support of Tito.

The remainder of the session was devoted to what Brooke called "pretty speeches."[20] Churchill emphasized the need to keep maximum pressure on the Germans. To do this, he said, the Big Three and their staffs needed close and intimate contact. In "closing on the wild beast," he added, "all parts of the narrowing circle should be aflame with battle."[21] To this end, campaigns in Turkey and Yugoslavia should be coordinated with the larger allied efforts.

The time of greatest danger for Overlord, predicted Stalin, would come at the beginning, because of the difficulties in overcoming the enemy's strongest defensive points. Suggesting that the Germans might try to transfer divisions from the eastern front, he announced that the Red Army would launch a large-scale offensive in a number of places during May. He had already made this promise, he explained, but it was important enough to repeat.[22]

Roosevelt said that Stalin's statement on the coordination of operations pleased him and forestalled the question that he had been about to ask. The conference had brought out the importance of the timing of operations in all theaters, and the three staffs should continue to work together.

Concerning Overlord, Roosevelt said that he had already told Stalin that the next step was the appointment of a commander. While he could not yet announce a decision, he promised to settle the issue within four days at the latest. And he proposed that both the British and American military staffs return to Cairo, because they had a "great deal of detail work to do in working out the decisions" reached at Tehran.[23]

The major remaining problem, said Churchill, was to find the necessary landing craft. He could not believe that the United States and Britain lacked the resources and ingenuity to make available what was needed. He had asked his staff to determine the total number of landing craft available in the Mediterranean and expected to have the answer upon returning home. Overlord should be delivered with smashing force to place "that man [Hitler] in a position where there was no way out for him," said Churchill.[24] So, if Hitler attempted to hold firmly in the west, he would be smashed on the Russian front, and, if he attempted to hold the east, he would be smashed in the west. Churchill's hopes would be fulfilled, he declared, if the armed forces of the three allies were in heavy action on the continent "by June."[25]

Roosevelt brought up the subject of a communiqué to be released to the press. He suggested releasing a document that would serve to weaken the enemy's resolve and strengthen home morale. The military staffs could draft a text concerning the military aspects and give it to the Big Three for review and amendment before release. Stalin agreed, on the condition that the communiqué only cover military plans. And, when Churchill said that any press release should emphasize the concerted nature of the allied offensives, Stalin agreed, but he warned that it should not be so specific as to enable the Germans to prepare for what was in store for them. Churchill suggested making the paper "brief and mystifying."[26] Without telling the Germans what to expect or when, the allies might give them a foretaste of doom. Stalin agreed, but he said that the allies should guard against turning the mystical tone of the communiqué into "mysticism."[27] Confusing the Germans was a good idea, Stalin carefully added, so long as one of the mysteries was not the second front.[28]

Also discussed during the third plenary session was the need to develop cover plans to keep the enemy guessing about impending operations. The Germans, warned Churchill, would soon learn of the preparations for the invasion of France, and they would begin countermoves that might well threaten the campaign's success. He asked if the Big Three could devise a plan to deceive them. Replying that a big operation such as Overlord could not be hidden in a sack, Stalin said that the Germans could be tricked by dummy tanks and aircraft, together with false landing fields and phony radio traffic, into expecting an attack in the wrong area.

"In wartime," said Churchill, "Truth is so precious that she should always be attended by a bodyguard of lies."[29] When Stalin replied that the Russians knew that but preferred to call it military cunning, the prime minister said that he liked to call it military diplomacy. But, whether it was called one thing or another, the allies agreed upon the necessity of shielding or disguising their plans.

Churchill concluded that the plenary meeting could now "break up as the military questions had been settled."[30] According to British minutes, the following were the points of agreement: (1) Overlord was to be launched in May with an invasion of southern France on the largest possible scale; (2) allied staffs were to keep "in closest touch from now onwards;" (3) a draft communiqué covering the military conversations was to be prepared, this task to be completed by the three staffs before the next day; (4) cover and deception plans were to be devised; and (5) the American and British staffs were to depart the following day for Cairo.[31] The third point was fulfilled by a brief statement which read: "The military Staffs of the three Powers concerted their plans for the final destruction of the German forces. They reached complete agreement as to the scope and timing of the operations which will be undertaken from East, West, and South, and arrangements were made to ensure intimate and continuous cooperation."[32]

But Churchill knew that the Big Three had unfinished business. He expressed the hope that the allies could discuss a number of "political" questions in meetings on 1 and 2 December. "Great value," he said, would derive from telling the world that "full agreement had been reached on all questions."[33] Roosevelt and Stalin agreed to stay in Tehran through 2 December.

At the close of the third plenary session, several of the Americans were pleased. "Everything went along as smooth as silk," recorded Arnold.[34] Roosevelt told his son Elliott that the choice of a date for Overlord was settled at last, and he added drily, "for the fourth time."[35] Leahy, more cautious, wrote that the journey halfway around the world would be justified if the decisions reached were actually carried out.[36]

Unfortunately, the allied chiefs left few clues behind as to their true intentions, perhaps due to a shared sense of political expediency. Brooke wrote: "One thing is quite clear. The more politicians you put together to settle the prosecution of the war, the longer you postpone its conclusion!"[37] Meanwhile, King had noticed that Stalin was a doodler. At the end of previous meetings, Stalin had folded the papers into a compact wad and put them in his pocket. When, following the third meeting, he forgot to take his doodling with him, King raced Hollis and Cunningham for the prize. But King was detained when the president asked him a question, and, when he looked up, the "page was gone since some Britisher got it."[38] Hollis, the victor, kept the contents to himself, and what the scribbling may have revealed about Stalin's state of mind did not come to light.[39]

Churchill's Birthday Dinner

30 November was Churchill's sixty-ninth birthday. During the forenoon, the British chiefs visited him in his bedroom to wish him many happy returns. Leery of how they might sound, recalled Cunningham, they had decided against singing "Happy Birthday."[40] Churchill grumpily claimed the right to host dinner, because, as he had told Harriman, his name came first alphabetically, because Britain had been the first of the allies at war with Germany, and because 30 November was his birthday.[41] Besides, Roosevelt and Stalin had already taken their turns. At 8:30 P.M. the prime minister hosted thirty-four dinner guests.[42]

Stalin posed for a photograph under the British embassy coat of arms before joining the other guests in the drawing room, where Roosevelt was mixing cocktails. The marshal seemed suspicious of the drinks and asked

Birse what was in them. Evidently not reassured by the explanation, Stalin asked for a simpler drink. Birse gave him whiskey, to which Stalin's reaction was that ordinary vodka was better.[43]

Dinner-jacketed, Churchill shepherded his guests to a long mahogany table flanked by portraits of Queen Victoria and King Edward VII. The sumptuous dinner featured boiled salmon trout from the Caspian Sea as well as soup, turkey, Iranian lantern ice, and cheese soufflé, accompanied by many wines and champagne, and, to commemorate Churchill's birthday, a small cake bearing the letter "V" and sixty-nine closely grouped candles.[44]

To Cadogan, Stalin seemed to be in "quite a good mood," but by other accounts, the marshal was hardly the model dinner guest.[45] Ignoring Churchill's outstretched hand of welcome, he had walked poker-faced to the table.[46] Perhaps he was uncomfortable. He reputedly asked Birse to help him choose the right silverware for each course.[47] In addition to whatever uneasiness his unfamiliarity with British dining customs may have caused, he was apparently a "frightening figure with the slit, bear eyes" and a poor table companion, who brooded much of the evening.[48]

An exchange of toasts began during the soup course and lasted until nearly midnight. The president later remarked that the Russians seemed to have a genius for thinking of things to toast. The more common themes, noted one American skeptic, were "abiding friendship with the Bolsheviks and our common hopes for a new order in the world."[49] As the only woman present, Sarah Oliver was repeatedly the object of gracious remarks, and, whenever she was toasted, Stalin would leave his chair, scuttle around the table, and clink glasses with her. The glasses were never permitted to stand empty, and enough champagne was consumed to have floated a battleship.[50] Most of those present, like Roosevelt, learned to make a small glass last for a dozen toasts, while Stalin drank only from his own bottle, which may have contained water.[51]

Although the duty was Churchill's, Roosevelt requested the privilege of proposing a toast to the king. Presenting his gift, a porcelain bowl purchased earlier in a local bazaar, Roosevelt also toasted a continued association with Churchill for many years to come. Churchill responded by paying tribute to the good experience the Big Three had enjoyed together in Iran. He commended Roosevelt, who had prevented revolution in the United States during the troubled 1930's and had "guided his country along the tumultuous stream of party friction and internal politics amidst the violent freedoms of democracy."[52] Next, Churchill proposed a toast to Stalin, who, he said, merited the title of "Stalin the Great."[53] Stalin replied that the honor really belonged to the Russian people, who would accept nothing less than heroic soldiers.

At his turn, Hopkins employed a witty speech to tease Churchill without offending him. After studying the British constitution, said Hopkins, he had discovered that it was whatever Churchill decided. Laughter greeted this remark, and Churchill laughed as loudly as the rest at the "best speech" of the evening.[54] To be sure, Churchill later wrote that Hopkins really had little foundation for his jocular statement.

The exchanges were occasionally barbed. Stalin offered a toast to his "fighting friend" Churchill and then added in a stage whisper, "if it is possible for me to consider Churchill my friend."[55] Later, Cunningham toasted Stalin as commander-in-chief of the Russian Navy. When his guests raised their glasses "To the Russian Navy," Churchill added, "coupled with the health of *Admiral* Stalin."[56]

The most discordant note of the evening occurred when Brooke proposed a toast to the British people, whom he described as having suffered more, lost more, fought more, and "done more to win the war" than either Russia or America.[57] Possibly interpreting Brooke's toast as a slight to the Russian people, Stalin remained standing and held his glass without drinking when Roosevelt toasted Brooke's health. Paying tribute to Brooke's greatness as a man, Stalin observed that Brooke had apparently adopted an unfriendly, grim, and distrustful opinion of the Russians, which was inconsiderate in the face of Russia's suffering. Stalin then drank to Brooke's health, with the hope that he would discover that the Russians were "quite good chaps."[58]

Brooke later wrote that he knew he would be finished for good in Stalin's eyes if he sat under Russian insults without responding. When Brooke replied, he said that he may have misjudged the Russians because of what he termed the "excellent Soviet cover plan" in the early part of the war, an obvious reference to Nazi-Soviet Pact.[59] He added that perhaps Stalin had, in turn, mistaken his real feelings of comradeship for the Russians. After four years of war and the continual cultivation of false appearances for the enemy's sake, Brooke asked, was it not possible that one's outward appearances might even deceive one's friends?[60] When this speech had been translated, Stalin chuckled, admitted that what Brooke said was possible, even probable, and shook Brooke's hand.

A layered ice cream dessert was already melting by the time it reached the table, where Pavlov was in the midst of translating one of Stalin's many toasts. The waiter lost control of his tray and the ice cream, just missing Stalin, cascaded over Pavlov's head. Without wiping the mess from his hair, Pavlov continued to speak without interruption. This greatly impressed the British, who regarded Pavlov's performance as a willingness to accept any discomfort rather than risk Stalin's wrath by ruining his speech.[61]

In what he intended to be the concluding toast, the prime minister referred to the great progress made by the Big Three at Tehran. He said that their efforts could be translated into the resolution of world problems. To this end, he offered a joint toast to Roosevelt and Stalin.

But Stalin asked for the opportunity to deliver a final word. He praised the United States for manufacturing eight thousand planes each month, a number greater than the combined production of Russia, Japan, and England. Russian production, he said, was twenty-five hundred, but would likely increase to three thousand a month. When the British began murmuring, Stalin guessed that they were discussing their capacity and announced, "I will tell you what your production is. It is twenty-five hundred a month and you can't increase it."[62] Claiming that the war would have been lost had the United States failed to deliver aircraft all over the world, he pointed out the greater power of America in a way that seemed "rather humiliating to the British."[63] Stalin concluded with a warm toast to the leadership of Roosevelt in implementing Lend-Lease.

Then Roosevelt asked to speak. Mindful of allied differences, he remarked:

> There has been discussion here tonight of our varying colors of political complexion. I like to think of this in terms of the rainbow. In our country the rainbow is a symbol of good fortune and of hope. It has many varying colors, each individualistic, but blending into one glorious whole. Thus with our nations. We have differing customs and philosophies and ways of life. Each of us works out our scheme of things according to the desires and ideas of our own peoples. But we have proved here at Tehran that the varying ideals of our nations can come together in a harmonious whole, moving unitedly for the common good of ourselves and of the world. So as we leave this historic gathering, we can see in the sky for the first time that traditional symbol of hope, the rainbow.[64]

Churchill and Stalin continued talking after the dinner party broke up. Churchill remarked that the political complexion of Britain, while by no means red, was undergoing an orderly change and had gone so far as to be termed pink. Stalin quickly replied: "That is a sign of health," but Churchill added that the process should not be carried so far as to "induce congestion."[65] When Stalin told Churchill that he wished to call the prime minister his friend, Churchill replied, "Call me Winston. I call you Joe behind your back."[66] Stalin said that he wanted to call Churchill a "good friend," and the two exchanged toasts to the proletarian masses and the Conservative Party.

Some participants believed that allied cordiality was never higher and that the banquet represented the high-water mark of allied collaboration.[67] Recording that the good effects were impossible to weigh, Boettiger wrote, "I am willing to put in the record my conviction that we should be friends, and that we can be friends, and more than that, we *must* be friends for the future salvation of the race."[68] Churchill described the dinner as one of the most memorable occasions of his life, and Birse wrote that Stalin, agreeably surprised by the spirit of good fellowship, went away in a happy state of mind.[69] Even Brooke, who had suffered several tense moments, reported that "it was a wonderful evening."[70]

Not all, however, were enthusiastic about the apparent harmony. Ismay could not forget that the Americans and Russians had not trusted the British enough to forego a thorough inspection of the embassy by their own security personnel, prior to the dinner.[71] For him, that put a different complexion on the toasts. And Leahy commented that the "monotonous exchange of international compliments" was irrelevant and largely insincere.[72] To pass muster, the cordiality would have to carry over into the military and political talks.

Chiang Kai-shek, Roosevelt, and Churchill during a pause at the Cairo Conference.
Wide World Photos

بندی بستش دو دست و میان
که نگشاید آن بند پیل ژیان

One of five postcards depicting the Tehran Conference; given by Churchill to Roosevelt.
Courtesy: Franklin D. Roosevelt Library

Eden with unidentified persons and guards in the garden at the British Embassy, 29 November.
Courtesy: Franklin D. Roosevelt Library

Left to right: George C. Marshall and Sir Archibald Clark-Kerr (shaking hands), Harry Hopkins, Ivan Pavlov, Stalin, Vyacheslav Molotov, and Kliment Voroshilov outside the Russian Embassy, 29 November.
Courtesy: Franklin D. Roosevelt Library

Churchill and Stalin saluting during the playing of the Russian national anthem at the Sword of Stalingrad Ceremony, 29 November.
Courtesy: Franklin D. Roosevelt Library

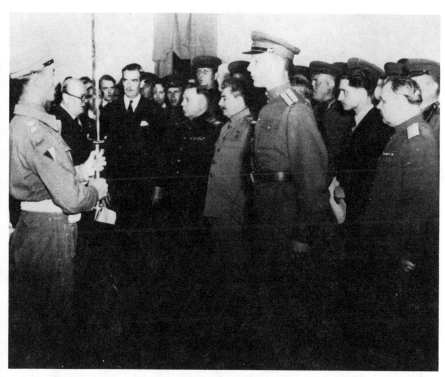

Churchill presenting the Sword of Stalingrad to Stalin, 29 November.
Courtesy: Franklin D. Roosevelt Library

Posing for photographs on the portico of the Russian Embassy, 29 November.
Courtesy: Franklin D. Roosevelt Library

Stalin, Roosevelt, and Churchill in somber pose; *second row, left to right:* Henry
H. Arnold (between Stalin and Roosevelt), Sir Alan Brooke, Sir Andrew B.
Cunningham, and William D. Leahy, 29 November.
Wide World Photos

Stalin, Roosevelt, and Churchill in relaxed pose; *second row, left to right:*
Voroshilov (partly hidden), Arnold, Brooke, Cunningham, and Leahy, 29 November.
Courtesy: Franklin D. Roosevelt Library

Stalin displaying charm in greeting Sarah Churchill Oliver; *behind her, left to
right:* Molotov (partly hidden), W. Averell Harriman, Arnold, Clark-Kerr, and
Eden, 29 November.
Courtesy: Franklin D. Roosevelt Library

Close-up of Stalin and Roosevelt, 29 November.
Courtesy: Franklin D. Roosevelt Library

Marshall and Sir John Dill on the front steps of the Russian Embassy, 29 November.
Courtesy: Franklin D. Roosevelt Library

Elliott Roosevelt, Michael Reilly, and Ross T. McIntire during the photograph
session, 29 November.
Courtesy: Franklin D. Roosevelt Library

Line-up on the Russian Embassy steps; *left to right:* Voroshilov, Clark-Kerr, Molotov, Eden, Dill, and Brooke, 29 November.
Courtesy: Franklin D. Roosevelt Library

The Shah of Iran and Churchill, 30 November.
Courtesy: Franklin D. Roosevelt Library

Churchill greeting his guards in the garden at the British Embassy, 30 November.
Courtesy: Franklin D. Roosevelt Library

Charles Bohlen, Roosevelt, Churchill, and Stalin at the prime minister's birthday dinner, 30 November.
Courtesy: Franklin D. Roosevelt Library

Roosevelt reviewing troops of the Persian Gulf Command, 2 December.
Courtesy: Franklin D. Roosevelt Library

John Winant, Hopkins, and Harriman pose before leaving Tehran, 2 December.
Courtesy: Franklin D. Roosevelt Library

10

INFORMAL POLITICAL DISCUSSIONS

> After all, allies could squeeze each other if they wanted to
> from time to time.
>
> —Joseph Stalin

Big Three Luncheon

The military staffs were not present when, on 1 December, the Big Three turned from strictly military issues to the "more treacherous terrain of postwar policies."[1] The American and British chiefs were en route to Cairo, ostensibly to make final preparations for Overlord. Churchill had once said that soldiers should not play at politics, because they entered a "sphere in which the values were quite different from those to which they had hitherto been accustomed."[2] He did not say, however, how one could separate military and political issues.

After the heated arguments at Tehran, the military chiefs welcomed a respite. When the British invited them to spend a day and night in Jerusalem before returning to Cairo, the Americans were "very happy to accept."[3] The British served as genial hosts, and the men of war paid tribute to the Man of Peace by tramping through all the Holy places to view such sights as Christ's footprints embedded in cement.[4] Photographs of the combined chiefs walking together over the sacred soil would yield "good publicity value before the crusade to Europe."[5] Marshall, Arnold, King, and Leahy, none of whom had been there before, greatly enjoyed Jerusalem, and the vacation partly restored them for the resumption of hard bargaining on Overlord and Buccaneer.

Meanwhile, the Big Three agenda was pushed into high gear by weather reports that forecast an approaching cold front, bringing poor flying conditions. Actually, the Big Three had decided earlier that any political discussions would be tentative. Nevertheless, the effect of the ominous weather predictions was to cram all remaining discussions into a short period.

At noon on 1 December, the Big Three lunched informally with their foreign ministers and with Hopkins in Roosevelt's quarters. They discussed a

132

wide range of political problems, but none of them seemed particularly concerned to resolve everything before them, because they agreed that political issues were less pressing than the military problems. They operated on the mutually accepted premise that, in case of disagreement, postponement was advisable.

The political discussions were marked by a spirit of congeniality and near frivolity, in contrast to the often heated exchanges of the military talks. Roosevelt apparently continued to do all that he could to establish good relations with Stalin. Having earlier warned Churchill not to take offense, Roosevelt said to Stalin, "Winston is cranky this morning. He got up on the wrong side of the bed."[6] When an answering smile passed over Stalin's face, Roosevelt poked fun at the prime minister's Britishness, cigars, and habits. Churchill glowered; Stalin finally broke out into a deep hearty guffaw, and Roosevelt seemed to believe that he had, at last, established rapport with Stalin.

Roosevelt quickly tested Stalin's good mood. Informing the marshal that his son commanded two hundred and fifty observation and scouting planes, Roosevelt asked if Elliott could have permission to fly through from Italy, photograph the Danube Basin, and land in the Soviet Union. Thus, Roosevelt subtly raised what was actually the shuttle bombing question. Stalin, agreeably, proposed to refer exact details to the military mission in Moscow. Also, he agreed to make fields available in northern Russia for flights from England to Russia. This seemed to settle the issue in some minds.[7]

Discussion on Turkey

The Turkish question came up again at the luncheon meeting. Deciding upon the best approach to use with the Turks was the bone of contention. After discussing the text of a proposed telegram, the allies agreed to invite President Inönü to visit Cairo when Roosevelt and Churchill returned to Egypt. Prior contacts with Turkey had indicated that Inönü would meet them if he could participate in a free discussion among equals. When Churchill expressed doubt that Inönü would automatically accept the invitation, Stalin asked, "He might fall ill?" and Churchill replied, "Easily."[8]

Determining what Inönü should be told, once bidden or lured to Cairo, was the key. Turkey would need more help than it could give. This can hardly have escaped Stalin's attention, especially when Hopkins made it clear that the Big Three should decide in advance what military assistance Turkey might be offered. Churchill listed twenty fighter squadrons, seventeen from Egypt and three from elsewhere in the Mediterranean, plus three anti-aircraft regiments. But, because Germany would probably not bother Turkey, no land forces would be needed, and the allies "should be satisfied with strained neutrality from Turkey."9 When Stalin asked what Churchill expected from the Russians, if Turkey declared war on Germany and Bulgaria intervened, the prime minister explained that he was "not asking for anything, but an advance through Odessa would create a great effect among the population in Bulgaria."10

The serious shortage of landing craft cast a pall over all planning. Explaining that he was only asking for enough shipping to carry out a "temporary operation" in March, the prime minister proposed to sandwich the Rhodes invasion into the time between Italy and Overlord.11 Roosevelt disagreed. Landing craft would have to be ready in Corsica and Sardinia by 1 April, he insisted, in order to be useful for Overlord on 1 May.12 Landing craft, of course, could be procured by various means. When Churchill asked if the Americans would divert landing craft from the Pacific, Roosevelt answered that "distance alone" and the needs of impending operations made it "absolutely impossible" to withdraw anything from the southwest Pacific.13 And Hopkins, perhaps suspecting that British commitment to Overlord was wavering and concerned about the unknown costs of Turkish operations, was so anxious to get the record straight that he wrote his own version of the conversation for inclusion in the conference minutes. "It should be clearly understood," wrote Hopkins, "that the American side believe[s] that there are no landing craft available for an attack on Rhodes—and more important still that even if the landing craft were available—no decision has been reached as to whether or not the landing craft could not be used to better advantage in some other operation."14 Churchill had touched the Americans' sore point.

The prime minister agreed to make no promises to Turkey beyond what was decided at Tehran. He suggested that the allies could present the "ugly case" that would result from a Turkish failure to join the allies, but, he lamented, the Big Three could offer only an "unappetizing picture" of help for Turkey.15 Nevertheless, if Inönü balked at coming to Egypt, Churchill offered to go to Ankara himself and try personal diplomacy.

But some of the Americans, still wary of courting the Turks, emphasized that the allied offer of help should not be presented in such a way as to give the Turks false hopes. Hopkins insisted that when Roosevelt and Churchill met with Inönü, no mention should be made, "implied or otherwise," about prospective operations in the eastern Mediterranean.16 No amphibious operations of any kind, added Roosevelt, should be discussed with the Turks.

How would Turkish participation in the war benefit both the Turks and the allies? For one thing, said Churchill, Turkey would gain the right to sit alongside the Soviet Union at the peace table and would fare better in the postwar world if she helped in the allied struggle for victory. And Turkish entry into the war would make available air bases that the allies could use to bomb Rumanian oil fields, which were vital to the German war machine.

Also, increased pressure on German forces in the Balkans would improve the chances of allied operations in other theaters. But, if he were Inönü, interjected Roosevelt, he would ask for "Crete and other islands to be taken," to which Churchill replied that "it paid [the allies] anyhow to lose one aircraft for every German machine shot down."[17]

Stalin did not regard Turkish participation in the war as an unmixed blessing. It might have drawn off ten German divisions earlier, he said, but it was not necessary in 1944. Neither Churchill nor Roosevelt questioned Stalin on this point or reminded him that, by his own admission, Russian troops were not advancing along the front, except in the Ukraine, where they were making only limited gains. Warning that a Turkish decision for the allies might be countered by a Bulgarian declaration of war on Turkey, Stalin asked Churchill to spell out in detail exactly what military assistance Turkey needed.[18]

Turkey had some definite needs, admitted Churchill, but these were not unreasonable. The brave infantry of the Turks, which would have been a "good army at the end of the last war," he explained, had begun to appear deficient when Bulgaria started to import modern weapons.[19] Turkey needed anti-tank guns and also sufficient forces to provide air cover. The allies had already invested nearly twenty-five million dollars' worth of mostly American military equipment. This effort, warned Churchill, would be wasted unless Turkey joined the war.

Churchill's insistence upon Turkish participation provoked a debate. Turkey did not need actually to attack Germany, argued Stalin, so long as she granted bases to the allies, thereby satisfying the prerequisites of both allied need and Turkish caution.[20] This proposal gained the support of Roosevelt, who said that Portugal was a good example of a nation providing indirect aid to the allies. But the British disagreed. Turkey would not give up bases without declaring war, but fear of Germany made such a declaration unlikely. As Churchill pointed out, Turkey preferred neutrality, so long as no greater advantage could be derived from going to war. When he tried to encourage Turkey to take a small role in the war, the Turks replied that they preferred a big role, and, if that were subsequently offered, they expressed regrets that they were not ready.[21] What if Turkey refused to meet allied terms? Then, Turkey would forfeit her chance to sit at the peace conference and would be treated as other neutrals, and, Churchill concluded, "we would say that Great Britain had no further interest in her affairs."[22]

Stalin thereupon suggested that Turkey declare war on Germany, but not on Bulgaria, and he promised that Russia would stop Bulgaria from invading Turkey. Then he asked what the allies would do if Germany occupied Bulgaria. Churchill replied that this would strain German forces, remove enemy troops from the eastern front, and generally improve the allied advantage.[23] What could be better?

Molotov asked the British to spell out what effects a Turkish rejection might have on the status of the Straits. Of course, control of that strategic waterway, roughly of the same importance to Russia as the mouth of the Mississippi is to the United States, has been a historic Russian objective. Claiming that he was "far from the cabinet" and unable to make a definite commitment, Churchill evasively replied that he "certainly thought that the regime deserved review; for instance, Japan was a party to the Treaty of Montreaux."[24] Roosevelt suggested making the Dardanelles free to the commerce of the world, whether or not Turkey entered the war. As a Black Sea power, said Molotov, following an inconclusive discussion, Russia had a special interest, but she "would not insist on this question today."[25]

Without really having decided what approach to use in negotiations with Turkey, Roosevelt and Churchill drafted a brief telegram to Inönü. They invited him to meet with them and a "representative of the Soviet Government" at Cairo.[26] At the close, Molotov announced that the Russians would take part. Overall, the Russians had good reason to participate. They had Churchill's promise that unfavorable Turkish behavior would open the door for a change in the Straits, and Turkey was not likely to abandon neutrality. When Churchill suggested that Turkey probably preferred to be "wheedled into the war by Great Britain rather than as a result of an ultimatum by the three powers," and that he was willing to use either method, Stalin replied, "All right."[27] Churchill later wrote that he dropped the Turkish subject, having gotten all he had thought it right to ask and with "fair hopes that it would not be insufficient."[28]

Discussion on Finland

One portion of the luncheon was devoted to Finland's status. In 1941 the Finns had joined in the German attack on the Soviet Union, and, at the same time as the Tehran Conference, they were retreating. Expressing American sympathy for Finland, Roosevelt said that he wanted to help get the Finns out of the war, and he asked Stalin and Churchill how this might best be accomplished.

The present lull in negotiations, said Stalin, was entirely Finland's fault. The Russians had recently told the Finns that they had no designs on their independence. "Only today," he claimed, the Russians had had word of Finland's reply and, although the full text was still to be delivered, the Finns apparently wanted restoration of the 1939 border, without Finnish disassociation from the Germans.[29] That, interjected Churchill, "was interesting."[30] But, Stalin continued, as the Finns well knew, such terms were not acceptable, and they were clearly not serious about negotiating, if this offer represented their thinking.

Evidently unhappy, Roosevelt commented that Stalin's interpretation was "most interesting but also unsatisfactory."[31] Something must be done, he said, to restore a basis for negotiations and to speed Finland's exit from the war. But Stalin insisted that "Finnish ruling groups" obviously nurtured hopes of an ultimate German victory.[32] When Roosevelt asked if the United States could help by encouraging the Finns to send a delegation to Moscow, Stalin replied that he had no objection.

Churchill described himself as being more inclined to take a severe attitude toward Finland than he had been in 1939 (at the time Russia had invaded Finland), when he had sympathized with the Finns. The first consideration seemed to be the security of Leningrad, because of its vulnerable position near the Russo-Finnish border. Russia should be secure as the leading naval and air power in the Baltic, but he warned against extracting an indemnity from a country as poor as Finland. "The Finns might cut down a few trees," he said, "but that would not do much good."[33] An excessively severe peace would impair the independence of Finland, a prospect that Churchill viewed with regret.

Stalin's insistence that Finland must pay war damages embroiled him in a debate with Churchill, who advised that "there were much bigger things to think about."[34] The marshal demanded payments of timber, paper, and other goods from Finland over a five-to-eight-year period, and even that would cover only a portion of the damages. Churchill said that his ears echoed with the noble slogan, "no annexations and no indemnities," and he "suggested that Marshal Stalin would not be pleased with him for having said that."[35] With a broad grin, Stalin replied, "I have told you that I am becoming a Conservative."[36] When Churchill expressed concern that a large indemnity would destroy Finland, Stalin consented to let the Finns live as they pleased, in exchange for payment of one half of the war damages.

This brought up the question of whether Finland was entirely responsible for her actions. Roosevelt suggested that Finland was Germany's hostage, rather than an accomplice, and was not, therefore, liable for damages. Could the Finns, he asked, expel the Germans from Finnish territory by their own efforts? Stalin answered quickly that the Finns had recently raised their strength from sixteen to twenty-one divisions, while simultaneously saying that they wanted to negotiate. This was because they wanted to bargain, said Churchill, who added, "Let us get the twenty-one divisions out," to which Stalin replied, "Yes, provided that it was not at the expense of Russia."[37] But Finland, insisted Molotov, had subjected Leningrad to artillery fire over a twenty-seven-month period, so the Finns could hardly be praised for having peaceful intentions.[38]

The president suggested that the Finns did not insist on maintaining a stranglehold on the approaches to Leningrad and were willing to move the frontier, but they hoped to keep control of Viborg. "Nothing doing about

Viborg," rebutted Stalin, so Roosevelt proposed an alternate "arrangement by which Hangö should be demilitarized and made into a bathing beach."[39]

When Churchill asked Stalin to list Russian conditions for ending the war with Finland, the marshal replied that the Russians had so informed the United States and Britain the previous February but had received no reply. He had to wonder if the terms had been passed on to the Finns. At that point, Roosevelt admitted that America had withheld the terms, because, he said, the Finns probably would not have been receptive "at that time."[40] The problem, said Stalin, was that Finland had signed a treaty and broken it, and now "everyone was ready to wage a war to modify a treaty."[41]

In answer to Churchill, Stalin repeated the February terms. They called for a restoration of the 1940 treaty, with some modifications. Whereas the 1940 treaty had awarded Hangö to Russia, Stalin offered to accept Petsamo instead. This would give Russia a common border with Norway, and Petsamo, said Stalin, had originally been a Russian gift to Finland.[42] Roosevelt called this a fair exchange. Churchill turned conciliatory, saying that he did not wish to press the Soviet government, that he was waiting for Russia to say what she needed, and that he might plead for leniency, but he "should leave it to the Soviet Union, which had suffered so much, to take the initiative."[43]

Insisting that the Russians and Finns at least resume negotiations, Roosevelt asked if it might be helpful for the Finns to go to Moscow without any preliminary conditions. Any subsequent breakdown would serve German propaganda, which was sure to exploit it as proof that the Russians were insincere, explained Stalin, and Finnish reactionaries would pretend that "it was impossible to talk with the Russians." But, Churchill interrupted, "that would be a lie . . . and we would all say so loudly."[44]

What did the British really want? According to the prime minister, they wished to see Russia satisfied with her frontiers and the Finns "free and independent," to live as well as they could "in those very uncomfortable regions."[45] Yet, the British did not want to give the impression that they were pressuring the Russians on this subject. "After all," replied Stalin, "allies could squeeze each other if they wanted to from time to time."[46] Let the Finns live, he offered, so long as they made good half the damage they had done.

But Roosevelt was preoccupied with making arrangements to send a Finnish delegation to Moscow. Reluctantly, Stalin said, "All right, let them come if you insist," but, he asked, whom could they send?[47] Roosevelt admitted that the present government was pro-German, but other Finns, he suggested, might be sent. Stalin agreed to accept anyone the Finns wanted to send, even the devil himself.[48] In any event, the Russian terms were not negotiable. With the exception of Petsamo being accepted in exchange for Hangö, Stalin called for restoration of the 1940 treaty. Petsamo would be an outright grant and not leased, as Hangö had been in the past. The Finns would have to make payments in kind for up to one half of war damages. If the Finns refused to pay, Stalin threatened to occupy "a region of Finland," but to withdraw "within the year," whenever the Finns complied.[49] Also, he said, the Finns must agree to break with Germany and to reorganize their army in accordance with Russian guidelines.

Churchill again questioned the advisability of reparations. While easy enough, he said, to cause damage, repair was very hard and "experience showed that large indemnities did not work."[50] Besides, claimed Churchill, the "Finns had only poor little musk rats and ermine and they had nothing to give." When Stalin, with a grin, asked, "What about your slogan against indemnities?" Churchill explained that his concern was reconstruction rather than indemnities.[51] Imposing harsh terms on Finland would undoubtedly influence Sweden to refuse to join the allied coalition in time for the May offensives. While he had not yet been elected a Soviet commissar, he said, he would advise treating the Finns with lenience.

At the end of the meeting, Stalin asked if the Finns would likely accept all other points, except reparations. Churchill, sidestepping a direct answer, replied that the allies should do nothing that would detract from the great May battles. Although it was not clear what had been or had not been resolved, Roosevelt offered to stand behind "all that had been said," and Churchill observed that he "liked all this talk."[52]

Third Roosevelt-Stalin Meeting

At 3:20 P.M., Stalin arrived at the president's rooms, where he and Roosevelt held their third private meeting. This time, Harriman and Molotov were present, but mostly they listened to the wide-ranging conversation. According to Bohlen, who interpreted, Roosevelt went alarmingly overboard in trying to establish rapport with Stalin.[53]

The purpose of their meeting, said Roosevelt, was to discuss internal American politics, "briefly and frankly."[54] While 1944 was a presidential election year, he said, he would rather not run again, and Bohlen believed that he was expressing his true feelings. But, "if the war was still in progress at the time of the election," Roosevelt explained, he would be forced to run.[55] And, in that case, six to seven million Americans of Polish descent would undoubtedly base their votes upon events in Poland. As a practical man, he did not wish to lose these votes. This, then, was the reason that America could not participate in any decisions concerning Poland at Tehran or during the following winter. Bohlen wondered why Roosevelt had decided to be "so frank," unless he was trying to provide himself with an excuse for opposing some part of the eventual Polish settlement, or unless he was trying to avoid altogether any entanglement in arguments about Poland.[56]

Nevertheless, Roosevelt proceeded to outline prospective territorial changes. Suggesting that he was sympathetic to the Russian desire to bring about boundary adjustments, he said that he would like to see the eastern border of Poland moved farther west and the western border shifted to the Oder River. When Roosevelt asked Stalin if he understood why the Americans could not openly support Russian claims, Stalin replied that he did. Harriman, who believed that it was absolutely essential to have an agreement ahead of the inevitable Russian "liberation" of Poland, was disappointed when Roosevelt did not press the issue before it was too late.[57]

Changing the subject, Roosevelt raised a discussion about the Baltic states and American citizens from Latvia, Estonia, and Lithuania. Roosevelt knew that these states had belonged to Russia "historically and more recently," and he joked that the United States would not go to war with Russia to prevent their reoccupation.[58] But Russia's eventual incorporation of this area, he said, ought to be based upon a referendum and self-determination of the Baltic peoples.

Stalin asked why the United States was interested in the Baltic. He reminded Roosevelt that the area had enjoyed no autonomy whatsoever under the last tsar, and nobody had protested then, even though both Britain and America had been allied with tsarist Russia. What had happened, he asked, to make public opinion a matter of concern now? Combined with his earlier burst of temper when he had disputed Roosevelt's proposal to internationalize the Baltic Sea, this query indicated that Stalin would not tolerate any suggestions about relaxing Russian influence in the region.

Roosevelt hastened to say that the Baltic states would naturally want to join the Soviet Union some day but that their absorption should not appear to be against the will of the people. Suggesting that the Russians release some sort of public declaration about popular elections, he added that he would not ask for more than a promise to hold future plebiscites. The root of the problem was that people "neither knew nor understood" what was going on.[59] Thus, a Russian declaration of good faith would soothe world public opinion.

But Stalin showed little interest in accepting the president's views on the Baltic. He told Roosevelt that people simply needed to be informed and that this could be accomplished through propaganda work. Ample opportunity for expression of the people's will would be granted in the future, but only in line with the Soviet constitution. Any problem would be settled by the Russians, without outside interference from a postwar international organization.

Concerning the latter, Roosevelt said that he had intended to outline a possible structure in his earlier conversation with Stalin. This plan, he said, was "just an idea" and the exact form of the organization would require further study.[60] But, because Churchill did not yet appreciate the finer points of the "Four Policemen" concept, said Roosevelt, discussing the idea with the British was not wise. Molotov interjected that Russia, at the Moscow conference of foreign ministers, had accepted the proposal for a world organization.

In other respects, the Russians were not so encouraging. Stalin told Roosevelt that he could not rush a decision on the position papers given to him the previous day. He could make no commitments about shuttle bombing, Yugoslavia, or the war in the Pacific, allegedly because he had not had enough time to study the issues as carefully as he wanted. He promised only to take up each of the proposals with Harriman in Moscow at some future, unnamed, date. This was disappointing news. In exchange for telling Stalin that America would take no interest in eastern Europe, Roosevelt got nothing. The president practically torpedoed his own United Nations plan. Moreover, telling Stalin that he could have his way in Poland was a mistake, bound to ruin prospects for a joint settlement in eastern Europe.[61] On the whole, this was not Roosevelt's finest hour.

11

FINAL POLITICAL TALKS

Well, Harry, all I can say is, nice friends we have now.
—William D. Leahy

Italian Shipping Issue

At 6:00 P.M. on 1 December 1943, the Big Three, joined by Hopkins, Eden, Molotov, and the interpreters, held a final plenary meeting. Two questions, Poland and Germany, made up the agenda, but before Roosevelt could get to the first item, Molotov, raising an issue previously discussed but not yet settled, asked if the Western allies were prepared to give the Russians their share of captured Italian shipping. This request, added Stalin, was both modest and reasonable.[1]

Earlier, the Russians had requested a list of all the Italian warships and civil vessels under Anglo-American control. Thereafter, they had asked for one battleship, one cruiser, eight destroyers, and four submarines, "to be dispatched right away to the northern ports."[2] When the West did not respond, Molotov had told Hull that the Russians were bitterly disappointed and desired the shipping "as a token," to convince their own people of Western "recognition of the part Soviet forces had played in Italy's collapse and as an indication that the Big Three were collaborating."[3]

Although reluctantly agreeing in principle that the Russians should be given part of the Italian fleet, neither Roosevelt nor Churchill had made plans for an actual turnover. As late as 10 November, the American joint chiefs had advocated Russian use of Italian shipping, "in furtherance of the war effort," without, at the same time, surrendering any vessel "by transfer of ownership and registry."[4] In other words, the Russians could borrow the ships.

Now agreeing that the Russian request for an outright grant was proper, Roosevelt said that the Italians had a large number of merchant ships and a lesser number of warships that should be used by the Big Three in their common offensives against the Axis. The vessels might be transferred on a temporary basis for the duration of the war, he suggested, and final disposition would properly follow the end of the war. Molotov interrupted to say that the Russians needed the ships, while Stalin "thought he could make good use of the ships and that he would hand them back after the war."[5]

Actually, Roosevelt was reluctant to carry out much more than a symbolic transfer of Italian ships to Russia. In a meeting on 30 November, his staff had warned him that the Italians might well resent and possibly resist giving their ships to Russia. Moreover, insisted the chiefs, Russia could not immediately man and employ the Italian vessels, which lacked spare parts and ammunition. Roosevelt agreed.[6]

Churchill, too, was reluctant to let the Italian ships go. Deciding where to deliver them, he said, was a difficult task, and he asked Stalin where the Russians would prefer. Stalin answered that either the Black Sea, if Turkey entered the war, or the northern ports in the Baltic would be suitable. Churchill conceded that delivery was a "small thing to ask" in the face of Russian sacrifices during the war.[7] The matter would have to be "so arranged that there would be no mutiny in the Italian fleet and no scuttling of ships," he said, and "a couple of months" should be sufficient for him and Roosevelt to "handle the Italians like a cat handling a mouse."[8] When Churchill asked, "In two months a battleship and a cruiser, would that do?" Stalin shot back, "What about the end of January?"[9] To carry out a transfer or to say anything about it to the Italians before their cooperation was no longer of operational importance, cautioned Churchill, would be dangerous to Big Three interests.[10]

Perhaps trying to make the fleet issue unappealing to the Russians, Churchill envisioned British ships at work in the Black Sea. Unperturbed, Stalin replied, "Good."[11] The Russians should not worry that the British nurtured ambitions in the Black Sea area, said Churchill, who proposed to use four or five submarines to clear the Black Sea. The Russians, replied Stalin, would be grateful for any help. If Turkey agreed, continued Churchill, the British could slip thirty to forty submarines already in the Mediterranean through the Straits, and he commented that the British "thought submarine warfare improper" but "had been forced to do a lot of it."[12]

Reluctantly, Roosevelt and Churchill promised to deliver Italian ships into Russian command by the end of January, "after refitting."[13] However, they did not decide whether to fulfill Russia's specific request or to follow Churchill's abbreviated list. Also unresolved was the port of delivery where the Russians would take possession of the ships. And the deal was conditional on Italian consent and Turkish cooperation, neither of which was likely.

The Polish Question

Bohlen later insisted that the question of Poland's government did not arise at Tehran, but the Big Three did briefly discuss the possibilities of patching up relations between Russia and the Polish government-in-exile.[14] Here, wrote Cadogan, was something important at last.[15] Despite earlier statements that he could not enter the Polish quagmire, Roosevelt asked if the conference might speed up efforts to reconcile the Poles and Russians. He may have believed that the allies could discuss this without slipping into a debate on frontiers.

According to Stalin, the break in relations was entirely Poland's fault. Why had the Poles slandered the Russians by blaming them for the Katyn Forest massacre? In spite of such allegations, Russia supported the restoration and strengthening of Poland—the true Poland, rather than the antagonistic government-in-exile. Insisting that neither Roosevelt nor Churchill could imagine what was really going on in Poland, he remarked, "We should like to have a guarantee that the agents of the Polish government will not kill partisans, that the emigré Polish government will really call for struggle against the Germans instead of engaging in machinations."[16]

The British, having gone to war expressly on Poland's account, said Churchill, had a special interest in what happened. This prompted a "great deal of discussion about the borders, but not the internal affairs, of Poland."[17] The most important issue, Churchill insisted, was to ensure absolute security along Russia's western frontier against future German pressure. Stalin asked Churchill to explain what he meant. Reminding Stalin how he had used three match sticks during their discussion the first night of the conference to show how the borders might be shifted, Churchill basically proposed to move Poland a few hundred miles to the west. Perhaps Churchill was preparing the way to sacrifice Polish territory as a *quid pro quo* for the restoration of relations between Russia and Poland. But Stalin insisted that the issue was not connected in any way to Russia's reestablishing relations with the Polish government-in-exile. Probably fearful of Russia's probable strength in the postwar world, Churchill wanted to reach a practical and definite agreement on the border between Russia and Poland. Moving Poland westward would presumably satisfy the Russians, penalize the Germans, pacify the Poles, and thus prove worthwhile all around.

Churchill asked Stalin to express the Russian view on Poland's borders and offered to relay any reasonable formula to the London Poles. He would like to be able, he said, to tell the Poles that the plan was a good one and the best that they were likely to get. Promising to wash his hands of the Polish affair if the Poles refused to accept a Big Three agreement, he pledged "not to oppose the Soviet government under any condition at the peace table," claiming that his only desire was to see a strong Poland friendly to Russia.[18]

Stalin evidently enjoyed teasing Churchill as a way of avoiding the subject. Addressing the prime minister, Stalin said, "I can't understand you at all; in 1919 you were so keen to fight and now you don't seem to be at all. What happened? Is it advancing age? How many divisions do you have in contact with the enemy? What is happening to all those two million men you have in India?"[19] But the question at hand was Russia's territorial demands, which Stalin, at last, outlined. The Poles, he said, should not attempt to gain control of the Ukraine and White Russia. And Russia would adhere to the "just and right" 1939 frontiers, for "they appeared to be ethnologically the righteous."[20]

Stalin's demand for lands claimed by Poland discomforted the British. Eden asked if what Stalin had described was not, in fact, the 1939 Ribbentrop-Molotov line. Bristling at this obvious reference to Russo-German collaboration, Stalin replied, "Call it whatever you like."[21] When Molotov suggested that the line was generally called the Curzon line, Eden rebutted that the two lines were entirely different, but Molotov insisted that he could find no differences in "essential points."[22] The allies turned to a painstaking map study. Churchill produced a map showing both the Curzon line, the south end of which was undefined, and the Oder line. The Americans offered their own map. Stalin took the latter, but when he learned that the data had come from Polish sources, he grunted, "took his red pencil, and somewhat contemptuously marked the map."[23]

Despite Roosevelt's attempt later to dissociate himself from the Polish question, the president did take part. "Did the frontiers of East Prussia and the territory east of the Oder approximate to the size of the eastern provinces of Poland itself?" he asked.[24] What he was suggesting was to give Stalin what he wanted and to make up the difference by giving German territory to Poland. Stalin replied that he could not say for sure, because the areas had not been measured.

Actually, the Curzon and Ribbentrop-Molotov lines were almost identical. The British contended that Lvov should be on the Polish side of the line, while the Russians were equally insistent that it must be part of Russian territory. Magnanimously offering to yield the point, Churchill commented that the value of German land proposed for Poland exceeded the value of the Pripet Marshes within the disputed area, the Poles should be satisfied, and he was "not prepared to make a great squawk about Lvov."[25]

When Eden asked if the Russians would accept the Curzon and Oder lines as a basis for negotiations, Molotov showed them the Russian version of the Curzon line and argument started anew. Stalin offered to withdraw the Russian claim, if the West could prove that the disputed districts were Polish, because, he said, the Russians had no desire to retain any regions primarily inhabited by Poles, "even though they were inside the 1939 line."[26] Although he had little reason to assume that the allies were close to agreement, the prime minister thereupon described the allies as "not very far apart in principle."[27]

If the populations of the disputed areas posed a problem, Roosevelt asked, would it be possible to have an involuntary transfer of people? Stalin, who demanded an area that he admitted was mainly Polish, an area south of Vilna and southwest of the Curzon line, replied that a transfer of that kind was entirely possible. Here, Roosevelt was certainly off base. An involuntary transfer of peoples was contrary to the Atlantic Charter; it would set a dangerous precedent, and the very idea revealed callousness to the sufferings of those to be moved.

Again separating into small groups, the allies gathered around the maps for a prolonged study of the Oder River as Poland's western frontier. Afterward, Churchill said that he liked the picture, expected the Poles to feel likewise, and promised to advise them to accept the new borders, adding that he was speaking only for the British.[28] The Poles would have ended up with nothing, he said, had it not been for the Red Army, but now they would have a fine place to live, and they should be quite content with the arrangements made in their behalf. Having reached implied acceptance of Stalin's demands, but not a formal written agreement, the allies, to the apparent satisfaction of everyone present, set aside the Polish issue. But, because the agreement was "entirely oral," it led to confusion later on.[29] Indeed, the Big Three talks on Poland led to "no concrete results," and the whole arrangement seemed a "bit woolly."[30] Moreover, indecision on the Polish question was bound to spill over to other issues. Certainly, Tehran foreshadowed Western inability, short of going to war, to block Russian expansion into eastern Europe.

The German Question

Roosevelt guided the discussion around to what would happen to Germany at the end of the war. This pleased Hopkins, who had worried that this issue might be postponed or ignored. For his part, Roosevelt favored imposing strict controls. As for air power, he had said shortly before the conference, the Germans should not be in a position to "fly anything larger than one of those toy planes that you wind up with an elastic."[31]

In January 1943 at the Casablanca Conference, insisting that peace would come only by the total destruction of Axis power, the president had announced that the United States and Britain would demand Germany's unconditional surrender. Harriman believed that Roosevelt had adopted this formula to avoid the misunderstanding and confusion that had been caused by Wilson's Fourteen Points at the close of the First World War.[32] It may also have been intended as an assurance that the West would not seek a separate peace with Germany at Russia's expense, and as a salve to take the sting out of further postponements of the second front.

If the policy was designed to cement allied unity and ruin enemy morale, it was not very successful. From the outset, it played into the hands of

12

THE CONFERENCE FOLLOW-UP

There would be plenty of time to make a final choice as the
general war shaped itself.
                                        —Winston S. Churchill

Declaration of the Three Powers

Before leaving Tehran, the Big Three signed the Declaration of the Three
Powers—a "stirring record of their beliefs and sentiments" and proof that
"allied might, growing steadily, was being cemented by allied unity."[1] This
communiqué went through a number of revisions that reveal a different
story. The first two drafts apparently never left the American legation.
Cadogan, responding to the third draft, prepared his own along "more (and
better) journalistic lines," but Cadogan's version, according to Boettiger,
was "appallingly dull."[2] Hopkins told Boettiger to revise the paper and both
Roosevelt and Churchill reviewed his work. Boettiger then prepared three
copies and delivered them on 1 December to Hopkins during the final
meeting. Twenty minutes later, Hopkins instructed Boettiger to prepare a
final corrected copy in a hurry, "because Stalin was tired and wanted to go."[3]

What had the four-day summit accomplished? According to the declaration,

> We—The President of the United States, the Prime Minister of Great
> Britain, and the Premier of the Soviet Union, have met these four days past
> in this, the capital of our ally, Iran, and have shaped and confirmed our
> common policy.
>
> We express our determination that our nations shall work together in war
> and in the peace that will follow. As to war—Our military staffs have
> joined in our round table discussions, and we have concerted our plans for
> the destruction of the German forces. We have reached complete agree-
> ment as to the scope and timing of the operations to be undertaken from
> the East, West, and South.
>
> The common understanding which we have here reached guarantees that
> victory will be ours. And as to peace—we are sure that our concord will

151

win an enduring peace. We recognize fully the supreme responsibility resting upon us and all the United Nations, to make a peace which will command the good will of the overwhelming mass of the peoples of the world, and banish the scourge and terror of war for many generations. With our diplomatic advisers we have surveyed the problems of the future. We shall seek the cooperation and the active participation of all nations, large and small, whose peoples in heart and mind are dedicated, as are our own peoples, to the elimination of tyranny and slavery, oppression and intolerance. We will welcome them, as they may choose to come, into a world family of democratic nations.

No power on earth can prevent our destroying the German armies by land, their U-boats by sea, and their war plants from the air. Our attack will be relentless and increasing. Emerging from these cordial conferences we look with confidence to the day when all peoples of the world may live free lives, untouched by tyranny, and according to their varying desires and their own conscience. We came here with hope and determination. We leave here, friends in fact, in spirit and in purpose.[4]

Many people had waited impatiently to learn what had taken place at Tehran. The *Chicago Tribune* editorialized that its readers deserved more than a recitation about dinner menus and Big Three wardrobes.[5] The *New York Times* bemoaned the "opera bouffe manner in which the news was released."[6] The Germans, too, were anxious to get the news, and everybody, observed Minister of Propaganda Josef Goebbels, was tense and full of expectation.[7]

A backdrop of inaccuracies and lies distorted the picture. On 1 December, for example, the press was told that Roosevelt and Churchill had left Cairo for "unannounced destinations," although they were actually preparing at that time for the return flight to Egypt.[8] One story quoted Churchill as having said on 2 December that he was hoping the "first" tripartite summit would take place before the first of the year.[9]

In part to dispel the cloud of rumors and in part to make a dramatic impact, the Big Three decided to release the communiqué simultaneously in Washington, London, and Moscow, at 8:00 P.M. Moscow time on 6 December 1943. But a 30 November Reuters dispatch from Lisbon leaked the news prematurely, prompting Boettiger to note, "It certainly looks as though the British have given us another good frigging."[10] By 3 December, rumors reached the front pages in America. The next day, Moscow newspapers and radio, announcing that the Big Three had discussed the "problems of the conduct of the war against Germany and also a number of political problems," released the text of the declaration.[11]

The Office of War Information, "frankly flabbergasted" by the premature release, asked why the British and Russians had not kept faith.[12] Like children anxious to tell a forbidden secret, the allies had simply found it difficult to keep their agreement. After a brief investigation, Harriman concluded that the Russians had apparently decided to state the "truth to end further rumors which were considered to affect adversely our mutual interests."[13] But American journalists were still incensed at having been scooped.

Under these circumstances, it is not surprising that the Tehran declaration played to mixed reviews. On the one hand, it was hailed as the "exception to the usual mixture of platitudes and generalities."[14] On the other hand, it seemed a "strange document" that ignored every concrete problem troubling the Grand Alliance, yet made reference to common policy and friendship in spirit.[15] For their part, as expected, the Germans made light of the communiqué. Dismissing it as "neither flesh nor fowl," Goebbels wrote that he would have expected a "little more" from the Big Three. He called the declaration a complete German victory, since it contained nothing dangerous and could be published almost verbatim. Moreover, he mocked the West for including such expressions as democracy, freedom of peoples, and elimination of intolerance and slavery in a document bearing Stalin's signature. In any event, verdicts would be settled on the battlefields, not in conferences.[16]

The communiqué probably did not have the effect the Big Three hoped. Its impact on home morale was uncertain; it raised more questions than it answered, and it had negligible effect on German morale. But what else could the allies have reported? They could hardly have announced something like: "We don't see eye to eye on many issues, so the Germans are in for quite a scrap." The specific Anglo-American need to downplay criticisms to the effect that they were letting the Russians do most of the fighting made it desirable to view Tehran as a benchmark in Grand Alliance diplomacy.

Declaration on Iran

The Iranians were understandably interested in the proceedings of the Tehran Conference. One of their goals was to win an allied promise that interference in Iran's affairs would end with the peace settlement. The importance of Iran's petroleum reserves and communications lines brought the British and Russians to Iran, which had been forced after 1941 to cooperate and to refrain from any act "contrary to British or Soviet interests."[17] And the problems of transporting Lend-Lease materiel to the Russians had led the Americans to violate Iranian sovereignty. This latter activity had prompted Eden pointedly to remind the Americans that the allies had "guaranteed the territorial integrity and the independence of Persia."[18] Overall, the heavy-handed behavior of the allies portended that Iran might have difficulty regaining control of her own affairs.

So, the Tehran Conference provided the Iranians with a golden opportunity to press their case. Prime Minister Ali Soheily and Minister for Foreign Affairs Mohammed Saed presented separate requests to get control of Iran's administration. In response, Roosevelt authorized Hurley "to work out something."[19] Eden agreed in principle, but he deferred to the American and Russian views. Soheily found Stalin reluctant, but not entirely opposed to the idea.

Roosevelt wanted to use Iran as a model to demonstrate what the United States could offer the less-favored associate nations in the Grand Alliance. America had earlier assisted Iran in the form of administrative and financial missions. Roosevelt hoped to create irrigation projects to water Middle Eastern deserts, and Iran, he liked to say, represented an ideal clinic for such efforts.[20] And American assistance could perhaps loosen the British and Russian economic stranglehold on Iran and gain oil concessions for the United States.

The Americans drew up a declaration for Stalin and Churchill to review. Elliott Roosevelt claimed modestly to have rendered "rather insignificant assistance," but Hurley was the main author.[21] On the last night of the conference, Harriman had shown the draft in English to Stalin, who then accepted a verbal translation and agreed to sign it, if Roosevelt would sign first.[22] Churchill wanted to substitute the word *Persia* for *Iran*, on the ground that some people might confuse Iraq with Iran. But Stalin refused to make this change; Roosevelt supported Stalin, and Churchill backed down. Stalin then insisted that Churchill sign first, so that the prime minister might know the "designation of the country that they were in" and the site where the conference had taken place.[23]

The next step was to get Iranian acceptance of the document. Hurley rushed the communiqué to the Iranian Foreign Office, where Saed was waiting. Telephoning Soheily, Saed read the declaration in full. Soheily approved it without amendment, Saed initialed two copies, and Hurley hurried back to the conference table, as "pleased as a small boy who had just landed a big fish in the mill pond."[24]

The communiqué acknowledged Iranian assistance to the war effort, promised continued economic aid, and guaranteed autonomy:

> The President of the United States, the Premier of the U.S.S.R., and the Prime Minister of the United Kingdom, having consulted with each other and with the Prime Minister of Iran, desire to declare the mutual agreement of their three Governments regarding their relations with Iran.
>
> The Governments of the United States, the U.S.S.R., and the United Kingdom recognize the assistance which Iran has given in the prosecution of the war against the common enemy, particularly by facilitating the transportation of supplies from overseas to the Soviet Union. The three Governments realize that the war has caused special economic difficulties for Iran, and they are agreed that they will continue to make available to the Government of Iran such economic assistance as may be possible, having regard to the heavy demands made upon them by their worldwide shortage of transport, raw materials, and supplies for civilian consumption.

With respect to the postwar period, the Governments of the United States, the U.S.S.R., and the United Kingdom are in accord with the Government of Iran that any economic problems confronting Iran at the close of hostilities should receive full consideration, along with those of other members of the United Nations, by conferences or international agencies held or created to deal with international economic matters.

The Governments of the United States, the U.S.S.R., and the United Kingdom are in one with the Government of Iran in their desire for the maintenance of the independence, sovereignty and territorial integrity of Iran. They count upon the participation of Iran, together with all other peace-loving nations, in the establishment of international peace, security and prosperity after the war, in accordance with the principles of the Atlantic Charter, to which all four Governments have subscribed.[25]

Especially pleased with the communiqué, Hurley believed that it defeated the forces of imperialism, reduced the Shah's fears about Britain and Russia, and put the United States on record as being the defender of the rights of all peoples to self-government and as the protector of the territorial integrity of smaller nations. The allies, he thought, had reaffirmed the Atlantic Charter.[26]

Like the Declaration of the Three Powers, the Declaration on Iran was broadcast prematurely. Although the Big Three had agreed to withhold publication until 6 December 1943, the Russians printed the full text in the 5 December morning edition of the communist organ, *Friend of Iran*. Thereupon, Iranian authorities released the news to their press agents.[27] When Americans inquired what had prompted the early release, the Russians claimed that they had heard that the Iranians were going to jump the starting line, so they had rushed into print in order not to be left behind. Besides, they explained, the allied agreement on simultaneous announcements by their understanding applied only to the Declaration of the Three Powers. Dreyfus privately accused the Russians just the same of having knowingly jumped the gun.[28]

The Declaration on Iran was not quite as effective as it might have been, because the allies chose to interpret the Atlantic Charter in accordance with selfish national interests, and increasingly they bent its principles and objectives. "So far as one could judge from the behavior of the three powers in Persia," the war effort came first, national aims a close second, and the projected "new internationalism" a distant third.[29] Britain wanted trade and investment opportunities; Russia sought warm water outlets; America feared either Britain or Russia gaining a free hand, and all three coveted Iranian oil.

Military Conclusions

Besides two communiqués, the Big Three prepared a secret paper, initialed on 1 December, on the military decisions reached at Tehran. This document provides the best measure for judging what the summit conference really achieved. In the words of the secret paper, the allies

(1) Agreed that the Partisans in Yugoslavia should be supported by supplies and equipment to the greatest possible extent, and also by commando operations;

(2) Agreed that, from the military point of view, it was most desirable that Turkey should come into the war on the side of the allies before the end of the year;

(3) Took note of Marshal Stalin's statement that if Turkey found herself at war with Germany, and as a result Bulgaria declared war on Turkey or attacked her, the Soviet [Union] would immediately be at war with Bulgaria. The Conference further took note that this fact could be explicitly stated in the forthcoming negotiations to bring Turkey into the war;

(4) Took note that Operation Overlord would be launched during May 1944, in conjunction with an operation against southern France. The latter operation would be undertaken in as great a strength as availability of landing craft permitted. The Conference further took note of Marshal Stalin's statement that the Soviet forces would launch an offensive at about the same time with the object of preventing the German forces from transferring from the Eastern to the Western front;

(5) Agreed that the military staffs of the three Powers should henceforward keep in close touch with each other in regard to the impending operations in Europe. In particular it was agreed that a cover plan to mystify and mislead the enemy as regards these operations should be concerted between the staffs concerned.[30]

Throughout the conference, the Americans had insisted on only limited support for Yugoslavian guerrillas, the British had proposed all possible aid, and the Russians had been, on the whole, strangely silent about the prospects of drawing off enemy divisions to the Balkans. Significantly, the Big Three did resolve part of the Yugoslav issue. Aid, more limited than the British preferred, would go to Tito, and Mihajlović would be left to fend for himself.

British persistence had kept the issue of Turkey's participation in the war before the conference, as Churchill tried to drum up allied interest in the eastern Mediterranean. The prime minister met strong resistance from the Americans, who suspected that a deeper involvement in the Mediterranean would prolong the war, and from the Russians, who insisted that Turkey would not abandon neutrality. Yet, the allies agreed to seek an early decision on this question.

Turkish participation could be more of a liability than a help, if Germany or Bulgaria invaded the Straits, forcing the allies to divert enough support to keep Turkey in the war. Stalin offered to handle Bulgaria. In offering to let his allies inform Turkey about promised Russian help, Stalin was likely trying to make a Turkish decision more unlikely, because the Turks were sure to be skittish about the prospects of a Russian presence closer to the Straits.

The Tehran Conference revolved around the Russian insistence upon opening a second front. The talks focused on Overlord. Three agreements followed. First, Overlord's date was named as "during May 1944."[31] Secondly, in conjunction with Overlord, the Americans and British promised to undertake the Anvil operation. Finally, Stalin promised to keep German forces occupied in the east, by launching an offensive about the same time Overlord got underway. Meanwhile, the Big Three placed a premium on cooperative planning. The military staffs should work together to strike Germany in unison, while deceiving the enemy about the timing and location of their offensives.

What the secret paper did not mention was nearly as important as the agreements it described. It did not record the Anglo-American decision to commit troops in Italy to a campaign to advance northward beyond Rome to the Pisa-Rimini line. Despite Stalin's aversion to "flyspeck diversions" in the Mediterranean, the chiefs decided to intensify their effort there.[32] Nor did the secret paper take note of the Western promise to transfer up to one-third of the Italian battle fleet to Russian control. No statement was made about shuttle bombing Germany. No reference was made to Stalin's promise to go to war with Japan, as soon as Germany was defeated. Also, the Big Three did not endorse Buccaneer and the Cairo Conference decisions.

That ensuing interpretations differed should come as no surprise. As Churchill put it, "There would be plenty of time to make a final choice as the general war shaped itself."[33] Ismay began to reevaluate the decisions almost immediately. That he was not alone in questioning the Tehran decisions was quickly evident when the British and Americans met in Egypt for the next round of discussions.

Second Cairo Conference

The purpose of the Second Cairo Conference, from 2 December to 7 December 1943, was to clean up a number of odds and ends.[34] The British and Americans, said Churchill, here resumed their "intimate discussions on the whole scene of the war."[35] But Moran, who was troubled by Churchill's persistent exhaustion and signs that he was close to total collapse, suspected that allied relations worsened because the prime minister lost his temper more frequently than he had in Iran.[36] And Marshall remarked on the friction that occurred when the agreements sketched at Tehran began to unravel.[37]

The British wasted little time reviving the issues supposedly settled at

Tehran. On 2 December, Ismay prepared a draft agenda including "agreement as to military conclusions of Eureka," Turkey, command of the forces operating against Germany, command in the Mediterranean, Rankin, operations against southern France, and the Pacific theater.[38] From the British perspective, the most troublesome obstacle was that the Americans "advocated doing marvels in all parts of the world; while [the British] took the line of first things first, and protested against *any* resources of any kind that were required to beat the Bosche being diverted at this juncture against the Yellow Man."[39] The combined chiefs, insisted Ismay, must be "quite clear as to the implications of these conclusions" before leaving Cairo.[40]

On 3 December many unsettled issues came up for discussion. The British proposed to interpret the Tehran agreements to retain landing craft in the Mediterranean until 15 January, to defer Overlord's date selection to the commander yet unnamed, to delay overt Turkish participation until mid-February, to invade Rhodes in March, and possibly to cancel Buccaneer. But the Americans announced that the conference must come to an end shortly. Dumbfounded, Brooke noted that the Americans had thereby "completely upset the whole meeting by wasting all our time with Chiang Kai-shek and Stalin before we had settled any points with them. And now . . . they propose to disappear into the blue and leave all the main points . . . unsettled."[41]

Nor did Roosevelt and Churchill agree about what they had or had not settled at Tehran. On 3 December, they stayed at the table past midnight discussing their differences. The next day, Roosevelt asked whether or not he was right in thinking that the Big Three had decided that nothing should hinder either Overlord or Anvil, that landing craft for operations in the eastern Mediterranean would have to be scraped up by hook or crook if Turkey entered the war, and that Buccaneer would have to make do with the resources at hand. Churchill replied that "there were still many questions of first-class importance to be settled."[42]

Two decisive events, in Churchill's judgment, had occurred at Tehran. Stalin's voluntary promise to declare war on Japan the moment Germany was defeated diminished the importance of Anglo-American operations in the Pacific. And the decision to cross the channel in May made Overlord the task above all else. But when Churchill suggested stripping resources from the Pacific, Roosevelt replied that the allies had a moral obligation to do something for China and that he would not forego Buccaneer "except for some very great and readily apparent reason."[43] Withdrawing landing craft from Buccaneer, said Churchill, would aid Overlord and make possible a two-division assault for Anvil.

Meanwhile, on 3 December, Brooke suggested that the whole landing craft situation must be examined to find necessary vessels to transport two divisions for Anvil. King objected, saying that the Tehran decision was "only that the operation should be undertaken in as great a strength as the availability of landing craft permitted and that there was no decision as to the strength of the assaulting force."[44] Nevertheless, in their final report to Roosevelt and Churchill, the chiefs agreed to recommend a two-division assault.

Buccaneer was the major stumbling block to Anglo-American harmony. Once operations had begun in North Burma, said Brooke, either the allies would have to continue them to complete the capture of the whole of Burma or forces would have to be withdrawn when the monsoon stopped. He warned that Burma might become a huge vacuum, where allied forces would be wasted to little advantage.[45] But the president had promised Chiang an amphibious operation, and Brooke noted privately that Roosevelt did not like to go back on his word.[46] The only way out of the impasse, or so it seemed to the British, was for Churchill to convince Roosevelt to change his mind.[47]

On 5 December, Buccaneer's fate was settled. When Portal asked if the invasion was essential on purely military grounds, Marshall admitted that it "would be of assistance but was not vital."[48] Cunningham warned that, unless Buccaneer was launched earlier than planned, operations in both Europe and the Pacific would suffer, and the allies would be in danger of "falling between two stools."[49] Leahy consented to the withdrawal of forces from Buccaneer, "only if they were essential to the success of Anvil," and he added that they "should not be taken for diversionary operations such as Rhodes."[50] In the afternoon, Roosevelt informed Churchill, "Buccaneer is off." Pleased with this decision, Churchill telephoned Ismay, quoting, "He is a better man that ruleth his spirit than he that taketh a city."[51] The next day, to Brooke's satisfaction, the chiefs agreed formally to delay amphibious operations in the Bay of Bengal and to divert landing craft previously assigned to Buccaneer to Overlord and Anvil.

With this decision, China was demoted from the ranks of the Big Four. American planners at last realized that Japan could be defeated without a major land campaign in Burma or China. Fast carrier task forces and long-range bombers, using what were later dubbed island-hopping tactics, took Japanese positions in the Gilbert and Marshall island chains and, the more islands that fell, the less need there was for China's help.[52] British insistence on landing craft for Anvil sealed the issue, and the Americans abandoned Buccaneer.

One of the main purposes of the Second Cairo meeting, said Churchill, was to bring about a Turkish decision to enter the war. In a plan he called Operation Saturn, Churchill proposed that British aircraft occupy Turkish airfields by 15 February 1944, that all preparations be made to seize Rhodes before the end of February, that Bulgaria be warned that two or three tons of bombs would be dropped upon Sofia for every ton dropped upon Constantinople (Istanbul) or Smyrna, and that Turkey allow the secret passage into the Black Sea of six to eight British submarines.[53] This was bad enough, but a proposal even more unpalatable to the Americans emerged in staff meetings. It called for Turkey to stand on the defensive and to protect the Straits, while Western forces invaded Rhodes towards the end of February, thus delaying Overlord until 15 July.[54]

When Turkish president Inönü agreed to meet with the allies on 4 December, Churchill and Roosevelt started a "mad race . . . for the honor of escorting the Belle of the Dardanelles." Both swains sent huge transport planes instead of flowers. Boettiger and Randolph Churchill went "racing off to Turkey almost simultaneously, and when both returned, Ismet stepped out of an American C-54 on Boettiger's arm."[55]

Promising that the British would not invoke their alliance or ask Turkey to join the war, "unless and until such action could be taken without unfair risk for Turkey," Churchill told Inönü that the moment had come for the Turks to consider seriously the advantages of associating themselves with the great allies. And he insisted that Inönü must permit the West to station troops in Turkey.[56]

A favorable decision, however, was hard to achieve. Some unknown wag circulated the story that all the Turks wore hearing devices so perfectly attuned to one another that they all went out of order at the same time whenever mention was made of the possibility of Turkey's entering the war.[57] On 5 December, Inönü disallowed the idea of a fixed date for Turkey's decision. His reluctance, he explained, was based upon the real possibility that Turkey might have to face Germany alone for several months if she entered the war.[58]

The Americans endorsed Turkey's cautious approach. Suggesting that Turkey should not enter the war until fully prepared, Roosevelt remarked that the Turks "did not want to be caught with their pants down."[59] Speculating that Turkish belligerency might not be useful after 1 January, Hopkins said that the United States wanted Turkey to enter the war "willingly and wholeheartedly."[60]

In the end, the Anglo-American talks with Inönü were inconclusive. Eden was not surprised, and he surmised that Turkey's caution was based upon unpreparedness.[61] Apparently impressed greatly by the German military machine, Turkey "shivered on the brink" of the war.[62] But Britain's ambassador to Turkey, Sir Hughe Knatchbull-Hugessen, gave the Turks credit for being "perfectly genuine in their fears and not stalling as some think."[63]

On 7 December, when Churchill and Eden went to see the Turks off, Inönü embraced the prime minister in farewell. Driving back to Cairo, Churchill turned to Eden and said, "Did you see, Ismet kissed me?" Eden replied that this seemed "to be the only gain from fifteen hours of hard argument."[64] That evening, when Sarah went to say good night to her father, she found him giggling quietly to himself. He explained, "The president of the Turks kissed me—twice. The trouble with me is that I am irresistible."[65] The Turks left Cairo to report to their parliament, Churchill later wrote; the British set about implementing Operation Saturn, and "there the matter rested."[66]

At Tehran, Roosevelt had promised Stalin that he would name Overlord's commander. On 4 December, the president decided tentatively to appoint Eisenhower and, on the day following, he so informed Stalin.[67] Then, on 6 December, the president casually informed Churchill that he could not spare Marshall and asked Churchill's opinion of Eisenhower. Churchill replied that the Americans should decide, but he added that the British had the warmest regard for Eisenhower and would trust their "fortunes to his discretion with hearty good will."[68]

On 6 December, the combined chiefs delivered to Roosevelt and Churchill a report outlining the conference's military decisions. The report named Overlord and Anvil the supreme operations for 1944 and stated they would be carried out during May. Anvil would be a two-division assault. The chiefs decided that Aegean operations were desirable, provided they could be fitted in without detriment to Anvil or Overlord. Also, they repeated their commitment to advancing to the Pisa-Rimini line in Italy, unifying command in the Mediterranean theater and providing support to the Balkans. Churchill called the report a "masterly survey of the whole military scene," and he predicted that military historians would find the Cairo decisions "fully in accordance with the classic articles of war."[69]

Toward the end of the conference, Churchill decided that he and the president should go sightseeing. Roosevelt agreed, and they traveled by car to see the pyramids and the Sphinx. Afterwards, Roosevelt wrote to his secretary, Grace Tully, "I've seen the pyramids and made close friends with the Sphinx. Congress should know her."[70]

The Second Cairo talks, from Brooke's perspective, "ended up with a complete triumph for the righteous." He looked forward to resting well and feeling "very satisfied at the final results."[71] This seems to suggest that the British believed that they had made up some of the ground lost at Tehran. At dinner on 7 December, Churchill asked everyone at the table to predict when Germany would be defeated. Marshall named March, or, if not then, November. Dill gave even money on March, Brooke gave six-to-four odds on March, and the remainder favored March or November.[72] The prime minister, not so optimistic, concluded that so much remained "unknown and immeasurable."[73]

13

WHAT TEHRAN ACHIEVED

I had an uneasy vision of a large balloon carrying in its
basket Marshal Stalin, President Roosevelt, and the Prime
Minister. The balloon's course was erratic, and it appeared
also to be losing height. However, Marshal Stalin stood up
and was soon in command of the situation.
—Alastair Forbes

Critical Impressions

From different perspectives, the conference participants and their contempo-
raries reached conflicting, sometimes contradictory, conclusions about the
significance of the Tehran Conference. For many Americans, Tehran was the
foundation rock of military collaboration and political harmony that ensured
Germany's defeat and marked the beginning of unprecedented allied cooperation in coalition warfare. The allies exchanged military information, and
Stalin's descriptions of Red Army operations gave Westerners a better estimate of conditions on the Russian front. In other words, the conference
brought about good effects that were "impossible to weigh adequately."[1]
Harriman believed that the summit laid to rest Russian suspicions that the
West was not doing enough.[2] To Bohlen, Tehran was the "high-water mark
of Soviet-Western cooperation" during the war.[3]

According to some analysts, the conference marked an American victory
over the British on Overlord. The British had insisted that Overlord could
not be successful unless German divisions withdrew from France, that the
best way to accomplish this was to increase pressure in the Mediterranean,
and that the Mediterranean must be strengthened at Overlord's expense.
Both the Americans and the British had sought to win Stalin's endorsement.
The outcome was clear to Roosevelt, at least, who told Stimson in mid-
December 1943 that he had "fought hard for Overlord and with the aid of
Stalin finally won out."[4]

Stalin's performance won him admiration and respect among American
observers. Everyone who had carefully considered overall allied strategy for
beating the Germans, wrote Arnold, had to agree with Stalin's views.[5] "I am

162

sold on Stalin," recorded Boettiger.[6] On 5 December 1943, after reviewing the conference minutes, Stimson noted in his diary, "I thank the Lord that Stalin was there. In my opinion, he saved the day. He was direct and strong and he brushed away the diversionary attempts of the prime minister with a vigor which rejoiced my soul. . . . In the end Stalin carried the day and I was delighted with it."[7]

Of all those who regarded Tehran as a success, none quite matched the early enthusiasm of the president, who apparently believed that he had established a firm foundation for friendship with the Russians. Insisting that the "actual fact" of meeting Stalin lived up to his highest expectations, Roosevelt described the marshal as a realist, rather than as an imperialist or communist.[8] On 3 December, he wired Stalin that the conference had been an "important milestone in the progress of human affairs."[9] In his 1943 Christmas Eve fireside chat, he described the meetings as "intense and consistently amicable." The Big Three, he said, had planned to talk to each other across the table, but they had discovered happily that they were "all on the same side."[10]

Outwardly, at least, the Russians seemed to have been pleased with the conference. According to some observers, Stalin returned to Moscow in a jubilant, "almost boisterous," mood.[11] On 6 December 1943, in a telegram to Roosevelt, he called the conference a "great success," and, on 20 December, he explained: "I also attach important significance to our meeting and to the conversations taken place there which concerned such substantial questions of accelerating of our common victory and establishment of future lasting peace between the peoples."[12] And when, in reply to a congratulatory message from Hopkins, Molotov wired that the allies had proven that they could work together and had established the foundation for continuing their work in the future, he was simply following the official line. The Russian press without exception praised the conference. *Pravda* described it as "heralding to the world, tortured by ruthless and devastating war, the approach of the desired hour of victory." *Izvestia* claimed that "the time of decisive battles had been fixed." *Red Star* reported that the allied decisions spelled doom for Nazi plans.[13]

The reaction of the Western press and public was mostly favorable. Describing the talks as "intensive, intimate, and frank," the *New York Herald Tribune* called Tehran a landmark in diplomatic history.[14] *Business Week* hailed what it called a "momentous conference."[15] The allies, editorialized the *Times* (London), had met with "common determination to end the war quickly and completely and to lead Europe back to security and freedom."[16] The *Christian Science Monitor* declared that allied decisions represented complete agreement that the war could not end in a soft peace for either end of the Axis.[17] And the *Washington Post* claimed that the conference rivaled the great military victories.[18]

While remaining optimistic, some observers had an uneasy feeling that
Tehran was a step in the wrong direction. For example, Bohlen found Stalin's
leaning toward German dismemberment, Soviet desires for warm water
ports, their disregard for Poland, and the hints of Russian demands in Asia
troubling indeed.[19] In the view of another, the "task of defeating Germany
remained so immediate and burdensome," the allies were forced to cooperate, though such harmony was expected to be short-lived.[20]

Churchill's attitude was ambivalent. Surveying the military decisions
reached, he was well content, but he admitted that the "political aspects were
at once more remote and speculative." Cooperation with the Russians was
necessary, because "it would not have been right for the Western democracies
to found their plans upon suspicions of the Russian attitude in the hour of
triumph and when all her dangers were removed."[21] Though he may well
have been temporarily troubled by the "disastrous involvements, obligations
and assumptions" of Tehran, he recovered quickly.[22] After the summit, he
was still "louder in praise of Russian courage than in criticism of Stalin's
surliness."[23]

For some, Tehran was a major disappointment. The only output of the
conference seemed to be a series of ambiguous policies, bound to cause
disagreement if anyone tried to implement them. The acid test, of course,
was whether the Big Three would really carry out what they had promised.
"Actually," wrote Martel, "we got nothing out of the Russians except what
they wanted to give."[24] The Grand Alliance had entirely too much residual
distrust to be relieved by a four-day excursion to Iran.[25] Brooke did not
share what he called the illusion that a meeting of minds had taken place.
Agreement had been reached only in principle, he wrote, and most of the
participants held reservations "regarding this or that."[26]

Meanwhile, Secretary of State Hull was given little evidence upon which
to judge the conference. On 3 December 1943, the president promised to
bring him the "minutes of all that was said and done."[27] But, on 7 December, Stimson was surprised to discover that Hull had not yet seen the
Tehran protocol. And three months later, when a subordinate explained that
foreign service officers would be stronger in their operations if they were
informed of Roosevelt's secret conversations at Tehran, Hull replied with a
touch of sarcasm, "Oh, you think so, do you? Well please know that the
operations of the secretary of state would also be strengthened if he knew
what happened at Tehran!"[28]

In the view of some, the most critical failing of the conference was that
Stalin had gotten the better of the president. Given Russia's standing in the
war effort, even a less astute negotiator than Stalin would have to have been
in the driver's seat.[29] The president was certainly mistaken in placing so
much weight upon the notion that Stalin just needed someone to whip him
into shape. Moreover, he may have fallen prey to the tactics Russians used to
throw their opponents off balance.[30] As one disgruntled American put it,

"After Bloody Joe got through laying down the law . . . we were lucky to get away with our shirts."[31]

Criticism, of course, surfaced in the press as well. The *Chicago Tribune*, looking in vain for momentous achievements, called Tehran a "great disappointment."[32] "Cut and dried solution of the manifold and intricate problems," ran one skeptical account, could hardly have been resolved during the short time the allies were together.[33] One reporter summoned up a rather ominous spectacle:

> I had an uneasy vision of a large balloon carrying in its basket Marshal Stalin, President Roosevelt, and the Prime Minister. The balloon's course was erratic, and it appeared also to be losing height. However, Marshal Stalin stood up and was soon in command of the situation. As he addressed his two companions, I thought I heard him saying that if the balloon continued to lose altitude he would have to bale out, but it would be preferable first to throw overboard some of the valuable cargo. Accordingly, Mr. Churchill and Mr. Roosevelt began, a little reluctantly perhaps, to heave over the side some cases variously labelled "Atlantic Charter," "Democracy," "Old Friends and Allies," "Four Freedoms," etc. After which the balloon began to gain height again but appeared to be travelling backwards.[34]

The German hope was that the Big Three would fall victim to fighting over the spoils before the victory was finally won. Calling the conference a farce, the Germans mocked the Big Three for wasting time. The mountain labored and brought forth a mouse, some German commentators exclaimed.[35] Many Germans believed that they were secure so long as the allies could not decide on how to assault Europe. Goebbels chided the West for stupidity and shortsightedness in thinking that Stalin would keep his word, described the Big Three relationships as being a far cry from staged photographs and flowery communiqués, and derided Big Three declarations as scraps of paper.[36]

Nevertheless, the Germans were forced, at least privately, to face harsh realities following Tehran. There were "nervous efforts" to draw parallels to Wilson's Fourteen Points.[37] It is never a promising sign, of course, when the enemy is confident enough of final victory to envision the nature of the postwar world. Despite virtually ignoring the conference in public, Hitler may have gotten a vivid picture of what was in store for the Reich. And, given the West's apparent concessions to Stalin, some Germans concluded that everything possible must be done to hasten the end of the war.[38]

Agreement in Principle

Since the war, it has become popular to view the Tehran Conference as having established a covenant among the Big Three. Under this rubric, the

sought to create a united Anglo-American front. But the Americans frustrated Churchill, and he may have left Tehran downcast, if not completely disheartened.

Thus, the pattern was consistent. Whether the issue related to Poland, the desirability of an international organization, or the second front, agreement in principle was what the allies really achieved. Perhaps the complexities of the diverse problems confronting the allied leaders precluded any cut and dried solutions. For whatever reasons, the decisions taken at Tehran were not fixed as unalterable, and, whether genuine adjustments to changing circumstances or selfish national interests were to blame, the Tehran accord quickly dissipated. Shortly after the conference, the cooperative mood was rocked by Russian allegations of bad faith on the part of the West. In January 1944, the Russians charged that the British and Americans were meeting secretly with German agents in the Spanish Pyrenees, and, in February, they added the accusation that the West had established contacts through Switzerland to arrange a separate peace with Germany.

But, for all that, the Tehran Conference was a useful exercise in summit diplomacy. The talks gave Stalin a chance to state his views, to deal firsthand with both Roosevelt and Churchill, and possibly the chance to relieve his suspicions that the West was not interested in contributing a greater share to the war effort. Moreover, the conference led to more confidence within the Grand Alliance, and this better prepared the allies for coming storms. And the overall diplomatic pattern was an ingenious application of agreement in principle. Given the nature of the allied coalition in 1943, the Tehran achievement may have been the best that could reasonably have been expected.

NOTES

Introduction

1. "Three Men of Destiny," *New York Times Magazine*, 21 November 1943.
2. Interview by author with Governor W. Averell Harriman, 2 July 1981 (hereafter cited as Harriman interview).
3. Keith Eubank, *The Summit Conferences, 1919–1960* (Norman: University of Oklahoma Press, 1966), 75; Robert Beitzell, *The Uneasy Alliance: America, Britain and Russia, 1941–1943* (New York: Alfred A. Knopf, 1972), 378; Khosrow Sadegni, "A Study of the Tehran Conference of 1943," (Ph.D. diss., Kent State University, 1975), iii.
4. See Keith Sainsbury, *The Turning Point. Roosevelt, Stalin, Churchill and Chiang Kai-Shek, 1943. The Moscow, Cairo, and Teheran Conferences* (New York: Oxford University Press, 1985).
5. "Where the West Really Began Its Retreat: Teheran, 1943," *U.S. News and World Report*, 26 June 1961, 84; Oswald G. Villard, "Roosevelt Postwar World," *Christian Century*, 31 May 1944, 668.
6. Felix Wittmer, *The Yalta Betrayal: Data on the Decline and Fall of FDR* (Caldwell, Idaho: The Caxton Printers, 1954), 54; Edward J. Rozek, *Allied Wartime Diplomacy: A Pattern in Poland* (New York: John Wiley and Sons, 1958), 51; Jan Ciechanowski, *Defeat in Victory* (Garden City, N.Y.: Doubleday and Co., 1947), 250.
7. Herbert Feis, *Churchill, Roosevelt and Stalin. The War They Waged and the Peace They Sought* (Princeton: Princeton University Press, 1957), 402; Joseph R. McCarthy, *America's Retreat from Victory* (New York: Devin-Adair Publishers, 1951), 39–40.

Chapter 1. The Need for a Summit

1. Beitzell, *Uneasy Alliance*, 366.
2. Ivan Maisky, *Memoirs* (New York: Charles Scribner's Sons, 1968), 101.
3. Anthony Eden, *The Reckoning* (Boston: Houghton Mifflin, 1965), 318.
4. Winston S. Churchill, *Grand Alliance* (New York: Bantam Books, 1962), 399.
5. Harriman interview.
6. Vojtech Mastny, "Stalin and the Prospects of a Separate Peace in World War II," *American Historical Review* 77 (1972): 1385.
7. Norman Longmate, *The GIs* (London: Hutchinson, 1975), 94.
8. James Leasor, *War at the Top* (London: Michael Joseph, 1959), 11, passim.
9. Charles Moran, *Churchill* (Boston: Houghton Mifflin, 1966), 141.
10. "Big Four Map Own Postwar Places as Well as Axis Annihilation," *Newsweek*, 13 December 1943, 24.

11. "Three Men of Destiny," *New York Times Magazine*, 21 November 1943.

12. Harriman interview.

13. John R. Deane, *Strange Alliance* (New York: The Viking Press, 1947), 42.

14. See Robert E. Sherwood, *Roosevelt and Hopkins. An Intimate History* (New York: Harper and Brothers, 1948), 443. Like many fanciful stories, this one may well have been apocryphal, but it was apparently one of Hopkins' favorites.

15. Lord Hastings Ismay, *The Memoirs of General the Lord Ismay* (London: Heinemann, 1960), 116.

16. Maisky, *Memoirs*, 271.

17. A. J. P. Taylor, *The War Lords* (London: Hamish Hamilton, 1976), 93–94.

18. Ella Winter, "Our Allies, the Russians," *Ladies' Home Journal*, February 1943, 37.

19. Harriman interview.

20. Ismay, *Memoirs*, 337.

21. Andrew B. Cunningham, *A Sailor's Odyssey* (London: Hutchinson, 1951), 587.

22. Harriman interview.

23. Wendell Willkie, *One World* (New York: Simon and Schuster, 1943), 3.

24. Nikita Khrushchev, *Khrushchev Remembers*, trans. and ed. Strobe Talbott (Boston: Little, Brown and Co., 1970), 258.

25. Harriman interview.

26. William D. Leahy, *I Was There* (London: Victor Gollancz, 1950), 243.

27. Deane, *Strange Alliance*, 43.

28. Harriman interview.

29. Forrest C. Pogue, *George C. Marshall*, vol. 3, *Organizer of Victory* (New York: The Viking Press, 1973), 313.

30. Ronald Hingley, *Joseph Stalin: Man and Legend* (New York: McGraw-Hill, 1974), 352–53.

31. Ross T. McIntire and George Creel, *White House Physician* (New York: G. P. Putnam's Sons, 1946), 16.

32. Summer Welles, *Where Are We Heading?* (New York: Harper and Brothers, 1946), 77.

33. Harriman interview.

34. Eleanor Roosevelt, *Autobiography* (New York: Harper and Brothers, 1958), 263.

35. W. Averell Harriman and Elie Abel, *Special Envoy to Churchill and Stalin, 1941–1946* (New York: Random House, 1975), 258.

36. Henry H. Arnold, *Global Mission* (New York: Harper and Row, 1972), 469.

37. Wartime diary of John D. Boettiger, 20 November 1943, John D. Boettiger Papers, Franklin D. Roosevelt Library, Hyde Park, New York (hereafter cited as Boettiger diary and FDRL).

38. William H. Standley and Arthur A. Ageton, *Admiral Ambassador to Russia* (Chicago: Henry Regnery, 1955), 63.

39. Deane, *Strange Alliance*, 84–85.

40. William C. Bullit, "How We Won the War and Lost the Peace," *Life*, 30 August 1948, 94.

41. As quoted in Raymond G. O'Connor, *Diplomacy for Victory* (New York: W. W. Norton, 1971), 44.

42. Estimate of Enemy Situation by Fronts, 18 November 1943, Modern Military Records, Record Group 218, Records of the U.S. Joint Chiefs of Staff, CCS 300/3, National Archives (hereafter records in the National Archives Building are indicated by the symbol NA).

43. Ibid.

44. Estimate of Enemy Situation as of 1 November 1943, RG 218, 18 November 1943, CCS 300/3, NA.

45. Estimate of Enemy Situation by Fronts, 18 November 1943, RG 218, CCS 300/3, NA.

46. Estimate of Enemy Situation, 1944—Pacific and Far East, 18 November 1943, RG 218, CCS 300/2, NA.

47. Chinese Capabilities and Intentions, 18 November 1943, RG 218, CCS 300/2, NA.

48. Telegram, Roosevelt to Churchill, 8 December 1941, Record Group 59, Archives of the State Department, Decimal File 740.0011Pacific War/854E:Telegram, NA.

49. Churchill, *Grand Alliance*, 609.

50. U.S. Department of State, Foreign Relations of the United States, *The Conferences at Washington, 1941–42 and Casablanca, 1943* (Washington, D.C.: Government Printing Office, 1968), 112 (hereafter cited as FRUS, WC).

51. Maxim Litvinov, "More Fronts to Win the War Now," *Vital Speeches* 8 (15 March 1942): 325.

52. Eden, *Reckoning*, 383.

53. FRUS, WC, 467.

54. Winston S. Churchill, *The Hinge of Fate* (New York: Bantam Books, 1962), 419.

55. FRUS, WC, 774.

56. Ibid.

57. Memoirs, Lawrence Franklin Burgis Papers, 43, Churchill College, Cambridge, England.

58. U.S. Department of State, Foreign Relations of the United States, *The Conferences at Washington and Quebec 1943* (Washington, D.C.: Government Printing Office, 1970), 284–85 (hereafter cited as FRUS, WQ).

59. Telegram, Stalin to Roosevelt, 11 June 1943, Franklin D. Roosevelt Papers, Map Room, FDRL.

60. Harriman, *Special Envoy*, 152.

61. Henry L. Stimson and McGeorge Bundy, *On Active Service in Peace and War* (New York: Harper and Brothers, 1947), 527.

62. Moran, *Churchill*, 36.

63. Leslie Hollis, *One Marine's Tale* (London: Andre Deutsch, 1956), 97.

64. Dwight D. Eisenhower, *Crusade in Europe* (Garden City, N.Y.: Doubleday and Co., 1953), 60.

65. Charles De Gaulle, *Complete War Memoirs*, vol. 2 (New York: Simon and Schuster, 1959), 594.

66. Henry Lewis Stimson Diaries, 45, 90–91, 6 December 1943, Manuscripts and Archives, Yale University Library, New Haven, Connecticut (hereafter cited as Stimson diaries).

67. General Sir John Kennedy, *The Business of War*, ed., Bernard Fergusson (New York: William Morrow and Co., 1958), 294–95.

68. Ibid., 309.

69. Eisenhower, *Crusade*, 194.

70. Harriman interview.

71. Eisenhower, *Crusade*, 199.

72. See FRUS, WQ.

73. Cordell Hull, *The Memoirs of Cordell Hull*, vol. 2 (New York: Macmillan, 1948), 1231.

74. Stimson, *Active Service*, 439.

75. FRUS, WQ, 1159.

76. Maisky, *Memoirs*, 275.

77. Telegram, Churchill to Roosevelt, 23 October 1943, FDR Papers, Map Room, FDRL.

78. U.S. Department of State, Foreign Relations of the United States, *The Conferences at Cairo and Tehran* (Washington, D.C.: Government Printing Office, 1961), 358 (hereafter cited as FRUS, CT).

79. British Memorandum on Overlord and the Mediterranean, 25 November 1943, RG 218, CCS 409, NA.

80. *A War Atlas for Americans,* Prepared with Assistance of the Office of War Information (New York: Simon and Schuster, 1944), 71.

81. See Janusz Zawodny, *Death in the Forest* (South Bend, Ind.: University of Notre Dame Press, 1962), 79.

82. Heinz Eulau, "As the Big Three Meet," *New Republic* 5 February 1945, 169.

83. Warren B. Walsh, "What the American People Think of Russia," *Public Opinion Quarterly* 8 (1944–45):519.

Chapter 2. Opening Moves

1. Standley, *Admiral,* 153.

2. See Harriman, *Special Envoy,* 176.

3. Telegram, Roosevelt to Churchill, 25 November 1942, FDR Papers, Map Room, FDRL.

4. FRUS, WC, 490–91. In Churchill's words, "I entirely agree in principle that there should be a conference with the Russians. . . ."

5. Telegram, Roosevelt to Churchill, 2 December 1942, FDR Papers, Map Room, FDRL. The reference was to the meeting of France's Napoleon I and Russia's Alexander I in July 1807 on a raft in the Niemen River at Tilsit, East Prussia, where they concluded a peace settlement highly unfavorable to Russia. It is not clear whether Roosevelt was referring to the distance he would have to travel, the facilities at the meeting site, or the possible outcome of the talks.

6. See Joseph P. Lash, *Roosevelt and Churchill* (New York: W. W. Norton, 1976), 182.

7. Sherwood, *Roosevelt and Hopkins,* 757.

8. Hull, *Memoirs,* 1:158.

9. Memorandum, 8 September 1944, Henry J. Morgenthau Jr. Papers, 770:120, FRDL.

10. Hull, *Memoirs,* 1:1109.

11. Robert D. Murphy, *Diplomat Among Warriors* (Westport, Conn.: Greenwood Press, 1964), 447.

12. Ministry of Foreign Affairs of the USSR, *Correspondence Between the Chairman of the Council of Ministers of the USSR and the Presidents of the USA and the Prime Ministers of Great Britain During the Great Patriotic War,* 2 vols. (Moscow: Foreign Languages Publishing House, 1958), 2:42 (hereafter cited as Stalin's Correspondence).

13. FRUS, WC, 496.

14. E. Llewellyn Woodward, *British Foreign Policy in the Second World War* (London: Her Majesty's Stationery Office, 1962), 239.

15. Stalin's Correspondence, 2:43.

16. Telegram, Roosevelt to Churchill, 8 December 1942, FDR Papers, Map Room, FDRL.
17. Telegram, Roosevelt to Churchill, 11 December 1942, FDR Papers, Map Room, FDRL.
18. Stalin's Correspondence, 1:82.
19. Ibid., 2:4.
20. FRUS, WC, 496.
21. Hull, *Memoirs*, 2:1249.
22. Telegram, Roosevelt to Stalin, 5 May 1943, FDR Papers, Map Room, FDRL.
23. FRUS, CT, 5.
24. Ibid., 8.
25. Ibid., 10–11.
26. FRUS, WQ, 391.
27. Ibid.
28. FRUS, CT, 20.
29. Stalin's Correspondence, 1:149–150; 2:85–86.
30. FRUS, WQ, 1306.
31. Stalin's Correspondence, 1:157.
32. Ibid., 163.
33. FRUS, CT, 26.
34. Standley, *Admiral*, 498.
35. Telegram, Churchill to Roosevelt, 5 October 1943, FDR Papers, Map Room, FDRL.
36. Telegram, Roosevelt to Churchill, 14 October 1943, FDR Papers, Map Room, FDRL.
37. Stalin's Correspondence, 2:99.
38. Telegram, Churchill to Roosevelt, 16 October 1943, FDR Papers, Map Room, FDRL.
39. Telegram, Foreign Office to Moscow, 2 October 1943, No. 1680, CAB 120/113, Public Records Office, London (hereafter cited as PRO).
40. Eden, *Reckoning*, 482.
41. Telegram, Moscow to Foreign Office, 21 October 1943, No. 1144, CAB 120/113, PRO.
42. Valentin Berezhkov, *History in the Making* (Moscow: Progress Publishers, 1982), 219.
43. Telegram, Foreign Office to Moscow, 22 October 1943, No. 1680, CAB 120/113, PRO.
44. Personal and Secret Telegram, Roosevelt to Hull, 21 October 1943, Cordell Hull Papers, No. 24, Library of Congress, Washington, D.C.
45. Stalin's Correspondence, 2:104.
46. Telegram, Churchill to Roosevelt, 2 November 1943, FDR Papers, Map Room, FDRL.
47. FRUS, CT, 51–52.
48. Ibid., 71.
49. Telegram, Churchill to Roosevelt, 12 November 1943, FDR Papers, Map Room, FDRL.
50. Diary, Sir Alexander George Montagu Cadogan Papers, ACAD 1/12, 13 November 1943, Churchill College, Cambridge (hereafter cited as Cadogan diary).
51. Telegram, Roosevelt to Churchill, 11 November 1943, FDR Papers, Map Room, FDRL.
52. Prime Minister's Personal Telegram No. T.1747/3, No. 476, 27 October 1943, CAB 120/113, PRO.

53. Telegram, Roosevelt to Churchill, 25 October 1943, FDR Papers, Map Room, FDRL.

54. Memorandum, Joint Chiefs of Staff to Roosevelt, 17 November 1943, RG 218, NA.

55. FRUS, CT, 63.

56. Ibid., 82.

57. Telegram, Roosevelt to Stalin, 20 November 1943, FDR Papers, Map Room, FDRL.

58. Telegram, Foreign Office to Moscow, No. 118 Extra, 23 October 1943, CAB 120/113, PRO.

59. Winston S. Churchill, *Closing the Ring* (New York: Bantam Books, 1962), 272.

60. Telegram, Churchill to Roosevelt, 21 November 1943, FDR Papers, Map Room, FDRL.

61. Diary, Lord Alanbrooke Papers, AB 5/8, 20 November 1943, Liddell Hart Centre for Military Archives, King's College, London (hereafter cited as Alanbrooke Papers).

62. War Cabinet Chiefs of Staff Committee "Sextant Minutes," Hastings L. Ismay Papers, Ismay 6/5, p. 53, COS Sextant 3, 21 November 1943, Liddell Hart Centre for Military Archives, King's College, London (hereafter cited as Ismay Papers).

63. "Conference Bits," *Newsweek*, 13 December 1943, 26.

64. Diary, Alanbrooke Papers, AB 5/8, p. 13; Cadogan diary, ACAD 1/12, 25 November 1943; Moran, *Churchill*, 139.

65. Moran, *Churchill*, 139; Arthur Bryant, *Triumph in the West* (Garden City, N.Y.: Doubleday and Co., 1959), 53. There is a different version in the Alanbrooke diary, AB 5/8, p. 13. Here, Brooke described Madame Chiang as a "study in herself, a queer character in which sex and politics seemed to predominate, both being used indiscriminately, individually, or unitedly to achieve her ends."

66. Churchill, *Closing Ring*, 279.

67. See Letter, "At Sea on Way Back from Sextant," Ismay Papers, Ismay 4/Som/4.

68. Barbara Tuchman, *Stilwell and the American Experience in China* (New York: Macmillan, 1971), 515.

69. FRUS, CT, 311.

70. Notes for My Memoirs, Alanbrooke Papers, AB 2/11, 23 November 1943.

71. Ernest J. King and Walter M. Whitehill, *Fleet Admiral King* (New York: W. W. Norton, 1952), 511. According to Joseph W. Stilwell, *The Stilwell Papers*, ed. Theodore H. White (New York: William Sloane, 1948), 245, "Brooke was insulting."

72. Arnold, *Global Mission*, 461.

73. Stilwell, *Papers*, 245.

74. Notes On My Life, Alanbrooke Papers, AB 3/A/10. Brooke's original reaction was that discussions were somewhat heated. See Diary, AB 5/8, 23 November 1943.

75. Churchill, *Closing Ring*, 279.

76. Moran, *Churchill*, 141.

77. British Memorandum on Effects of Weather on Overlord, 25 November 1943, RG 218, CCS 410, NA.

78. Minutes of Joint Chiefs Meeting, 22 November 1943, RG 218, NA.

79. Combined Chiefs of Staff Minutes, Ismay Papers, Ismay 6/7, p. 77, 25 November 1943.

80. FRUS, CT, 329.

81. Robert W. Coakley and Richard M. Leighton, *Global Logistics and Strategy, 1943–1945* (Washington, D.C.: Office of the Chief of Military History, 1968), 275.

82. Diary, Alanbrooke Papers, AB 5/8, p. 17, 26 November 1943.
83. FRUS, CT, 358.
84. Minutes of Joint Chiefs Meeting, JCS 129th Meeting, 24 November 1943, RG 218, NA.
85. Churchill, *Closing Ring*, 286.
86. Bryant, *Triumph*, 56.
87. Churchill, *Closing Ring*, 290.
88. "FDR's Jam Session," *Newsweek*, 13 December 1943, 26.
89. Eden, *Reckoning*, 491; Diary, Alanbrooke Papers, AB 5/8, 25 November 1943.
90. Leasor, *War at Top*, 258.

Chapter 3. Bringing the Big Three Together

1. Telegram, Stalin to Roosevelt, 25 November 1943, Telegram, Roosevelt to Stalin, 26 November 1943, FDR Papers, Map Room, FDRL.
2. Standley, *Admiral*, 105.
3. Alexander Cadogan, *The Diaries of Alexander Cadogan*, ed. David Dilks (New York: G. P. Putnam's Sons, 1971), 579.
4. "Trip to Sextant," Journal, 29 November 1943, Henry H. Arnold Papers, Box 272, Library of Congress, Washington, D.C. (hereafter cited as Arnold journal).
5. Harriman interview.
6. Adam B. Ulam, *Stalin* (New York: The Viking Press, 1973), 587.
7. "How Three Men Kept Their Date with Destiny," *Washington Times-Herald*, 7 December 1943.
8. Boettiger diary, 47, 27 November 1943, FDRL.
9. Arthur H. Birse, *Memoirs of an Interpreter* (New York: Coward and McCann, 1967), 154.
10. Cunningham, *Odyssey*, 587.
11. Harriman, *Special Envoy*, 266.
12. Cadogan diary, ACAD 1/12, 26 November 1943.
13. Eden, *Reckoning*, 494.
14. Churchill, *Closing Ring*, 292.
15. Walter H. Thompson, *Assignment: Churchill* (New York: Popular Library, 1955), 273.
16. Sarah Churchill, *A Thread in the Tapestry* (New York: Dodd and Mead, 1967), 64. According to other accounts, the prime minister savored taking risks. See Thompson, *Assignment*, 273; and Churchill, *Closing Ring*, 292–93.
17. Ismay, *Memoirs*, 337; Sarah Churchill, *Thread*, 65.
18. George Greenfield, "An Observer at Teheran," *History of the Second World War*, vol. 4, ed. Barrie Pitt (Hicksville, N.Y.: Marshall Cavendish, 1973), 1524.
19. Ernest J. King Diaries, 27 November 1943, Ernest J. King Papers, Library of Congress, Washington, D.C. (hereafter cited as King diaries).
20. William D. Leahy Diaries, 27 November 1943, William D. Leahy Papers, Library of Congress, Washington, D.C. (hereafter cited as Leahy diaries).
21. Churchill, *Closing Ring*, 293.
22. Boettiger diary, 43, 28 November 1943, FDRL.
23. Memorandum for Chief of Staff, 19 November 1943, George C. Marshall Papers, George C. Marshall Research Foundation, Lexington, Virginia.
24. Boettiger diary, 28 November 1943, FDRL.
25. Sarah Churchill, *Thread*, 65.

26. Boettiger diary, 28 November 1943, FDRL.

27. FRUS, CT, 373.

28. Beitzell, *Uneasy Alliance*, 296. Churchill, *Closing Ring*, 277–94, is mute.

29. William M. Rigdon and James Derieux, *White House Sailor* (Garden City, N.Y.: Doubleday, 1962), 78.

30. Boettiger diary, 44, 27 November 1943, FDRL.

31. Harriman, *Special Envoy*, 262.

32. I. G. Edmonds, *The Shah of Iran* (New York: Holt, Rinehart and Winston, 1976), 101.

33. Harriman interview.

34. Moran, *Churchill*, 164.

35. Harriman interview.

36. FRUS, CT, 440.

37. Leahy, *I Was There*, 240.

38. Harriman, *Special Envoy*, 263.

39. Frances Perkins, *The Roosevelt I Knew* (New York: Harper and Row, 1946), 83.

40. Harriman, *Special Envoy*, 264.

41. Norman Cousins, "Proportion and the Press," *Saturday Review of Literature*, 18 December 1943, 14.

42. *New York Times*, 22 November 1943.

43. Laslo Havas, *Hitler's Plot to Kill the Big Three* (New York: Cowles Book Co., 1969), 143.

44. Harriman, *Special Envoy*, 264; Leahy, *I Was There*, 240.

45. Michael F. Reilly and William J. Slocum, *Reilly of the White House* (New York: Simon and Schuster, 1947), 178.

46. Cadogan, *Diaries*, 579.

47. Churchill, *Closing Ring*, 293.

48. Letter, "At Sea on Way Back from Sextant," Ismay Papers, Ismay 4/Som/4b.

49. *Reilly*, 178.

50. Boettiger diary, 28 November 1943, FDRL.

51. Leahy, *I Was There*, 240.

52. Boettiger diary, 46, 28 November 1943, FDRL.

53. Leahy, *I Was There*, 240.

54. Ismay, *Memoirs*, 337; Also, see George N. Crocker, *Roosevelt's Road to Russia* (Chicago: Henry Regnery, 1959), 213.

55. Harriman interview.

56. Elliott Roosevelt, *As He Saw It* (New York: Duell, Sloan and Pearce, 1946), 178.

57. *Reilly*, 179.

58. Perkins, *Roosevelt I Knew*, 83.

59. Havas, *Hitler's Plot*, 144.

60. "Personal Contact Close at Teheran," *New York Times*, 7 December 1943.

61. "GI View of Teheran," *The Best from Yank* (New York: E. P. Dutton, 1945), 200.

Chapter 4. Raising the Curtain

1. Stalin's Correspondence, 2:43.

2. Ibid., 1:81, 175.

3. Eden, *Reckoning,* 465.

4. Harriman interview.

5. Memorandum of Conversation, Harriman-Bohlen-Molotov-Pavlov, 16 November 1943, Record Group 43, Records of International Conferences, Commissions, and Expositions, NA.

6. Agenda for Sextant, 22 November 1943, RG 218, CCS 404, NA.

7. Combined Chief Minutes, Combined Chiefs 129th Meeting, 24 November 1943, RG 218, NA.

8. Eden, *Reckoning,* 489.

9. Harriman, *Special Envoy,* 263.

10. Cadogan diary, ACAD 1/12, 27 November 1943.

11. Harriman, *Special Envoy,* 263.

12. See Henry Field, "How FDR Did His Homework," *Saturday Review of Literature,* 8 July 1961, 9. According to this unsubstantiated and unlikely account, the president studied numerous memoranda prior to the summit. These papers supposedly included a personality profile on Stalin and an outline of probable strategems the Russians might employ at the bargaining table.

13. Charles Bohlen, *Witness to History, 1929–1969* (New York: W. W. Norton, 1973), 136.

14. Ibid., 138.

15. Record of British Chiefs of Staff Proceedings, Ismay Papers, Ismay 6/5, p. 22, COS Sextant 6th Meeting, 28 November 1943.

16. Ibid.

17. Diary, Alanbrooke Papers, AB 5/8, p. 19, 28 November 1943.

18. Ray S. Cline, *Washington Command Post: The Operations Division* (Washington, D.C.: Office of the Chief of Military History, 1951), 227. Sextant was devoted to this purpose: "Quadrant commitment to Overlord, which was nearly irrevocable—in short, whether they were at last going 'to fish or cut bait.' "

19. FRUS, CT, 480.

20. Ibid.

21. Ibid., 481.

22. Boettiger diary, 46, 28 November 1943, FDRL.

23. FRUS, CT, 483.

24. Berezhkov, *History,* 254.

25. See Roosevelt, *As He Saw It,* 174; Rigdon, *Sailor,* 81; Berezhkov, *History,* 254.

26. Bohlen, *Witness,* 41.

27. *Reilly,* 179.

28. Memorandum of Conference, 28 November 1943, Harry L. Hopkins Papers, Sherwood Collection, No. 332, p. 1, FDRL.

29. Robert Beitzell, ed., *Tehran. Yalta. Potsdam. The Soviet Protocols* (Hattiesburg, Mississippi: Academic International, 1970), 338 (hereafter cited as Soviet Protocols).

30. Ibid.

31. Ibid.

32. FRUS, CT, 484.

33. Soviet Protocols, 339.

34. Memorandum on Conference, 28 November 1943, Hopkins Papers, Sherwood Collection, No. 332, p. 2, FDRL.

35. FRUS, CT, 484. The original minutes, before editing, had "sympathetic" in place of "symbolic."

36. Memorandum on Conference, 28 November 1943, Hopkins Papers, Sherwood Collection, No. 332, p. 2, FDRL; FRUS, CT, 509.

66. FRUS, CT, 513.
67. Bohlen Supplementary Memorandum, 28 November 1943, RG 43, NA.
68. Ibid.
69. FRUS, CT, 511.
70. Ibid.
71. Eden, *Reckoning*, 495.
72. See Leahy diaries, 63, 28 November 1943.
73. McIntire, *Physician*, 173.
74. Churchill, *Closing Ring*, 308.
75. Record of Conversation between Churchill and Stalin, 28 November 1943, PREM 3/136/8, PRO.
76. Ibid.
77. Harriman interview.
78. Churchill, *Closing Ring*, 309.
79. Record of Conversation between Churchill and Stalin, 28 November 1943, PREM 3/136/8, PRO.
80. Ibid.
81. Churchill, *Closing Ring*, 310.
82. PREM 3/136/8, PRO.
83. Ibid.
84. *Reilly*, 180.
85. Moran, *Churchill*, 151, has the incident occuring during dinner on 29 November when Churchill turned sixty-nine.
86. Eden, *Reckoning*, 495.
87. Boettiger diary, 29 November 1943, FDRL.
88. Roosevelt, *As He Saw It*, 179.
89. Churchill, *Closing Ring*, 310.
90. Standley, *Admiral*, 495.

Chapter 6. Second-Day Warm-Up Talks

1. Cunningham, *Odyssey*, 587.
2. Military Conference, 29 November 1943, RG 218, NA. According to FRUS, CT, 514, Pavlov was present, but CAB 80/77, PRO, lists "Berejkov" instead.
3. King diaries, 28 November 1943.
4. FRUS, CT, 515.
5. Ibid.
6. See Meetings of International Conferences, 18 November 1943, RG 218, CCS 300/3, NA.
7. FRUS, CT, 516.
8. Ibid.
9. Coakley and Leighton, *Global Logistics and Strategy*, 272.
10. FRUS, CT, 517.
11. Diary, Alanbrooke Papers, AB 5/8, p. 21, 29 November 1943.
12. CAB 80/77, PRO; Minutes of Military Experts Meeting, 29 November 1943, RG 218, CCS Minutes, NA.
13. Soviet Protocols, 12.
14. FRUS, CT, 518.
15. CAB 80/77, PRO.
16. FRUS, CT, 518.

17. CAB 80/77, PRO.
18. See Sherwood, *Roosevelt and Hopkins*, 783.
19. FRUS, CT, 519.
20. CAB 80/77, PRO
21. FRUS, CT, 520.
22. CAB 80/77, PRO.
23. FRUS, CT, 521.
24. Soviet Protocols, 15.
25. FRUS, CT, 523.
26. CAB 80/77, PRO.
27. Ibid. The Soviet minutes put the query in a different form. Whereas the British version portrays Voroshilov as rude and somewhat overbearing, the Russian version merely has the marshal asking if the British regarded Overlord as the primary operation to be undertaken.
28. See CAB 80/77, PRO.
29. FRUS, CT, 524.
30. Ibid., 528.
31. Soviet Protocols, 17. The quotation is taken from FRUS, CT, 526.
32. CAB 80/77, PRO.
33. Ibid.
34. King diaries, 29 November 1943.
35. Sherwood, *Roosevelt and Hopkins*, 783.
36. Leahy diaries, 63, 29 November 1943.
37. Bryant, *Triumph*, 63.
38. Moran, *Churchill*, 146.
39. Roosevelt, *As He Saw It*, 179.
40. Harriman interview.
41. FRUS, CT, 614.
42. Arnold, *Global Mission*, 467.
43. FRUS, CT, 529.
44. Ibid.
45. Ibid., 530.
46. Ibid.
47. See FRUS, CT, 622. Because the sketch was originally undated, it is unclear when it was done. For example, Sherwood placed the sketch at sometime preceding the Big Three dinner on 28 November. See Sherwood, *Roosevelt and Hopkins*, 789.
48. FRUS, CT, 530.
49. Soviet Protocols, 341.
50. FRUS, CT, 530.
51. Ibid.
52. Soviet Protocols, 342.
53. Ibid.
54. FRUS, CT, 531.
55. William H. McNeill, *America, Britain and Russia. Their Co-operation and Conflict, 1941–1946* (New York: Oxford University Press, 1953), 356.
56. Bohlen, Witness, 145.
57. Soviet Protocols, 343.
58. FRUS, CT, 532.
59. Soviet Protocols, 343.
60. Ibid.
61. FRUS, CT, 532.
62. Moran, *Churchill*, 146.

Chapter 7. Second-Day Meetings of the Big Three

1. Leahy diaries, 29 November 1943.
2. Greenfield, "Observer," *History of the Second World War,* 1529.
3. Bryant, *Triumph,* 63.
4. Hollis, *One Marine,* 106.
5. King diaries, 24, 29 November 1943; Arnold, *Global Mission,* 467.
6. Hollis, *One Marine,* 107.
7. Boettiger diary, 29 November 1943, FDRL.
8. Birse, *Memoirs,* 157.
9. King diaries, 24, 29 November 1943.
10. Thompson, *Assignment,* 274.
11. "Big Little Man," *Time,* 20 December 1943, 23.
12. Roosevelt, *As He Saw It,* 180.
13. Cadogan diary, ACAD 1/12, 29 November 1943; Hollis, *One Marine,* 107; Churchill, *Closing Ring,* 311; Diary, Alanbrooke Papers, AB 5/8, p. 22, 29 November 1943.
14. Birse, *Memoirs,* 158.
15. King diaries, 29 November 1943.
16. Moran, *Churchill,* 146.
17. Cadogan diary, ACAD 1/12, 29 November 1943.
18. Perkins, *Roosevelt I Knew,* 85.
19. Arnold, *Global Mission,* 466. CAB 80/77, PRO, deletes Harriman, Clark-Kerr, and Berezhkov. The last mentioned is probably the "secretary" noted in the American minutes. See FRUS, CT, 533.
20. See Arnold, *Global Mission,* 466.
21. Boettiger diary, 49, 29 November 1943, FDRL.
22. Soviet Protocols, 19. Also, see Roosevelt, *As He Saw It,* 178; FRUS, CT, 533–34.
23. CAB 80/77, PRO.
24. Leahy diaries, 64, 29 November 1943.
25. Moran, *Churchill,* 147.
26. FRUS, CT, 535.
27. CAB 80/77, PRO.
28. Leahy, *I Was There,* 245.
29. CAB 80/77, PRO.
30. FRUS, CT, 535.
31. CAB 80/77, PRO.
32. FRUS, CT, 536.
33. Soviet Protocols, 27.
34. CAB 80/77, PRO.
35. FRUS, CT, 537.
36. CAB 80/77, PRO.
37. Soviet Protocols, 26.
38. Hollis, *One Marine,* 108.
39. CAB 80/77, PRO.
40. Churchill, *Closing Ring,* 317.
41. Ibid., 316.
42. FRUS, CT, 539. According to Soviet Protocols, 29, Roosevelt offered to stay as long as Stalin remained in Tehran.
43. Bohlen, *Witness,* 148.
44. FRUS, CT, 539.

45. King diaries, 22, 29 November 1943.
46. Churchill, *Closing Ring*, 318.
47. CAB 80/77, PRO.
48. Diary, Alanbrooke Papers, AB 5/8, p. 23, 29 November 1943.
49. Bryant, *Triumph*, 67.
50. Rigdon, *Sailor*, 87.
51. Bohlen, *Witness*, 147.
52. Sherwood, *Roosevelt and Hopkins*, 790.
53. Cadogan diary, ACAD 1/12, 29 November 1943.
54. Leahy, *I Was There*, 244.
55. Churchill, *Closing Ring*, 319.
56. Bohlen, *Witness*, 146.
57. Harriman, *Special Envoy*, 274.
58. Boettiger diary, 50, 29 November 1943, FDRL.
59. *Reilly*, 181.
60. Harriman interview.
61. Churchill, *Closing Ring*, 320.
62. Bohlen, *Witness*, 147.
63. Interview with Prime Minister Churchill at Chequers, March 1944, Sir Victor Alexander Louis Mallet Papers, Memoirs, 147B, Churchill College, Cambridge.
64. FRUS, CT, 554.
65. Ibid., 554–555.
66. Memorandum by Bohlen, Moscow, December 1943, Bohlen Collection, RG 59, NA.
67. Moran, *Churchill*, 151.
68. Bohlen, *Witness*, 148. In this account, the conversation took place "after the dinner." However, there is reason to suppose that the talks did not take place until the following day. See Henry Hitch Adams, *Harry Hopkins: A Biography* (New York: Putnam, 1977), 347.
69. Cadogan diary, ACAD 1/12, 29 November 1943.
70. Moran, *Churchill*, 148.
71. Ibid., 149.

Chapter 8. Third-Day Staff and Private Meetings

1. Diary, Alanbrooke Papers, AB 5/8, p. 23, 30 November 1943; Bryant, *Triumph*, 65.
2. Record of British Chiefs of Staff Proceedings, Ismay Papers, Ismay 6/5, COS (Sextant) 8th Meeting, 30 November 1943.
3. Ibid.
4. Leahy, *I Was There*, 247.
5. FRUS, CT, 555.
6. Minutes of CCS 132nd Meeting, 30 November 1943, CAB 99/25, PRO (hererafter cited as CAB 99/25).
7. FRUS, CT, 556.
8. Ibid., 557.
9. Notes on My Life, Alanbrooke Papers, AB 3/A/10, 30 November 1943.
10. CAB 99/25, PRO.
11. Ibid.
12. FRUS, CT, 560.
13. CAB 99/25, PRO.

14. FRUS, CT, 558.

15. CAB 99/25, PRO.

16. Ibid.

17. John Ehrman, *Grand Strategy,* vol. 5, *August 1943 to September 1944* (London: Her Majesty's Stationery Office, 1956), 181.

18. CAB 99/25, PRO.

19. FRUS, CT, 562.

20. CAB 99/25, PRO.

21. Ibid.

22. FRUS, CT, 561.

23. CAB 99/25, PRO.

24. FRUS, CT, 563.

25. Arnold journal, 20, 30 November 1943.

26. Programme of Conferences at Eureka, Ismay Papers, Ismay 2/3/162, p. 2, 30 November 1943.

27. FRUS, CT, 564.

28. Bryant, *Triumph,* 67.

29. Ismay, *Memoirs,* 340.

30. Bryant, *Triumph,* 67.

31. Churchill, *Closing Ring,* 321.

32. Records of the Anglo-American-Russian Conversations in Tehran . . . , PREM 3/136/8, PRO (hereafter cited as Records).

33. Ibid.

34. Harriman interview.

35. Records, PREM 3/136/8, PRO.

36. Churchill, *Closing Ring,* 324.

37. Records, PREM 3/136/8, PRO.

38. Churchill, *Closing Ring,* 323.

39. Soviet Protocols, 345.

40. Churchill, *Closing Ring,* 322.

41. Records, PREM 3/136/8, PRO.

42. Churchill, *Closing Ring,* 324.

43. Soviet Protocols, 345.

44. Churchill, *Closing Ring,* 325.

45. Soviet Protocols, 347.

46. Birse, *Memoirs,* 159.

47. Records, PREM 3/136/8, PRO.

48. Moran, *Churchill,* 153.

49. Harriman, *Special Envoy,* 276. Nothing of this meeting is to be found in Soviet Protocols.

50. Records, PREM 3/136/8, PRO.

51. FRUS, CT, 570.

52. Records, PREM 3/136/8, PRO.

53. FRUS, CT, 571.

54. Records, PREM 3/136/8, PRO.

55. Ibid.

56. Ibid.

57. Ibid.

58. FRUS, CT, 575.

59. Records, PREM 3/136/8, PRO.

60. Ibid.

Chapter 9. Third-Day Meetings of the Big Three

1. Harriman, *Special Envoy,* 274.
2. Birse, *Memoirs,* 159.
3. See Soviet Protocols, 347.
4. Sherwood, *Roosevelt and Hopkins,* 791.
5. Minutes of Big Three Luncheon, 30 November 1943, Hopkins Papers, FDRL.
6. Records, PREM 3/136/8, PRO.
7. Churchill, *Closing Ring,* 326.
8. Minutes of Big Three Luncheon, 30 November 1943, Hopkins Papers, FDRL.
9. Ibid.
10. Ibid.
11. Records, PREM 3/136/8, PRO.
12. FRUS, CT, 322; Meeting of Chiang Kai-shek with Roosevelt, 23 November 1943, RG 43, NA.
13. Churchill, *Closing Ring,* 326.
14. Ibid.
15. Ibid.
16. Minutes of Big Three Luncheon, 30 November 1943, Hopkins Papers, FDRL.
17. Arnold journal, 30 November 1943; CAB 80/77, PRO.
18. Beitzell, *Uneasy Alliance,* 340.
19. FRUS, CT, 576; CAB 80/77, PRO.
20. Bryant, *Triumph,* 66.
21. FRUS, CT, 576.
22. Soviet Protocols, 32.
23. FRUS, CT, 577.
24. Ibid., 578.
25. Soviet Protocols, 33.
26. Ibid.
27. Ibid.
28. Note: Kennedy, *Business of War,* 314, has Stalin making the remark to Martel at Churchill's birthday banquet.
29. Churchill, *Closing Ring,* 328.
30. FRUS, CT, 578.
31. CAB 80/77, PRO.
32. Ibid.
33. FRUS, CT, 578.
34. Arnold journal, 21, 30 November 1943.
35. Roosevelt, *As He Saw It,* 193.
36. Leahy diaries, 30 November 1943.
37. Diary, Alanbrooke Papers, AB 5/8, p. 25, 30 November 1943.
38. King diaries, 30 November 1943.
39. Hollis, *One Marine,* 109.
40. MSS of Book, Andrew B. Cunningham Papers, CUNN 1/1, p. 336, Churchill College, Cambridge.
41. Churchill, *Closing Ring,* 328.
42. Boettiger diary, 51, 30 November 1943, FDRL.
43. Birse, *Memoirs,* 160.
44. *Times* (London), 7 December 1943.
45. Cadogan diary, ACAD 1/12, 30 November 1943.
46. Greenfield, "Observer," *History of the Second World War,* 1529.

47. Birse, *Memoirs*, 160.
48. Sarah Churchill, *Thread*, 65.
49. Leahy diaries, 65, 30 November 1943.
50. Boettiger diary, 51, 30 November 1943, FDRL.
51. Arnold, *Global Mission*, 468.
52. Sherwood, *Roosevelt and Hopkins*, 793.
53. FRUS, CT, 583.
54. Arnold, *Global Mission*, 469; See Churchill, *Closing Ring*, 330.
55. FRUS, CT, 837.
56. Gerald S. Pawle, *The War and Colonel Warden* (New York: Alfred A. Knopf, 1963), 270.
57. Berezhkov, *History*, 288; According to Brooke's biographer, no such toast was offered. See Bryant, *Triumph*, 67.
58. Diary, Alanbrooke Papers, AB 5/8, p. 26, 30 November 1943.
59. Bohlen, *Witness*, 149.
60. Bryant, *Triumph*, 68.
61. Astley, *Inner Circle*, 124; Birse, *Memoirs*, 161; Hollis, *One Marine*, 109; Cadogan, *Diaries*, 581; Bryant, *Triumph*, 69. Curiously, American memoirs make no reference to this episode, which, if true, reveals something of Stalin's despotism. But Harriman could not recall such a thing happening—Harriman interview.
62. Arnold journal, 22, 1 December 1943.
63. Stimson diaries, 45, 120, 16 December 1943.
66. FRUS, CT, 585.
65. Ibid., 837.
66. Moran, *Churchill*, 153.
67. Roosevelt, *As He Saw It*, 194; Bohlen, *Witness*, 149; Harriman interview.
68. Boettiger diary, 30 November 1943, FDRL.
69. Churchill, *Closing Ring*, 329; Birse, *Memoirs*, 161.
70. Bryant, *Triumph*, 69.
71. Ismay, *Memoirs*, 340; Astley, Inner Circle, *123*.
72. *Leahy, I Was There*, 250.

Chapter 10. Informal Political Discussions

1. Harriman, *Special Envoy*, 278.
2. Winston S. Churchill, *The Gathering Storm* (New York: Bantam Books, 1961), 123.
3. King diaries, 24, 1 December 1943.
4. Astley, *Inner Circle*, 127; Memoirs, Burgis Papers, 51.
5. Letter, Ismay to Churchill, Further Points on Cairo Tehran Conference, Ismay Papers, Ismay 2/3/214/a.
6. Perkins, *Roosevelt I Knew*, 83.
7. Standley, *Admiral*, 307.
8. Soviet Protocols, 36.
9. Churchill, *Closing Ring*, 335.
10. Records, PREM 3/136/8, PRO.
11. FRUS, CT, 586.
12. Records, PREM 3/136/8, PRO.
13. FRUS, CT, 587.
14. Minutes of Luncheon, 1 December 1943, Hopkins Papers, FDRL.
15. Ibid.

16. Ibid.
17. Records, PREM 3/136/8, PRO.
18. FRUS, CT, 588.
19. Ibid.
20. Soviet Protocols, 38.
21. Churchill, *Closing Ring*, 335.
22. Records, PREM 3/136/8, PRO.
23. FRUS, CT, 589.
24. Records, PREM 3/136/8, PRO.
25. Ibid.
26. FRUS, CT, 632.
27. Records, PREM 3/136/8, PRO.
28. Churchill, *Closing Ring*, 335.
29. FRUS, CT, 590; There is no mention of this meeting in Soviet Protocols.
30. Records, PREM 3/136/8, PRO.
31. FRUS, CT, 590.
32. Ibid.
33. Churchill, *Closing Ring*, 340.
34. Records, PREM 3/136/8, PRO.
35. Churchill, *Closing Ring*, 341.
36. Records, PREM 3/136/8, PRO.
37. Ibid.
38. Ibid.
39. Ibid.
40. FRUS, CT, 592.
41. Records, PREM 3/136/8, PRO.
42. FRUS, CT, 592.
43. Records, PREM 3/136/8, PRO.
44. Churchill, *Closing Ring*, 341.
45. Records, PREM 3/136/8, PRO.
46. Ibid.
47. Ibid.
48. FRUS, CT, 592.
49. Records, PREM 3/136/8, PRO.
50. Churchill, *Closing Ring*, 342.
51. Records, PREM 3/136/8, PRO.
52. Ibid.
53. Bohlen, *Witness*, 151.
54. FRUS, CT, 594.
55. Roosevelt-Stalin Meeting, 1 December 1943, Hopkins Papers, FDRL.
56. Bohlen, *Witness*, 151.
57. Harriman interview.
58. Harriman, *Special Envoy*, 279.
59. Roosevelt-Stalin Meeting, 1 December 1943, Hopkins Papers, FDRL.
60. FRUS, CT, 595.
61. Harriman interview.

Chapter 11. Final Political Talks

1. FRUS, CT, 597; Records, PREM 3/136/8, PRO.
2. See FRUS, CT, 112.

3. Telegram, Hull to Roosevelt, 30 October 1943, FDR Papers, Map Room, FDRL.

4. FRUS, CT, 173.

5. Records, PREM 3/136/8, PRO.

6. FRUS, CT, 622; Allocation of Italian Ships to USSR, Joint Chiefs of Staff to Roosevelt, 30 November 1943, RG 218, NA.

7. FRUS, CT, 597.

8. Records, PREM 3/136/8, PRO.

9. Ibid.

10. Churchill, *Closing Ring*, 336–37.

11. Records, PREM 3/136/8, PRO.

12. Ibid.

13. Ibid.

14. Bohlen, *Witness*, 151.

15. Roger Parkinson, *A Day's March Nearer Home* (New York: David McKay Co., 1974), 224.

16. Soviet Protocols, 41.

17. Harriman interview.

18. FRUS, CT, 599.

19. Cadogan, *Diaries*, 581.

20. FRUS, CT, 599; Records, PREM 3/136/8, PRO.

21. Records, PREM 3/136/8, PRO. No reference to this exchange appears in Soviet Protocols.

22. FRUS, CT, 600.

23. Bohlen, *Witness*, 151.

24. Records, PREM 3/136/8, PRO.

25. Churchill, *Closing Ring*, 339.

26. FRUS, CT, 600.

27. Churchill, *Closing Ring*, 339.

28. Records, PREM 3/136/8, PRO.

29. Bohlen, *Witness*, 152.

30. Hull, *Memoirs*, 2:1317; Cadogan, *Diaries*, 581.

31. FRUS, CT, 177.

32. Harriman interview.

33. Ibid.

34. Records, PREM 3/136/8, PRO.

35. Churchill, *Closing Ring*, 342.

36. Records, PREM 3/136/8, PRO.

37. Ibid.

38. FRUS, CT, 602.

39. Ibid.

40. Soviet Protocols, 43.

41. Churchill, *Closing Ring*, 344.

42. Harriman, *Special Envoy*, 280.

43. Records, PREM 3/136/8, PRO.

44. FRUS, CT, 253.

45. Memorandum of Meeting, 18 August 1944, Morgenthau papers, 763:202, FDRL.

46. John M. Blum, *Years of War* (Boston: Houghton Mifflin, 1967), 338.

47. Memorandum of Meeting, 18 August 1944, Morgenthau Papers, 763:202, FDRL.

48. Stimson Diaries, 48, 21, 23 August 1944.

49. Soviet Protocols, 144.

50. Records, PREM 3/136/8, PRO.

51. Ibid.

52. U.S. Department of State, Foreign Relations of the United States, *The Conference of Berlin, 1945*, 2 vols. (Washington, D.C.: Government Printing Office, 1960), 2:305.

53. Churchill, *Closing Ring*, 345.

54. FRUS, CT, 634.

55. Don Lohbeck, *Patrick J. Hurley* (Chicago: Henry Regnery, 1956), 219.

56. FRUS, CT, 838.

57. Ibid., 634.

58. See Sherwood, *Roosevelt and Hopkins*, 798.

59. Rigdon, *Sailor*, 88.

60. Leahy diaries, 67, 1 December 1943.

61. William M. Rigdon, *Log of the President's Trip to Africa and the Middle East, November–December 1943* (n.p., 1943?), Rare Book Collection, Library of Congress, Washington, D.C.

62. Bohlen, *Witness*, 152.

63. Lohbeck, *Hurley*, 219.

64. Havas, *Hitler's Plot*, 253.

65. Cadogan diary, ACAD 1/12, 1 December 1943.

66. Sarah Churchill, *Thread*, 66.

67. Moran, *Churchill*, 155.

Chapter 12. The Conference Follow-Up

1. *New York Times*, 12 December 1943.

2. Cadogan diary ACAD 1/12, 1 December 1943; Boettiger diary, 53, 1 December 1943, FDRL.

3. Boettiger diary, 53, 1 December 1943, FDRL.

4. "Meeting at Teheran: Roosevelt-Stalin-Churchill Declaration," *Current History* 6 (January 1944):54.

5. *Chicago Tribune*, 2 December 1943.

6. *New York Times*, 6 December 1943.

7. Joseph Goebbels, *Goebbels Diaries, 1942–1943*, ed. Louis P. Lochner (Garden City, N.Y.: Doubleday, 1948), 544.

8. Boettiger diary, 49, 29 November 1943, FDRL.

9. *New York Times*, 2 December 1943; 7 December 1943.

10. Boettiger diary, 53, 2 December 1943, FDRL.

11. See Telegram, Harriman to Hull, 4 December 1943, RG 59, DF 740.0011EW1939/32176, NA.

12. *Atlanta Constitution*, 4 December 1943.

13. Telegram, Harriman to Hull, 8 December 1943, RG 59, DF 740.0011EW 1939/32243, NA.

14. Ismay, *Memoirs*, 340.

15. "Teheran Declaration: If It Can Be Believed, It Solves Everything; If It Cannot, It is a Colossal Fraud," *Life*, 20 December 1943, 32.

16. Goebbels, *Diaries*, 544.

17. T. H. Vail Motter, *The Persian Corridor and Aid to Russia* (Washington, D.C.: Office of the Chief of Military History, 1962), 10.

18. FRUS, CT, 113.

19. Ibid., 841.
20. Arthur C. Millspaugh, *Americans in Persia* (New York: Da Capo Press, 1976), 206.
21. Roosevelt, *As He Saw It*, 197.
22. FRUS, CT, 885.
23. As quoted in Beitzell, *Uneasy Alliance*, 355.
24. Leahy, *I Was There*, 249.
25. "Two Meetings of Allied Chiefs," *Catholic World*, January 1944, 403.
26. Motter, *Persian Corridor*, 445.
27. Telegram, Dreyfus to Hull, 5 December 1943, RG 59, DF 891.00/2068, NA.
28. FRUS, CT, 651.
29. Millspaugh, *Americans in Persia*, 156.
30. Military Conclusions of the Teheran Conference, PREM 3/136/10, PRO.
31. FRUS, CT, 652.
32. Omar N. Bradley, *A Soldier's Story* (New York: Henry Holt, 1951), 201.
33. Churchill, *Closing Ring*, 346.
34. Ismay, *Memoirs*, 341.
35. Churchill, *Closing Ring*, 349.
36. Moran, *Churchill*, 155.
37. Pogue, *Organizer*, 316.
38. Memoranda Circulated at Cairo and Tehran, Ismay Papers, Ismay 6/7, p. 66, Draft Agenda, CCS 404/2, 2 December 1943.
39. Letter, Ismay to Somerville, Ismay Papers, Ismay 4/Som/4b.
40. Record of British Chiefs of Staff Proceedings, Ismay Papers, Ismay 6/5, p. 75, COS Sextant 19, 2 December 1943.
41. Diary, Alanbrooke Papers, AB 5/8, p. 30, 3 December 1943.
42. Churchill, *Closing Ring*, 350.
43. FRUS, CT, 680.
44. Ibid., 668.
45. Ibid., 681.
46. Bryant, *Triumph*, 73.
47. Letter, Ismay to Churchill, Ismay Papers, Ismay 2/3/214a, 17 May 1950.
48. FRUS, CT, 699.
49. Ibid., 719.
50. Ibid.
51. Churchill, *Closing Ring*, 352.
52. See Tuchman, *Stilwell*, 523.
53. Churchill, *Closing Ring*, 355–57.
54. Memoranda Circulated at Cairo and Tehran, Ismay Papers, Ismay 6/7, pp. 107–108, CCS 418/1, 3 December 1943.
55. *Reilly*, 182.
56. FRUS, CT, 711.
57. Sherwood, *Roosevelt and Hopkins*, 799.
58. FRUS, CT, 741.
59. Ibid., 711.
60. Ibid., 732.
61. Eden, *Reckoning*, 497.
62. Sarah Churchill, *Thread*, 67.
63. Diary, 1943–45, Sir Hughe Knatchbull-Hugessen Papers, KNAT 1/14/81, 7 December 1943, Churchill College, Cambridge.
64. Eden, *Reckoning*, 497.
65. Sarah Churchill, *Thread*, 67.

66. Churchill, *Closing Ring,* 357.

67. Telegram, Roosevelt to Stalin, 6 December 1943, FDR Papers, Map Room, FDRL.

68. Churchill, *Closing Ring,* 357.

69. FRUS, CT, 749.

70. Grace Tully, *FDR. My Boss* (New York: Charles Scribner's Sons, 1949), 270.

71. Letter, Ismay to Somerville, Ismay Papers, Ismay 4/Som/4c; Bryant, *Triumph,* 76.

72. Diary, Alanbrooke Papers, AB 5/8, p. 35, 7 December 1943.

73. Churchill, *Closing Ring,* 358.

Chapter 13. What Tehran Achieved

1. Boettiger diary, 52, 3 December 1943, FDRL.

2. Harriman, *Special Envoy,* 283.

3. Charles E. Bohlen, *The Transformation of American Foreign Policy* (London: MacDonald, 1970), 25.

4. Stimson diaries, 45, 128–30, 18 December 1943.

5. Arnold, *Global Mission,* 481.

6. Boettiger diary, 52, 3 December 1943, FDRL.

7. Stimson diaries, 45, 88, 5 December 1943.

8. Samuel I. Rosenman, comp., *The Public Papers and Addresses of Franklin D. Roosevelt. 1943. The Tide Turns* (New York: Harper and Brothers, 1950), 549.

9. Stalin's Correspondence, 2 : 111.

10. Rosenman, *Public Papers,* 553, 555.

11. See Beitzell, *Uneasy Alliance,* 382.

12. FRUS, CT, 849.

13. As reported in *New York Times,* 8 December 1943.

14. *New York Herald Tribune,* 7 December 1943.

15. "We Shall Work Together," *Business Week,* 11 December 1943, 14.

16. *Times* (London), 6 December 1943.

17. *Christian Science Monitor,* 6 December 1943.

18. *Washington Post,* 26 December 1943.

19. Bohlen, *Witness,* 153.

20. Cadogan, *Diaries,* 561.

21. Churchill, *Closing Ring,* 346.

22. Sarah Churchill, *Thread,* 83.

23. Sir John Wheeler-Bennett, ed., *Action This Day* (New York: St. Martin's Press, 1969), 90.

24. "From Notes on Russia," Sir Giffard Martel Papers, GMQ 4/4, p. 3, Department of Documents, Imperial War Museum, London. Martel added that the "result was worth it," because the atmosphere was friendly and the Russians "could not now possibly back out of the war."

25. Leasor, *War at Top,* 259.

26. Bryant, *Triumph,* 287.

27. FRUS, CT, 784.

28. Murphy, *Diplomat,* 447.

29. Harry C. Butcher, *My Three Years with Eisenhower* (New York: Simon and Schuster, 1946), 453.

30. Deane, *Strange Alliance,* 44.

31. Stilwell, *Papers,* 260.

32. *Chicago Tribune,* 7 December 1943.

33. *Egyptian Gazette,* 5 December 1943.

34. *Daily Mail,* 8 December 1943.

35. As reported in *New York Times,* 8 December 1943.

36. Goebbels, *Diaries,* 543.

37. Ulrich von Hassell, *The Von Hassell Diaries* (Garden City, N. Y.: Doubleday, 1947), 327.

38. Franz von Papen, *Memoirs* (New York: E. P. Dutton, 1953), 517.

39. Letter from Churchill to Ismay, Ismay Papers, 17 June 1949, Ismay 2/3/160.

›40. Letter from Ismay to Churchill, Ismay Papers, 30 June 1949, Ismay 2/3/162/1.

41. William D. Hassett, *Off the Record with FDR, 1942–1945* (New Brunswick, N.J.: Rutgers University Press, 1958), 248.

42. Harriman interview.

43. Eisenhower, *Crusade,* 229.

44. Kennedy, *Business of War,* 312.

45. Harriman, *Special Envoy,* 272.

46. Winston S. Churchill, "War Memoirs: Mounting History's Greatest Invasion," *Life,* 22 October 1951, 75.

47. Harriman interview.

48. Ibid.

49. Rozek, *Allied Wartime Diplomacy,* 280.

50. See Sir John Wheeler-Bennett and Anthony Nicholls, *The Semblance of Peace* (London: Macmillan, 1972), 194.

51. Arthur B. Lane, *I Saw Poland Betrayed* (New York: Bobbs-Merrill, 1948), 255; Stalin's Correspondence, 2:133.

52. A. A. Gromyko and B. N. Ponomorev, eds., *Soviet Foreign Policy, 1917–1980,* 2 vols. (Moscow: Progress Publishers, 1981), 1:442.

BIBLIOGRAPHY

Manuscripts

British Library (London)
    Andrew Browne Cunningham MSS

Churchill College Archives (Cambridge)
    Lawrence Franklin Burgis MSS
    Sir Alexander George Montagu Cadogan MSS
    Winston S. Churchill MSS (closed)
    Sir Hughe Knatchbull-Hugessen MSS
    Sir Victor Alexander Louis Mallet MSS

Harriman, Governor W. Averell. Interview with author. Washington, D.C., 2 July 1981.

Imperial War Museum (London)
    Sir Giffard Martel MSS

Library of Congress (Washington, D.C.)
    Henry H. Arnold MSS
    Cordell Hull MSS
    Ernest J. King MSS
    William D. Leahy MSS
    Henry L. Stimson MSS (microfilm)

Liddell Hart Centre for Military Archives (King's College, London)
    Lord Alanbrooke MSS
    Sir Hastings L. Ismay MSS

George C. Marshall Research Foundation (Lexington, Virginia)
    George C. Marshall MSS

National Archives (Washington, D.C.)
    Record Group 43, Records of International Conferences, Commissions, and Expositions.
    Record Group 59, Archives of the State Department; Decimal File Series 740.00 and 891.00.
    Record Group 218, Records of the United States Joint Chiefs of Staff.

Public Record Office (London)
    CAB 80/77, Minutes of Proceedings at Cairo and Tehran Between 22nd November and 7th December 1943.
    CAB 99/25, Minutes of Combined Chiefs of Staff Meetings.

PREM 3/136/8, Records of the Anglo-American-Russian Conversations in Tehran and of the Anglo-American-Turkish Conversations in Cairo.
PREM 3/136/10, Military Conclusions of the Teheran Conference.

Franklin D. Roosevelt Library (Hyde Park, New York)
John D. Boettiger MSS
Harry L. Hopkins MSS
Ross T. McIntire MSS
Henry J. Morgenthau, Jr. MSS
Franklin D. Roosevelt MSS

Serial Publications

Atlanta Constitution
Chicago Tribune
Christian Science Monitor
Daily Mail
Egyptian Gazette
Manchester Guardian
New York Herald Tribune
New York Times
Philadelphia Inquirer
Times (London)
Washington Post
Washington Star
Washington Times-Herald

General Works

Adams, Henry Hitch. *Harry Hopkins: A Biography.* New York: The Putnam Publishing Corp., 1977.

Arnold, Henry H. *Global Mission.* New York: Harper and Row, 1972.

Arnold-Foster, William. *Charters of the Peace. A Commentary on the Atlantic Charter and the Declarations of Moscow, Cairo, and Teheran.* London: Victor Gollancz, 1944.

Astley, Joan B. *The Inner Circle: A View of War at the Top.* Boston: Little, Brown and Co., 1971.

A War Atlas for Americans. Prepared with Assistance of the Office of War Information. New York: Simon and Schuster, 1944.

Balfour, Michael. *The Adversaries: America, Russia, and the Open World 1941–62.* Boston: Routledge and Kegan Paul, 1981.

Beitzell, Robert, ed. *Tehran. Yalta. Potsdam. The Soviet Protocols.* Hattiesburg, Mississippi: Academic International, 1970.

———. *The Uneasy Alliance: America, Britain and Russia, 1941–1943*. New York: Alfred A. Knopf, 1972.

Berezhkov, Valentin. *History in the Making. Memoirs of World War II Diplomacy.* Moscow: Progress Publishers, 1982.

The Best from Yank, the American Weekly. New York: E. P. Dutton and Co., 1945.

Birse, Arthur H. *Memoirs of an Interpreter.* New York: Coward and McCann, 1967.

Blum, John Morton. *From the Morgenthau Diaries.* 3 vols. Boston: Houghton Mifflin, 1967.

Bohlen, Charles E. *The Transformation of American Foreign Policy.* London: MacDonald, 1970.

———. *Witness to History, 1929–1969.* New York: W. W. Norton, 1973.

Bradley, Omar N. *A Soldier's Story.* New York: Henry Holt, 1951.

Browder, Earl R. *Moscow, Cairo, Teheran.* New York: Workers Library, 1944.

———. *Teheran and America: Perspectives and Tasks.* New York: Workers Library, 1944.

———. *Teheran. Our Path in War and Peace.* New York: International Publishers, 1944.

Brown, Anthony C. *Bodyguard of Lies.* 2 vols. New York: Harper and Row, 1975.

Bruce, George. *Second Front Now! The Road to D-Day.* London: MacDonald and Jane's, 1979.

Bryant, Arthur. *Triumph in the West.* Garden City, N.Y.: Doubleday and Co., 1959.

Butcher, Harry C. *My Three Years with Eisenhower.* New York: Simon and Schuster, 1946.

Cadogan, Alexander. *The Diaries of Alexander Cadogan.* Edited by David Dilks. New York: G. P. Putnam's Sons, 1971.

Chamberlin, William H. *America's Second Crusade.* Chicago: Henry Regnery, 1950.

Churchill, Sarah. *A Thread in the Tapestry.* New York: Dodd and Mead, 1967.

Churchill, Winston S. *Closing the Ring.* New York: Bantam Books, 1962.

———. *Grand Alliance.* New York: Bantam Books, 1962.

———. *The Hinge of Fate.* New York: Bantam Books, 1962.

Ciechanowski, Jan. *Defeat in Victory.* Garden City, N.Y.: Doubleday and Co., 1947.

Cline, Ray S. *Washington Command Post: The Operations Division.* Washington, D.C.: Office of the Chief of Military History, 1951.

Coakley, Robert W., and Richard M. Leighton. *Global Logistics and Strategy, 1943–1945*. Washington, D.C.: Office of the Chief of Military History, 1968.

Crocker, George N. *Roosevelt's Road to Russia*. Chicago: Henry Regnery, 1959.

Cunningham, Andrew B. *A Sailor's Odyssey. The Autobiography of Admiral of the Fleet Viscount Cunningham of Hyndhope*. London: Hutchinson, 1951.

Dallek, Robert. *Franklin D. Roosevelt and American Foreign Policy, 1932–1945*. New York: Oxford University Press, 1979.

Dallin, David J. *The Big Three. The United States, Britain, Russia*. New Haven: Yale University Press, 1945.

Deane, John R. *The Strange Alliance: The Story of Our Efforts at Wartime Cooperation with Russia*. New York: The Viking Press, 1947.

De Gaulle, Charles. *The Complete War Memoirs of Charles De Gaulle*. 3 vols. New York: Simon and Schuster, 1955–59.

Dennett, Raymond, and Joseph E. Johnson, eds. *Negotiating with the Russians*. Boston: World Peace Foundation, 1951.

Dulles, Foster R. *The Road to Teheran. The Story of Russia and America, 1781–1943*. Princeton: Princeton University Press, 1944.

Eden, Anthony. *The Reckoning*. Boston: Houghton Mifflin, 1965.

Edmonds, I. G. *The Shah of Iran*. New York: Holt, Rinehart, and Winston, 1976.

Ehrman, John. *Grand Strategy*. Vol. 5, *August 1943 to September 1944*. London: Her Majesty's Stationery Office, 1956.

Eisenhower, Dwight D. *Crusade in Europe*. Garden City, N.Y.: Doubleday and Co., 1948.

Eisenhower, John S. D. *Allies: Pearl Harbor to D-Day*. Garden City, N.Y.: Doubleday and Co., 1982.

Eubank, Keith. *Summit at Teheran. The Untold Story*. New York: William Morrow and Co., 1985.

———. *The Summit Conferences, 1919–1960*. Norman, Oklahoma: University of Oklahoma Press, 1966.

Feis, Herbert. *Churchill, Roosevelt and Stalin. The War They Waged and the Peace They Sought*. Princeton: Princeton University Press, 1957.

Fischer, Louis. *The Road to Yalta: Soviet Foreign Relations, 1941–1945*. New York: Harper and Row, 1972.

Goebbels, Joseph. *Goebbels Diaries, 1942–1943*. Edited by Louis P. Lochner. Garden City, N.Y.: Doubleday and Co., 1948.

Grigg, John. *1943. The Victory That Never Was*. London: Eyre Methuen, 1980.

Gromyko, A. A., and B. N. Ponomarev, eds. *Soviet Foreign Policy, 1917–1980*. 2 vols. Moscow: Progress Publishers, 1981.

Hamzavi, Abdol H. *Persia and the Powers: An Account of Diplomatic Relations, 1941–1946*. New York: Hutchinson, 1946.

Harriman, W. Averell, and Elie Abel. *Special Envoy to Churchill and Stalin, 1941–1946*. New York: Random House, 1975.

Harrison, Gordon. *The Cross-Channel Attack*. Washington, D.C.: Government Printing Office, 1961.

Hassell, Ulrich von. *The Von Hassell Diaries, 1938–44. The Story of Forces Against Hitler Inside Germany*. Garden City, N.Y.: Doubleday and Co., 1947.

Hassett, William D. *Off the Record with FDR, 1942–1945*. New Brunswick, N.J.: Rutgers University Press, 1958.

Havas, Laslo. *Hitler's Plot to Kill the Big Three*. New York: Cowles Book Co., 1969.

Higgins, Trumbull. *Soft Underbelly: The Anglo-American Controversy over the Italian Campaign, 1939–1945*. New York: Macmillan, 1968.

———. *Winston Churchill and the Second Front, 1940–1943*. Westport, Conn.: Greenwood Press, 1957.

Hingley, Ronald. *Joseph Stalin: Man and Legend*. New York: McGraw-Hill, 1974.

Hollis, Leslie. *One Marine's Tale*. London: Andre Deutsch, 1956.

Hoska, Lukas E. *A Critical Analysis of the Summit Conferences of Teheran, The Crimea, and Berlin*. Cambridge: Center for International Affairs, 1960.

Hull, Cordell. *The Memoirs of Cordell Hull*. 2 vols. New York: Macmillan, 1948.

Ismay, Lord Hastings. *The Memoirs of General the Lord Ismay*. London: Heinemann, 1960.

Issrealjan, Victor. *The Anti-Hitler Coalition: Diplomatic Cooperation Between the USSR, USA, and Britain During the Second World War, 1941–1945*. Moscow: Progress Publishers, 1971.

Kennedy, General Sir John. *The Business of War: The War Narrative of Major-General Sir John Kennedy*. Edited by Bernard Fergusson. New York: William Morrow and Co., 1958.

Khrushchev, Nikita. *Khrushchev Remembers*. Edited and translated by Strobe Talbott. Boston: Little, Brown and Co., 1970.

King, Ernest J., and Walter M. Whitehill. *Fleet Admiral King. A Naval Record*. New York: W. W. Norton, 1952.

Kuniholm, Bruce R. *The Origins of the Cold War in the Near East. Great Power Conflict and Diplomacy in Iran, Turkey, and Greece*. Princeton: Princeton University Press, 1980.

Lane, Arthur B. *I Saw Poland Betrayed. An American Ambassador Reports to the American People.* New York: The Bobbs-Merrill Co., 1948.

Lash, Joseph P. *Roosevelt and Churchill 1939–1941: The Partnership that Saved the West.* New York: W. W. Norton, 1976.

Leahy, William D. *I Was There. The Personal Story of the Chief of Staff of Presidents Roosevelt and Truman Based on His Notes and Diaries Made at the Time.* London: Victor Gollancz, 1950.

Lenczowski, George. *Russia and the West in Iran, 1918–1948: A Study in Big Power Rivalry.* Ithaca, N.Y.: Cornell University Press, 1949.

Leasor, James. *War at the Top.* London: Michael Joseph, 1959.

Levering, Ralph B. *American Opinion and the Russian Alliance, 1939–1945.* Chapel Hill: University of North Carolina Press, 1976.

Loewenheim, Francis L., Harold D. Langley, and Manfred Jonas, eds. *Roosevelt and Churchill: Their Secret Wartime Correspondence.* New York: Saturday Review Press, 1975.

Lohbeck, Don. *Patrick J. Hurley.* Chicago: Henry Regnery, 1956.

Longmate, Norman. *The GIs. The Americans in Britain, 1942–1945.* London: Hutchinson, 1975.

Louis, William R. *Imperialism at Bay. The United States and the Decolonization of the British Empire, 1941–1945.* New York: Oxford University Press, 1978.

Lukacs, John A. *The Great Powers and Eastern Europe.* New York: American Book Co., 1953.

Lukas, Richard C. *The Strange Allies. The United States and Poland, 1941–1945.* Knoxville: University of Tennessee Press, 1978.

Maisky, Ivan M. *Memoirs of a Soviet Ambassador. The War: 1939–1943.* New York: Charles Scribner's Sons, 1968.

Matloff, Maurice, and Edwin M. Snell. *Strategic Planning for Coalition Warfare.* 2 vols. Washington, D.C.: Office of the Chief of Military History, 1953–59.

McIntire, Ross T., and George Creel. *White House Physician.* New York: G. P. Putnam's Sons, 1946.

McCarthy, Joseph R. *America's Retreat from Victory.* New York: Devin-Adair Publishers, 1951.

McNeill, William H. *America, Britain and Russia. Their Co-operation and Conflict, 1941–1946.* New York: Oxford University Press, 1953.

Millspaugh, Arthur C. *Americans in Persia.* New York: Da Capo Press, 1976.

Moran, Charles M. W. *Churchill. Taken from the Diaries of Lord Moran. The Struggle for Survival, 1940–1965.* Boston: Houghton Mifflin, 1966.

Motter, T. H. Vail. *The Persian Corridor and Aid to Russia.* Washington, D.C.: Office of the Chief of Military History, 1952.

Murphy, Robert D. *Diplomat Among Warriors.* Westport, Conn.: Greenwood Press, 1963.

Neumann, William L. *Making the Peace 1941–1945.* Washington, D.C.: Foundation for Foreign Affairs, 1950.

Nicholas, H. G., ed. *Washington Despatches 1941–45.* London: George Weidenfeld and Nicolson, 1981.

O'Connor, Raymond G. *Diplomacy for Victory: Franklin D. Roosevelt and Unconditional Surrender.* New York: W. W. Norton, 1971.

Papen, Franz von. *Memoirs.* New York: E. P. Dutton and Co., 1953.

Parkinson, Roger. *A Day's March Nearer Home. The War History from Alamein to VE Day Based on the War Cabinet Papers of 1942 to 1945.* New York: David McKay Co., 1974.

Pawle, Gerald S. *The War and Colonel Warden.* New York: Alfred A. Knopf, 1963.

Perkins, Frances. *The Roosevelt I Knew.* New York: Harper and Row, 1946.

Pogue, Forrest C. *George C. Marshall.* 3 vols. New York: The Viking Press, 1963–1973.

Reilly, Michael F., and William J. Slocum. *Reilly of the White House.* New York: Simon and Schuster, 1947.

Rigdon, William M. *Log of the President's Trip to Africa and the Middle East, November–December 1943.* N.p., 1943? Washington, D.C.: Rare Book Collection, Library of Congress.

Rigdon, William M., and James Derieux. *White House Sailor.* Garden City, N.Y.: Doubleday and Co., 1962.

Roberts, Walter R. *Tito, Mihailović and the Allies, 1941–1945.* New Brunswick, N.J.: Rutgers University Press, 1973.

Roosevelt, Eleanor. *The Autobiography of Eleanor Roosevelt.* New York: Harper and Brothers, 1958.

Roosevelt, Elliott. *As He Saw It.* New York: Duell, Sloan and Pearce, 1946.

Rosenman, Samuel I. *Working with Roosevelt.* New York: Harper and Brothers, 1950.

———, comp. *The Public Papers and Addresses of Franklin D. Roosevelt, 1943. The Tide Turns.* New York: Harper and Brothers, 1950.

Rozek, Edward J. *Allied Wartime Diplomacy. A Pattern in Poland.* New York: John Wiley and Sons, 1958.

Sadegni, Khosrow. "A Study of the Tehran Conference of 1943." Ph.D. diss., Kent State University, 1975.

Sainsbury, Keith. *The Turning Point. Roosevelt, Stalin, Churchill, and Chiang Kai-Shek, 1943. The Moscow, Cairo, and Teheran Conferences.* New York: Oxford University Press, 1985.

Sharp, Tony. *The Wartime Alliance and the Zonal Division of Germany.* Oxford: Clarendon Press, 1975.

Sherwood, Robert E. *Roosevelt and Hopkins: An Intimate History.* New York: Harper and Brothers, 1948.

Skrine, Sir Clarmont Percival. *World War in Iran.* London: Constable, 1962.

Standley, William H., and Arthur A. Ageton. *Admiral Ambassador to Russia.* Chicago: Henry Regnery, 1955.

Stettinius, Edward R. *Roosevelt and the Russians: The Yalta Conference.* Edited by Walter Johnson. Garden City, N.Y.: Doubleday and Co., 1949.

Stilwell, Joseph W. *The Stilwell Papers.* Edited by Theodore H. White. New York: William Sloane, 1948.

Stimson, Henry L., and McGeorge Bundy. *On Active Service in Peace and War.* New York: Harper and Brothers, 1947.

Stoler, Mark A. *The Politics of the Second Front: American Military Planning.* Westport, Conn.: Greenwood Press, 1977.

Taylor, A. J. P. *The War Lords.* London: Hamish Hamilton, 1976.

Thompson, Walter H. *Assignment: Churchill.* New York: Popular Library, 1955.

Tuchman, Barbara W. *Stilwell and the American Experience in China, 1911–45.* New York: Macmillan, 1971.

Tully, Grace. *FDR. My Boss.* New York: Charles Scribner's Sons, 1949.

Ulam, Adam B. *Stalin: The Man and His Era.* New York: The Viking Press, 1973.

U.S. Department of State. Foreign Relations of the United States. *The Conference of Berlin, 1945.* 2 vols. Washington, D.C.: Government Printing Office, 1960.

———. *The Conferences at Cairo and Tehran.* Washington, D.C.: Government Printing Office, 1961.

———. *The Conferences at Washington, 1941–1942 and Casablanca, 1943.* Washington, D.C.: Government Printing Office, 1968.

———. *The Conferences at Washington and Quebec, 1943.* Washington, D.C.: Government Printing Office, 1970.

U.S.S.R. Ministry of Foreign Affairs of the U.S.S.R. *Correspondence Between the Chairman of the Council of Ministers of the USSR and the Presidents of the USA and the Prime Ministers of Great Britain During the Great Patriotic War of 1941–1945.* 2 vols. Moscow: Foreign Languages Publishing House, 1958.

———. "Tehran Conference of the Leaders of the Three Great Powers (November 28 to December 1, 1943), Documents." *International Affairs* 7 (July 1961): 133–45; 8 (August 1961): 110–122.

Walker, Gregg B. "Franklin D. Roosevelt as Summit Negotiator at Teheran, 1943, and Yalta, 1945." Ph.D. diss., University of Kansas, 1983.

Weber, Frank G. *The Evasive Neutral: Germany, Britain, and the Quest for a Turkish Alliance in the Second World War.* Columbia: University of Missouri Press, 1979.

Welles, Sumner. *Where Are We Heading?* New York: Harper and Brothers, 1946.

Wheeler-Bennett, Sir John, ed. *Action This Day. Working with Churchill. Memoirs by Lord Normanbrook, John Colville, Sir John Martin, Sir Ian Jacob, Lord Bridges, and Sir Leslie Rowan.* New York: St. Martin's Press, 1969.

Wheeler-Bennett, Sir John, and Anthony Nicholls. *The Semblance of Peace: The Political Settlement After the Second World War.* London: Macmillan, 1972.

Willkie, Wendell L. *One World.* New York: Simon and Schuster, 1943.

Wittmer, Felix. *The Yalta Betrayal: Data on the Decline and Fall of FDR.* Caldwell, Idaho: The Caxton Printers, 1954.

Woodward, E. Llewellyn. *British Foreign Policy in the Second World War.* London: Her Majesty's Stationery Office, 1962.

Zawodny, Janusz. *Death in the Forest: The Story of the Katyn Forest Massacre.* South Bend, Indiana: University of Notre Dame Press, 1962.

Articles

Bateman, Herman E. "Observations on President Roosevelt's Health During World War II." *Mississippi Valley Historical Review* 43 (June 1956): 82–102.

Beaverbrook, Lord. "Opportunity to Win the War in 1942: A Second Front in Europe to Aid Russia." *Vital Speeches* 8 (15 May 1942): 459–461.

"Big Four Map Own Postwar Places as Well as Axis Annihilation." *Newsweek*, 13 December 1943, 23–27.

Bullitt, William C. "How We Won the War and Lost the Peace." *Life*, 30 August 1948, 82–97.

Chase, John L. "Unconditional Surrender Reconsidered." *Political Science Quarterly* 70 (June 1955): 258–279.

Churchill, Winston. "War Memoirs: Mounting History's Greatest Invasion." *Life*, 22 October, 1951, 86–90.

"City Without a Plumber." *Christian Science Monitor Magazine*, 16 November 1946, 18–19.

"Conference Bits," *Newsweek*, 13 December 1943, 26.

Cousins, Norman. "Proportion and the Press." *Saturday Review of Literature*, 18 December 1943, 14.

Eulau, Heinz. "As the Big Three Meet." *New Republic*, 5 February 1943, 168–170.

Fay, Sidney B. "What Does Stalin Want?" *Current History* 4 (November 1943): 199–208.

"FDR's Jam Session." *Newsweek*, 13 December 1943, 26.

Field, Henry. "How FDR Did His Homework." *Saturday Review of Literature*, 8 July 1961, 8–10.

Franklin, William M. "Yalta Viewed from Tehran." In *Some Pathways in Twentieth Century History: Essays in Honor of Reginald Charles McGrane*, edited by Daniel R. Beaver. Detroit, Mich.: Wayne State University Press, 1969.

Gillis, J. M. "That Teheran Drinking Bout." *Catholic World* 164 (March 1947): 458–488.

Greenfield, George. "An Observer at Teheran." In *History of the Second World War*, edited by Barrie Pitt, 4:1710–1717. Hicksville, N.Y.: Marshall Cavendish, 1973.

Leighton, Richard. "Overlord Revisited: An Interpretation of American Strategy in the European War, 1942–1944." *American Historical Review* 68 (July 1963): 919–937.

———. "Overlord versus the Mediterranean at the Cairo-Tehran Conferences." In *Command Decisions*, edited by Kent R. Greenfield. Washington, D.C.: U.S. Department of the Army, 1960.

Litvinov, Maxim. "More Fronts to Win the War Now." *Vital Speeches* 8 (15 March 1942): 325–326.

Mastny, Vojtech. "Stalin and the Prospects of a Separate Peace in World War II." *American Historical Review* 77 (1972): 1365–1388.

"Meeting at Teheran: Roosevelt-Stalin-Churchill Declaration." *Current History* 6 (January 1944): 54–55.

Padmore, George. "Race Relations: Soviet and British." *Crisis*, November 1942, 345–348.

Pegler, Westbrook. "What Strange Bedfellows." *American Legion Magazine*, April 1939, 10–11.

Romine, C. W. "President Didn't Like Egyptian Flies; Other Notes from an Observer's Diary." *Newsweek*, 20 December 1943, 36.

Roosevelt, Eleanor. "A President's Planning." *Saturday Review of Literature*, 8 July 1961, 10.

"Spotlight Hovers on Balkans as Result of Big Four Parley." *Newsweek*, 20 December 1943, 28.

Taylor, A. J. P. "War at the Top." In *History of the Second World War*, edited by Barrie Pitt, 4: 455–478. Hicksville, N.Y.: Marshall Cavendish, 1973.

"Teheran Declaration: If It Can Be Believed, It Solves Everything; If It Cannot, It Is A Colossal Fraud." *Life*, 20 December 1943, 32.

"The Strange Death of President Roosevelt." *News Story* 3 (August 1945): 5.

"Three Men of Destiny." *New York Times Magazine*, 21 November 1943, 5.

"Two Meetings of Allied Chiefs." *Catholic World* 158 (January 1944): 402–404.

Villard, Oswald G. "Roosevelt Postwar World: (Reply to Forrest Davis)." *Christian Century,* 31 May 1944, 668–669.

Visson, Andre. "The Big Three in the Near East." *American Mercury* 60 (May 1945): 570–575.

Walsh, Warren B. "What the American People Think of Russia." *Public Opinion Quarterly* 8 (1944–45): 513–522.

"We Shall Work Together." *Business Week,* 11 December 1943, 14.

"Where the West Really Began Its Retreat: Teheran, 1943." *U.S. News and World Report,* 26 June 1961, 84–86.

Winter, Ella. "Our Allies, the Russians." *Ladies' Home Journal,* February 1943, 37.

INDEX

Boldface page numbers indicate references to maps.

Adriatic Sea, 70, 71, 73

Aegean Sea, 47, 70, 81, 98, 101, 161

Agreement in principle: Bismarck's definition of, 19; British, to Buccaneer, 34, 62; Brooke's assessment of, 164; Churchill on, 60, 74, 106, 109, 145, 172 n.4; on Danubian federation issue, 31; on disposal of Italian fleet, 142; Eden on, 154; on Gymnast issue, 29; on importance of military cooperation, 29; between Little Three, on Turkey, 106; pattern of, at Tehran Conference, 20–21, 165–168; Roosevelt's desire to move beyond, 85; on shuttle bombing, 42, 85; Stalin on, 37, 38, 39, 43; on Supreme World Council, 31; as a working formula, 12

Alexander, Harold, 49

Alexandria, 46

Amirabad airport, 52, 150

Anakim operation: accepted at Casablanca Conference, 30

Ancona line, **15**, 63

Andaman Islands, 34, 47, 64

Ankara, 43, 134

Anvil (proposed invasion of southern France): Anglo-American promise to undertake, 157; British desire to postpone, 98, 99; British reluctance to support, 89, 92; debated at Second Cairo Conference, 158, 161; discussed at Quadrant, 33; Marshall's support of, 82, 100; raised at Tehran Conference, 84, 108, 109; scrapped at Second Cairo Conference, 167; Stalin's endorsement of, 93

Arcadia, 29. *See also* First Washington Conference

Archangel, 36, 40

Arctic convoys: suspension of, 34

Arnold, General Henry H., 53, 54, 89, 91; absent from first plenary session, 68, 69; at

First Cairo Conference, 47, 48; impression after third plenary session, 113; on Overlord's commander, 166; on Russian policy, 26; on Stalin, 76, 162; visit to Jerusalem, 132

Asmara, 43

Astrakhan, 36, 40

Atlantic Charter, 29, 30, 146, 150, 155, 165

Baghdad, 38, 41–43, 150

Baku, 52

Balkans, 28, 63, 81, 161; as second front location, 28, 32, 75, 92, 93, 135

Baltic Sea, 27, 77, 109, 137, 140, 143

Bangkok, 64

Basra, 43

Bay of Bengal, 34, 47, 48, 102, 159

Berezhkov, Valentin, 52, 68, 80, 91

Bering Straits, 36, 39

Birse, Arthur H., 52, 68, 91; at Churchill's birthday dinner, 114, 116, 117; at Churchill-Stalin meeting, 102, 104; on debate over cross-channel invasion, 108; on Stalin, 70

Bizerte, 104

Black Sea, 73, 81, 136, 143, 160

Boettiger, John D., 54, 58, 90; on Anglo-American friction, 55, 152; on communiqué, 151; on effects of Tehran Conference, 116; on Russian embassy, 52; at Second Cairo Conference, 160; on Stalin, 162, 163

Bohlen, Charles, 53, 68, 91, 150; on effects of Tehran Conference, 162, 164; on Polish government issue, 143; at Roosevelt's first private meeting with Stalin, 64; on Roosevelt's frankness with Stalin regarding Poland, 139; on Stalin's embarrassment, 149; on Stalin's joke about liquidating German officers, 95–96; on Stalin's proposal for